BEYOND REALISM AND MARXISM

Also by Andrew Linklater

* MEN AND CITIZENS IN THE THEORY OF
  INTERNATIONAL RELATIONS

  NEW DIMENSIONS IN WORLD POLITICS
  (*editor with G. Goodwin*)

* Also published by Macmillan

BEYOND REALISM AND MARXISM

Critical Theory and International Relations

Andrew Linklater
Senior Lecturer in Politics
Monash University
Clayton, Victoria, Australia

palgrave

Published by
MACMILLAN PRESS LTD
Houndmills, Basingstoke, Hampshire RG21 2XS
and London
Companies and representatives
throughout the world

ISBN 0–333–32497–8 hardcover
ISBN 0–333–51720–2 paperback

A catalogue record for this book is available
from the British Library.

Transferred to digital printing 2001
Printed and bound by Antony Rowe Ltd, Eastbourne

Contents

Acknowledgements

Research for this book began at the point where an earlier work left off. The book in question, *Men and Citizens in the Theory of International Relations*, which was published by Macmillan in 1982, presented a philosophical defence of ethical universalism. There was no scope within that work to deal with the empirical question of how moral communities have expanded (and contracted) in the past. But a brief section on Marx's analysis of this subject led me to think that it would be profitable to begin by surveying Marxism with this theme in mind.

As my research proceeded it became necessary to take account of two important developments in the literature. In international relations, first of all, Marxism was invoked in an attempt to add the call for critical theory to earlier arguments for a political economy of international relations. In sociology a rather different trend drew upon realism to highlight the inadequacies of Marxism as a critical theory of society. The significance of these two developments - the Marxist, or Marxist-inspired, critique of realism in international relations, and the "realist" critique of Marxism in sociology - then became the main reason for writing this book.

I have incurred many debts in the process. Monash University granted me six months sabbatical from the middle of 1984 to concentrate on research for the present work. Most of this period was spent at the Centre for International Studies at The London School of Economics. I am grateful to the Centre for providing numerous facilities and a congenial environment. It was my good fortune to visit the London School of Economics at the same time as Hidemi Suganami from Keele University. As in the past, I derived immense benefit from his perceptive comments on an earlier draft of this manuscript. I would also like to thank Kenneth Waltz for several stimulating discussions and for his generosity during my visit to Berkeley in the early part of 1985.

Several colleagues at Monash University have provided the right blend of criticism and encouragement. Ian Bell, Tony Jarvis and Peter Lawler taught in the course which was the main vehicle for the development of the themes set out below. Each of them helped me to shape my argument. Peter Lawler in particular has been a valued source of encouragement and advice. Students in my third year seminar, *Problems in International Political Economy*, contributed their enthusiasm and the vital ingredients of debate and discussion.

Finally, without Tony Jarvis and Aubrey Townsend I could not have acquired my admittedly tenous grip on the world of word processing; and without Pauline Bakker's humour and expertise the manuscript would have taken much longer to complete.

A. L.

November 1988
Melbourne

Introduction

In his famous essay on the poverty of international theory Martin Wight referred to the tension between the language of Western political thought and the actual world of international relations. Wight argued that the vocabulary of political theory and law had been impregnated with the belief that human beings could perfect their social and political arrangements. The Marxist tradition developed this theme in the statement that history was a process in which human beings acquired increasing mastery of their social and political environment. The relevance of this language for the international system was clearly problematical in Wight's view. In an oft-quoted passage, Wight maintained that international politics was "the realm of recurrence and repetition", or the sphere of politics in which human "action is most regularly necessitous". For this reason, the history of international thought had been concerned simply with the goal of state survival. The attempt to construct philosophical visions of the good society had been the exclusive preserve of political theories of the state.[1]

The conflict to which Wight referred is no more evident than in the emerging debate between realism and the critical theory of international relations, a debate which resembles a much earlier controversy between "traditional" and "critical" approaches to sociology.[2] Realism begins with the premise that states must act to preserve their security in the only way possible - by accumulating the instruments of physical violence. It is a study of how this attempt to solve the problem of national security inevitably generates suspicion, competition and war, and an account of how states necessarily reproduce the constraining conditions which are unique to the international realm. The dominant category in realist theory is, in consequence, the concept of necessity - the necessity of recognising the existence of inescapable constraints on political choice, of working within rather than pressing against the limits on change, and of abandoning the search for the international good life in order to protect the immediate goals of security and survival.

Horkheimer's essay on traditional and critical theory anticipated the basic themes in the most recent critique of realism. Horkheimer argued that traditional theory (positivism) was distinguished from critical theory by its attempt to explain social laws and regularities. The aim of critical theory was to understand how these socially-created constraints upon the freedom of human subjects could be reduced and, where possible, eliminated.[3] Marx's point that human beings make their own history, but not under conditions of their own choosing, was central to Horkheimer's critique of positivism. This theme also encapsulated Rousseau's claim that the transformation of society in order to achieve the highest level of human autonomy is the major problem of modern politics.[4] But despite this similarity Marx and Marxism disputed Rousseau's account of the tragic nature of international politics. The Marxist tradition rejected the belief that an international kingdom of necessity would continue to surround and threaten to engulf domestic kingdoms of freedom. It assumed that the expansion of capitalism would dissolve not only class constraints but the constraints inherent in inter-state relations. The purpose of social theory was therefore to understand and overcome the greatest range of domestic and international constraints upon human autonomy. Alternative forms of theory of the state and international relations which left everything exactly as it was, with the exception of concepts, simply compounded inherited forms of oppression and domination.

Until recently, supporters of critical theory have rarely discussed international relations. This neglect has seemed to confirm Wight's argument that the search for the good society ends, so to speak, at the water's edge. By contrast, the realist tradition contains much that is clearly hostile to the idea of critical international theory. Most accounts of the ascent of realism note that its principles were shaped in response to the two perspectives which were the main heirs of the Enlightenment: liberalism and Marxism. Arguments which had been developed in an earlier epoch in reaction to the universalism of Christianity and the Enlightenment were resurrected in response to the belief that the "expanding circle"[5] of industrial and commercial cooperation would weaken the grip of nationalism and the state. The realists took issue with the Marxist view that the spread of capitalism would unify the human race. They disputed the notion that a revolution of the international proletariat would eventually triumph over the divisive nature of relations between states. Still later they argued that the rate at which Marxism in power had succumbed to the methods of traditional diplomacy further confirmed realist theory. The merits of political realism had been exemplified by the role that international relations had played in the transformation of Marxist politics in the twentieth century. What had been intended as an instrument of revolutionary change had become an agent of the reproduction of the international system. The appeal of nationalism and the principle of state sovereignty in the oppressed regions of the socialist bloc was the most striking illustration of this transformation of Marxism.[6]

The realist critique of the project of the Enlightenment effectively thwarted the development of a critical tradition of international theory. However the recent emergence of a critical voice in international theory suggests that this may be about to change. That is not to suggest that the importance of the realist critique of past theories of emancipation is in any way diminished. Indeed, the influence of that critique has increased recently outside the study of international relations and especially in sociology where it now forms an important part of the "contemporary critique of historical materialism".[7] At first glance, it may seem ironic that a sympathetic reappraisal of Marxism and the tradition of critical social theory should occur in international relations at the very moment when the realist critique of Marxism has begun to appear in modern social theory. It is possible, however, to place a quite different interpretation upon these developments. To do so it is worth discussing recent developments in both areas, beginning with such trends in the study of international relations.

The most important of these changes have disturbed, although they have not displaced, the hegemony of realism. The current challenge to realism began with the revival of the liberal tradition of international political economy. All of the main versions of the liberal approach questioned the realist practice of analysing the states-system as an autonomous domain. All argued that a more comprehensive theoretical approach which took account of the effects of industrialisation and modernisation upon contemporary state structures had become essential in the age of global interdependence. The growing importance of economic factors in world politics made students of international relations more sensitive to the need to analyse the phenomenon of change. It made them more aware of the possibility that the state might become obliged to be responsive to an ethical constituency which was broader than its own citizenry, and more cognisant of the possibility that international cooperation would be strengthened by the need to solve a number of emerging global problems.[8]

The resurgence of liberal political economy also re-opened the discussion of the purpose of international political inquiry and its relationship with political practice. One of the main conclusions to emerge from this discussion was that realism was not only guilty of offering a one-dimensional account of international relations but, on a deeper level, of advocating a political practice which stifled the forces which revealed that new patterns path of historical development might be possible. Because it bolsters the status quo realism has been accused of performing an ideological role in world politics which the protestation of value-neutrality has concealed.[9]

These challenges to the hegemony of realism inevitably brought Marxism into the discussion. In the early stages of this process some liberals called for a dialogue with Marxism while indicating that they did not believe that Marxism could itself construct a post-realist theory of international relations.[10] More recent versions of liberalism have acknowledged the importance of the Marxist account of dominance and dependence in the world economy. This changed attitude towards Marxism reflects the more general trend of recognising that Marxism captured important dimensions of world politics which liberalism and realism had neglected.[11]

Initially the move towards the rehabilitation of historical materialism was part of the trend towards developing a conceptual framework which could explain the relationship between classical power politics and global social and economic change.[12] The emphasis has shifted more recently to attempts to understand the implications which developments in current social theory may have for the theory of international relations. In the course of the 1970s it became customary in social theory to distinguish between three modes of sociological inquiry: positivism with its commitment to a scientific understanding of social regularities; the hermeneutic approach which focused upon the cultural and linguistic dimensions of human conduct; and critical sociology with its interest in freeing human subjects from unnecessary social constraints and distorted patterns of culture and communication. In one strand of the literature the third perspective was held to be superior to the other two. The promotion of human emancipation was regarded as the principal objective of social inquiry.[13]

In the 1980s this discussion has become relevant for the theory of international relations. It has been argued that the main strands of international theory resemble either positivism or hermeneutics. In other words, these strands of thought have either analysed the repetitive and the recurrent dimensions of world politics or focused upon the language and culture of diplomatic interaction. What they have overlooked is the possibility of a critical theory of international relations which analyses the prospects for universal emancipation.[14]

What is novel about this line of argument is the point that the realist critique of Marxism has been too preoccupied with determining the relative influence of economic and political factors in international history. In so doing, realists undoubtedly exposed major weaknesses in the Marxist contention that the expansion of capitalism would revolutionise the nature of world politics. They successfully demonstrated that Marxism overestimated the importance of class and production and underestimated the impact of strategic competition and war on human history. But they did not invalidate the Marxian claim that political theory ought to strive for the emancipation of the species. It is precisely this critical dimension of the Marxian project which has been turned against realism in recent international theory.

The emergence of a critical-theoretical approach to world politics is only one manifestation of the growing importance of Marxism in the study of international relations. As previously noted, an interest in Marxist political economy developed as the field became more concerned with the economic and social context of inter-state relations. In one branch of the literature, critical theory and political economy have been linked in the study of different forms of world order. This approach signifies the search for a perspective which transcends one of the main dualisms in the history of international theory - the dualism which opposes realism to idealism.[15] This perspective encapsulates Marx's important theme that history is a process in which human beings deepen their understanding of their possibility of achieving freedom. Marx's philosophical history therefore denied that there were permanent moral truths which allowed human beings to judge human conduct without taking account of differences of time or place. By the same token, it repudiated the proposition that the social world consisted of incommensurable ethical codes, and on the same grounds it rejected the judgment that history was devoid of meaning.

Marx's critical theory was concerned with analysing immanent developments within the process of history: with understanding the moments in which human beings grasped the higher possibilities which were latent within their forms of life, and the epochs in which they acted to realise the vision which evolved out of their reflection upon their historical experience. From the perspective of critical social theory, the classical distinction between realist and idealist approaches to international relations is a false dichotomy.

On these grounds, it has been suggested that the critical theory of world politics may prove to be the next stage in the development of international relations theory.[16] If so, it is necessary to ask whether the new critical paradigm ought to be post-Marxist by virtue of the necessity of retaining some of the themes of statecentric realism. This is a question which has not received the attention it deserves in recent international theory. In part, this is because the attempt to break down the traditional resistance to Marxism in the field of international relations has been largely concerned with methodological issues. It has mainly sought to defend the method of critical theory and to proclaim the merits of Marxist and neo-Marxist approaches to international political economy. The rehabilitation of Marxism and critical theory has been based upon the critique of the realist account of the nature and purpose of theory. Much less attention has been devoted to the question of whether Marxism may have run its course as a critical theory of the modern world precisely (but not only) because it has failed to appreciate the importance of relations between states; and much less attention has been devoted to the possibility that while the critical theory of international relations must absorb the main strengths of realism and Marxism its development is ultimately a matter of their joint transcendence.

This issue has been explored more directly in contemporary sociology where current trends indicate a growing sympathy with the realist critique of Marxism. The context for this development is worth considering in some detail. There has not been the same need in sociology as in international relations to weaken any long-standing resistance to Marxism. In contrast, neither the contribution of Marxist sociology nor the merits of critical social theory has been in serious doubt. It has been generally agreed that Marxism seized the initiative in several areas of sociological inquiry, the most recent being the theory of the state. As a result, one strand of contemporary sociology has been less concerned with defending Marxism from its critics than with revealing its limitations as a critical theory of the modern world. The increased sympathy with realism is part of this trend. The higher profile which realist themes now possess in sociological theory does not reflect any weakening of commitment to the idea of a critical sociology. In fact, the emphasis on realism is linked with the argument that a modern critical theory must outflank Marxism from the "left".[17]

This development is connected with the role that Marxism has played in analysing the modern state. The renaissance of Marxist political theory in recent years has been centred on the theory of the state. The literature in this area has been part of a larger project of breaking with earlier forms of economistic and reductionist political analysis. The attempted break with the past gave rise to a literature which sought to explain the (relative) autonomy of the state. Most of the literature argued that the autonomy of the modern state was a consequence of the structural needs of the capitalist mode of production. Initially, the Marxist theory of the state failed to raise the question of whether the state's strategic role in the context of anarchy might be an equally, and even a more important, reason for the state's independence from domestic class forces. This point has been raised in criticism of Marxism in more recent sociological analysis of the state, and its importance has been conceded by a growing number of analysts in the Marxist tradition.[18] As a result, the success that Marxism has enjoyed in retrieving the state for modern social theory has begun to rebound upon it in the form of a "contemporary critique of historical materialism" which argues that Marxism has exhausted its potential and promise as a critical theory of society.

The contemporary critique of historical materialism has restated the realist critique of Marxist approaches which commented on international relations. It has been noted that Marx's analysis of the imminent development of world communism abstracted the logic of capitalist expansion from the logic of competition and conflict between sovereign states. It has been claimed that this problem was part of a more basic flaw in the Marxian theory of history: its assumption that a crucial element in the modern world - class conflict - had been the decisive form of struggle throughout human history as a whole. At the level of practice, this failure to recognise the historical importance of the state and war was reflected in a failure to analyse means of reducing the power of nationalism and the state. Having underestimated the importance of these phenomena, socialist states were unprepared for the process in which Marxism was fragmented by, and assimilated within, the system of states.[19]

The critique of Marxism in sociology therefore focuses upon the failure to recognise the significance of "geopolitical militarism".[20] All strands of the critical literature endorse realism to that extent. The more sophisticated approaches observe that the realist predilection for dealing with the states-system in isolation from other domains is as one-sided as the classical sociological account of society which failed to consider the impact of world political and economic forces upon social development. The upshot of this argument is that a contemporary critical sociology ought to explain the interaction between the multiple logics which have shaped the development of the modern world. In this discussion, particular emphasis is placed upon the relations between the growth of state power, strategic interaction, capitalist development and industrialisation.[21]

This argument concludes that realists and Marxists have analysed particular dimensions of the modern world which exponents of the other perspective have tended to overlook. Since neither perspective has developed a comprehensive account of modernity the question then becomes how to incorporate their most compelling observations within a more synoptic form of social and political analysis. The additional observation that neither perspective has offered a convincing prognosis for dealing with the manifold ills of the modern world - including the likely global consequences of continuing militarisation and industrialisation - is equally central to the argument for exploring the territory which lies beyond realism and Marxism.

The argument for moving beyond realism and Marxism has emerged in sociology and in the study of international relations. It has been argued in both areas that such a move is crucial for the development of an adequate critical account of the nature of the modern world. What has yet to be constructed is a critical theory which follows the spirit if not the letter of Marx's inquiry into capitalism - a critical theory, in other words, which identifies the prospects for realising higher levels of human freedom across world society as a whole.

Some observers may respond that this project is undermined by the primacy of strategic competition. They may argue that a critical sociology which endorses so much of realism must surrender any hope of realising any emancipatory objectives. It is worth noting that E. H. Carr's comments on the weaknesses of realism and idealism point towards a quite different conclusion. *The Twenty Years' Crisis* is renowned for its defence of realism. It was a powerful assault on the "naivety" and "exuberance" of classical idealism but it was also a warning against the "barrenness" and "sterility" of classical realism. Carr's method of resolving the antinomy between realism and idealism was set forth in a defence of national policy which aimed at the extension of moral obligation and the enlargement of political community.[22]

Various perspectives have used a similar theme. This point has been crucial in functionalist and neo-functionalist approaches to international cooperation, and it has been equally important in the Marxist tradition as succeeding chapters aim to show. However it will be argued in the present work that neither Marxism nor any other tradition of social and political thought possesses an adequate account of this dimension of historical experience. For this reason the present work accepts Habermas' call for a new "empirical philosophy of history" which recognises the significance of moral development and seeks to explain the main advances in the evolution of universal moral norms.[23] This mode of historical inquiry is part of a larger project which would, when complete, include a philosophical defence of the notion of universal emancipation and a practical inquiry into the measures which may be capable of advancing this ideal in the modern system of states. These are the main concerns of a critical international theory which endeavours to incorporate and yet to supersede the main achievements of realism and Marxism.

1 Power, Order and Emancipation in International Theory

Power, order and emancipation are the primary concerns of the three main traditions of international theory - the realist, rationalist and revolutionist perspectives. Realism maintains that the struggle for power and security is the dominant logic in world politics; rationalism places particular emphasis on the high level of order which states can achieve in the context of anarchy; and revolutionism contends that a "Cosmopolis" which will realise the moral potential of the species is already "immanent" within the international system of states.[1]

Martin Wight, who first described the history of international thought in these terms, argued that the "mutual tension and conflict" between these three schools of thought would continue to shape the evolution of international theory.[2] The revolutionist tradition - the perspective which most closely approximates the idea of a critical international theory - would therefore survive as a reminder of the moral imperfection of the system of states. It would ensure that the tension between ethics and politics would remain important in the theory and practice of international relations. Most works of international theory have reached the very different conclusion that revolutionism is a distraction from the central issues in world politics which concern the preservation of national security and the maintenance of order between sovereign states. The dominant realist and rationalist perspectives have been skeptical of the revolutionist's attempt to attain ethical and philosophical certainty, and they have added that while the goal of achieving universal harmony may be a noble aspiration, it is almost certainly an unattainable one.

Because of the influence of such criticisms revolutionism has been the least important of the three main traditions of international thought. In recent years, however, there has been a revival of the spirit - if not of the letter - of revolutionism. It has been argued that a critical approach to world politics which is interested in promoting human emancipation is superior to traditional perspectives which deal exclusively with order or power. The contemporary argument for a critical theory of international relations differs from the earlier defence of revolutionism in one major respect. The former does not start from the philosophical contention that there are immutable and universal moral principles of international relations which other perspectives have overlooked. The crucial point is that the critical project is based on a method which avoids the epistemological and methodological limitations of other modes of inquiry. By the terms of this argument, the only adequate theory of international relations is one which is committed to the emancipation of the human species.

The contemporary opposition between traditional and critical theories of international relations is reminiscent of earlier controversies in sociology. Furthermore, the modern case for a critical theory of international relations rests on crucial similarities between the main traditions of international thought and "the three sociologies": positivism, hermeneutics and critical sociology. It is important to consider these similarities in some detail.

Positivism emulates the method of the natural sciences. Its exponents employ what they regard as the more advanced methodological techniques of the natural sciences in their attempt to construct an equally rigorous science of society. The exponents of the second perspective, the hermeneutic tradition of sociology, are opposed to the proposition that the natural sciences are a worthy model for the study of society. They argue that social actors differ from the objects of natural-scientific investigation by virtue of their capacity to interpret their own actions and invest them with meaning. The hermeneutic approach insists therefore on the distinction between the cultural and the natural sciences. Critical social theory is distinguished from these perspectives by the supposition that human subjects possess a unique capacity to transform their social environment in the attempt to achieve a higher level of self-determination. A critical approach to society aims to determine how far social relations are a superfluous constraint upon the freedom of human subjects, and it seeks to understand how far the dominant culture is an impediment to human autonomy.[3]

Habermas has argued that each of these traditions of inquiry is predicated upon a particular "knowledge-constitutive interest". The positivist strand of sociology is constituted by a technical interest in increasing the control of social behaviour. Positivism therefore resembles the physical sciences which produce knowledge that enables human beings to acquire mastery of nature. The hermeneutic analysis of the values and meanings which structure human conduct reflects a practical interest in preserving social consensus. Critical social theory is possible because subjects have an interest in transcending the limits upon their capacity for self-determination. It is constituted by an emancipatory cognitive interest in understanding the possibility of freeing social actors from unnecessary constraints and from institutionalised forms of distorted thought and communication.[4]

One of the main developments of this line of argument suggests that positivism, hermeneutics and critical sociology form a dialectical sequence of approaches to society. Positivism emerged because of a growing confidence that human beings could acquire a level of self-understanding which would equal the knowledge which science gave them of nature. However it obscured the distinction between conscious action and unreflective behaviour which necessitates the division between the cultural and the natural sciences. The hermeneutic approach is a more advanced perspective because it stresses the cultural and linguistic dimensions of social behaviour. Its main shortcoming is the failure to search the cultural realm for evidence of distorted thought and communication. Critical theory surpasses both perspectives because its inquiry is oriented towards the realisation of truth and freedom. Its proponents do not deny that those working within other traditions are capable of making perfectly valid observations about the nature of society. They are more concerned to take issue with the philosophical foundations of other approaches and to contest the social purposes which their observations tend to promote.[5]

It has been argued that the idea of a dialectical sequence of approaches to sociology also applies to the three patterns of international theory. Richard Ashley has developed this argument in the following way. One branch of realism - technical realism - resembles positivism because it analyses the recurrent and repetitive patterns of international relations. The technical realist has a cognitive interest in understanding how far states can influence the constraints which most deeply affect their security and survival. A second kind of realism - practical realism - resembles hermeneutic sociology because it analyses the language and culture of diplomatic practice and the conventions which states obey as members of an international society. The practical realist has a cognitive interest in strengthening the consensual foundations of international order. Ashley argues that a third approach to international relations is present in Herz's argument that a series of interlocked crises may bring about the transformation of the modern international system. Herz's claim that a radically different form of world order may already be immanent within the existing states-system is, Ashley argues, reminiscent of the method of critical social theory. A cognitive interest in freedom and universalism underlies both analyses.[6]

The three dominant perspectives in international relations do not merely disagree about the empirical nature of world politics - they possess radically different conceptions of the nature of international theory and contrasting notions of the right relationship between theory and practice. The idea of a dialectical development of the three sociologies suggests one method of resolving the differences between realism, rationalism and revolutionism. It suggests that realism, rationalism and revolutionism (for which critical international theory will be substituted below) form a sequence of progressively more adequate approaches to world politics. If this is so, a theory which analyses the language and culture of diplomatic interaction in order to promote international consensus is an advance beyond a theory of recurrent forces constituted by an interest in manipulation and control. And an account of world politics which seeks to understand the prospects for extending the human capacity for self-determination is an even greater advance in this sequence of approaches. The remainder of this chapter defends this proposition by examining realism, rationalism and the critical theory of international relations in greater detail.

REALISM: FREEDOM AND NECESSITY

The idea that there is an inevitable antinomy between the moral principles which apply within the relatively secure world of the sovereign state and the political maxims which the state must respect if it is to protect itself from its adversaries recurs throughout the history of realist thought. It has been a major argument in Western political theory since Machiavelli's attack on Christian universalism. In the nineteenth century, German realists extended this perspective in their critique of the cosmopolitanism of the Enlightenment. They rejected the modern belief that universal moral obligations are embedded in the structure of the individual mind. The inevitability and desirability of maximum cultural diversity was the starting point for this strand of realist political theory. Earlier this century the crisis of idealism gave rise to a new genre of realist analysis which set the conventional argument about the inevitability of the tension between ethics and power within a more empirical or scientific discussion of world politics. Several commentators have argued that the most recent statements of realism are reminiscent of positivist sociology. They have emphasised the extent of the realist's commitment to a technical interest in determining what states can and cannot control. However the modern form of realism reiterates the traditional argument that any serious extension of moral and political community beyond the boundaries of the sovereign state is inconceivable in the context of anarchy.[7]

The crucial text in this regard is Kenneth Waltz's *Theory of International Politics.* For present purposes the most important aspects of that work are captured in the distinction between reductionist and systemic theories of international relations. The former, which include the Marxist theory of imperialism, contend that the international system can be explained by analysing the domestic organisation of its constitutive national parts. The reductionist assumes that foreign policy directly reflects internal factors such as the nature of the domestic regime, the dominant ideology, the mode of production, or other internal characteristics. Waltz argues that the historical evidence reveals that this alleged correspondence between domestic structures and the international system simply does not exist. Reductionism cannot explain this discrepancy between the diversity of regimes and the similarity of foreign policy approaches and outcomes. Waltz argues that an explanation of this phenomenon is bound to assume that systemic constraints are interposed between state structures and policy outcomes. It must posit the existence of systemic factors which thwart the state's efforts to translate its domestic ideological preferences into a distinctive programme of foreign policy. The nature of these "constraining conditions" is the main concern of the systemic theory of international politics.[8]

Waltz proceeds to argue that the specific properties of domestic political systems can be omitted from a systemic theory of international relations. He also claims that it is permissible to analyse the states-system in isolation from other world structures such as the international economic and legal systems which possess their own systemic properties. This decision to abstract the states-system is not based on the assumption that these "domains" exist in mutual isolation; nor does it imply that detailed studies of the foreign policy-making process of particular societies can ignore their complex interconnections. The abstraction of the states-system from these related domains is justified on the very specific grounds that the recurrent features of world politics are intelligible without them.[9]

According to Waltz, the differences between domestic and international politics are traceable to their contrasting principles of organisation. Domestic political systems are "hierarchic" as they are based upon relations of "super- and subordination". The international system is anarchic because no agency other than the state has the legal right to use violence. In hierarchic systems the state assumes responsibility for the protection of citizens. In an anarchic system, where there is no systematic provision of security, the operative principle is the principle of self-help.[10] This is the key to the unique and irreducible logic of strategic rivalry which realists regard as inevitable in the context of anarchy and which Herbert Butterfield captured so elegantly in his analysis of the "tragic" nature of international relations.[11] Under conditions of anarchy no state can escape the struggle to accumulate military power without running the risk of physical sanction. For each state the decision to accumulate the instruments of violence necessarily overrides any ambition of establishing a new form of world order which might institutionalise its highest moral aspirations, including any universalistic themes which are present in its ethical discourse. Accordingly, rational behaviour in the context of anarchy inevitably reproduces the very condition of distrust and insecurity which threatens all states.

To repeat, the decision to regard the states-system as "a domain apart" is a function of Waltz's principal aim of explaining the reproduction of the states-system. A theory of the reproduction of the states-system can ignore all of the state's characteristics apart from the level of military power at its disposal. The state's position in the international configuration of power is the sole consideration of the systemic approach. On this basis, a systemic approach can explain why states are forced to reproduce the condition of anarchy.

Waltz's critique of the liberal belief that interdependence would unify the human race illustrates the significance of the distinction between hierarchic and anarchic political systems. Within the comparative security of hierarchic systems, individuals have acquired specialised roles within a complex social division of labour. The liberal theorists of interdependence assumed that the same trend towards economic specialisation and social differentiation would occur in the realm of international relations and bring about a concomitant increase in the level of international consensus. This prophecy failed to realise that anarchy prevents the development of a complex international division of labour. In this context all states fear that interdependence will encroach upon their autonomy and provide them with an insufficient share of the economic benefits of international specialisation. Strategic considerations necessarily prevent compliance with liberal economic rationality. As a result, "national politics" comprise "differentiated units performing specialised functions", whereas international politics consist "of like units duplicating one another's activities".[12] States are not distinguished by their specialised roles but by their unequal ability to perform similar functions. The states-system is hierarchical only in the sense that inequalities of economic and military power inevitably exist.

This explanation of the "dismaying persistence" of the states-system, of "the striking sameness of international life for millennia", strengthens the foundations for the practical conclusions which Waltz reached in his earlier study of the causes of war.[13] The claim that a structure must be interposed between agents and outcomes reaffirms the case against the "second image" solution to international conflict. From the vantage-point of a systemic theory of international relations, the transformation of domestic structures must fail to have an impact upon the problem of war.[14] This analysis of the necessitous character of world politics also reaffirms the traditional realist critique of the emancipatory project which lies at the heart of the liberal and Marxist traditions. It is expressly committed to what Ashley calls the "impossibility theorem" which maintains that there is "no actual or immanent universal consensus that will or can for a long time satisfy the real and emerging needs of all states and peoples".[15] In this approach one may detect echoes of Burke's famous hostility to the radical temperament. Similarities are suggested by the realist argument that fragile international arrangements will be disturbed if states pursue normative aspirations without regard for the constraints of anarchy. Nevertheless, it would be a mistake to assume that Waltz's critique of liberalism and Marxism - the joint heirs of the Enlightenment - is basically amoral. Waltz argues that the international system is inhospitable to the aspirations of liberalism and Marxism, but he also maintains that states can exercise some control over their propensity to use violence by endeavouring to maintain strategic equilibrium between the major powers. Through the skilful operation of the balance of power it is possible for states to reduce, but not to abolish, the incidence of war. The balance of power is rational as long as there is no realistic alternative to the states-system. Moreover, to the extent that states comply with the principles of the balance of power they can enjoy a limited yet significant influence over the international-systemic forces around them.[16]

The conventional realist argument that strategic equilibrium is the most effective constraint on the state's propensity to use violence is preserved in Waltz's argument. Nevertheless, Ashley argues that Waltz's argument signifies the emergence of a new phase of realist thought. The term "neo-realism" is designed to emphasise the positivism of Waltz's approach and the centrality of its technically rational conception of foreign policy.[17] In this context, it is worth noting that the traditional realist argument that foreign policy ought to be concerned with promoting consensus between adversaries is marginal to Waltz's argument. Morgenthau's argument that an enlightened diplomacy ought to take account of the legitimate security interests of other states, and Kissinger's claim that the acceptance of equivalent levels of insecurity is a precondition of stability between the super-powers belong to a classical form of realism from which Waltz's approach must be distinguished.[18] There is an even greater break with that strand of realism which combined skepticism about the possibility of short-term international change with a defence of its longer term desirability. Two illustrations may suffice: E. H. Carr's argument that the sterility of realism could be overcome in a politics which aimed to extend political community, and Morgenthau's argument that the supersession of the sovereign state has become essential in the nuclear age.[19]

Waltz's argument is distinctive because it is chiefly concerned with providing an account of the reproduction of the international system and with revealing that no state can avoid engaging in the politics of manipulation and control. This systemic approach helps to explain important dimensions of world politics which no serious account of international relations can realistically ignore. Moreover, one of the most important developments in recent social theory concedes that most sociological accounts of the origins and development of the modern world have seriously underestimated the part that strategic interaction has played in frustrating the universalist potential which many nineteenth century theorists thought was inherent in modern European civilisation.[20] (Marx's thought is frequently cited as one of the clearest examples of this limited form of explanation.) But, as previously noted, mainstream international theory contains various arguments which suggest that Waltz's perspective is insufficient. These criticisms are developed more fully in the rationalist and revolutionist (or critical) theories of international relations.

Rationalism accepts the realist point that the struggle for power and security will continue while the international system remains anarchic. However it criticises realism for neglecting the extent to which relations between states are regulated by normative conventions. For this reason the rationalist tradition has been especially interested in analysing the origins and reproduction of the normative underpinnings of international order. It also contains a quite different account of the right relationship between theory and practice. While the realist argues that the state cannot opt out of the struggle to manipulate and control others under conditions of anarchy, the rationalist argues that states also have the choice of acting to strengthen or to weaken the normative principles which bind states in an international society. Rationalists suggest that an adequate theory of international relations must recognise the existence of an international community, while a properly-constructed foreign policy must attempt to ensure its preservation.

Although some realists and rationalists have argued for the transformation of world politics, most nevertheless emphasise the limited opportunities for significant reform. On these grounds, most members of these traditions have been dismissive of the revolutionist tradition. As noted above, several recent attempts to apply critical theory to international relations accept the realist's point that Marxism and critical sociology failed to recognise the importance of international systemic constraints.[21] From the perspective of critical theory, however, realism can only be true if the species is unfree. What realism offers is an account of historical circumstances which human subjects have yet to bring under their collective control. What it does not possess is an account of the modes of political intervention which would enable human beings to take control of their international history. That is the ultimate task facing the critical theory of international relations.

An inquiry into alternative forms of foreign policy behaviour cannot be divorced from the question of how to construct a post-realist analysis of international relations. Rationalism and the critical theory of world politics have a similar approach to this second problem. Both reject the method of analysing the states-system as if it were a domain apart. Both regard the abstraction of the states-system as a barrier to understanding one of the crucial dimensions of international relations: the universalisation of the basic principles of international order, and the universalisation of the demand for self-determination respectively. As for Waltz's realism, the problem is not that it fails as an account of the reproduction of the states-system, or that it errs by emphasising the need for a technically-rational dimension of foreign policy. The issue is whether the decision to abstract the states-system from other domains ignores the existence of actual or potential logics of system-modification which may strengthen the bonds of international community; and it is whether the preoccupation with systemic reproduction ends in a practice which suppresses the tendencies inherent in alternative logics. Consequently, although realism succeeds in explaining the necessitous character of international relations it fails to explicate its role in reproducing the power relations which it regards as the objective foundation for the "impossibility theorem".[22]

RATIONALISM: ORDER AND JUSTICE

Martin Wight's writings demonstrate that rationalism can incorporate the strengths of realism within a more comprehensive explanatory framework. Although Wight's rationalism stresses the importance of the struggle for power and security it maintains that a complete account of the propelling principles of world politics cannot focus on strategic competition alone.[23] Consequently, whereas the realist analyses the systemic constraints which are unique to the condition of international anarchy, the rationalist includes the normative principles which link states together in an "anarchical society". In its study of the normative dimensions of international relations rationalism therefore resembles the hermeneutic study of society.

The nature of its "knowledge-constitutive interest" reveals that this affinity runs even deeper. The rationalist perspective has an unmistakably practical cognitive interest in preserving legitimacy, consensus and order.[24] This practical interest is especially evident in recent considerations of the Third World's revolt against the West. Bull and Watson have argued that the emergence of a global states-system in which there are unaccustomed cultural differences and unparalleled inequalities of economic and military power has weakened the idea of a community of states. In this context it has become necessary to modify the principles of international relations which contributed to order in the European system.[25] At this point, it will be noted below, the rationalist tradition begins to converge with the critical theory of international relations.

The goal of explaining the high level of order which exists between political entities which are not subject to a higher authority pervades the entire rationalist exercise. The existence of international order suggests that it is unwise to make a sharp distinction between anarchic and hierarchic political systems. In each system there are mechanisms for solving the problem of order. Moreover, rationalism challenges the realist contention that an equilibrium of military power explains the reproduction of the international system. It is also important to recognise that for the most part states display a normative commitment to international order. The assumption that the states-system is legitimate explains international cooperation to check threats to the balance of power. The mechanisms for preserving international order presuppose the sovereignty of the state, but they include normative conventions which seek to control the exercise of sovereign power. As a result, international relations are characterised by frequent conflicts of national interest and by the prospect of generalised warfare, but there are counterbalancing normative constraints on sovereign states which resemble the moral conventions which operate in hierarchic systems.

In Wight's judgement, there have been three states-systems in the whole of human history - in Ancient China between 771 and 221 B.C., in the Hellenic and Hellenistic periods and now in the modern world.[26] This is the basis for Wight's claim that the study of international relations should attempt to develop a comparative sociology of states-systems.[27] The scope of the inquiry distinguishes this approach from realism. Whereas realism has principally been concerned with explaining the survival of the system of states, Wight's rationalist agenda referred to the need to explain the origins, reproduction and transformation of different states-systems. Wight foreshadowed the possibility that such an inquiry might uncover evidence of commonalities in all states-systems: of common patterns of international thought, of the gradual destruction of the weak and the concentration of power in fewer hands, of a common susceptibility to destruction because of inter-state war or as a result of conquest by a neighbouring empire.[28] But the inquiry was also designed to highlight the particular structures and beliefs which lent each system of states its individual identity.

One of the central problems raised by Wight is the question of how a states-system is possible. Wight argued that there was reason to suppose "that a states-system will not come into being without a degree of cultural unity among its members".[29] Each of the three examples of states-systems mentioned above developed within a common civilisation. In each case, consciousness of difference from, and superiority to, the external "uncivilised" world was highly developed. The existence of a common culture made it possible for states to determine their rights and duties as members of an international system. Hedley Bull argued that Wight's approach failed to distinguish international systems from international societies.[30] According to Bull's definition, independent political communities form a states-system if they have permanent international relations and if they confront the common danger of generalised war. For states to form an international society they must share an "intellectual and moral culture that determines the attitudes towards the states-system of those societies that compose it".[31] In opposition to Wight, Bull argued that order can exist between states which lack the sense of belonging to a common civilisation. However, on this argument, international order is more likely to develop and to survive if states share an "international political culture".[32]

Bull maintained that international order is made possible by the state's desire to protect certain primary goals.[33] In a formulation which is reminiscent of Hart's minimum concept of natural law, Bull argued that three primary goals are constitutive of social order at all times and places. These are the goal of ensuring respect for property, the need for conventions governing the use of force and the goal of preserving a sufficient level of confidence and trust. Order within society is made possible by the individual's desire to realise these central objectives. The importance of these objectives for nation-states explains order at the international level.[34]

In some respects international order is no different from any other political order, and in other respects it is unique. The absence of a higher sovereign power is the main feature which distinguishes "the anarchical society" from domestic social systems, acephalous societies excepted. As the contractarians once argued, it is possible for states to preserve order among themselves without surrendering their rights to a supreme sovereign body.[35] The uniqueness of international order is also manifested in the existence of primary goals which are peculiar to sovereign states. The principle which asserts that sovereignty is a precondition of membership of the international system, the conviction that the system of states is the only legitimate form of world political organisation (which explains collective action to prevent empire), the belief that the sovereignty of each state should be respected, and the desire to maintain peace are the most important of these goals.[36]

Because these goals may come into conflict with one another, states have developed a hierarchy of purposes. When states sacrifice the independence of a small power to preserve the balance of power they indicate that the preservation of the system as a whole has priority over the survival of every one of its parts. Peace is not superior to the goal of ensuring the survival of the states-system, although it may override the use of force to preserve the territorial integrity of any one state. This hierarchy of goals indicates that order, which depends upon the stability of great power relations, can conflict with justice, which demands that states and individuals should be treated equally in relevantly similar circumstances. The vulnerability of the weak is evidence that an antinomy between order and justice is inherent in international relations.[37]

To use Waltz's phraseology, rationalism is a systemic theory of international relations but one that shifts the emphasis from systemic forces to systemic principles. Moreover, its account of the normative principles of international relations avoids the ahistoricism of which neo-realism has been accused.[38] Wight's seminal essay on international legitimacy reveals further differences between the methods of rationalism and neo-realism.

There have been, according to Wight, three main epochs in the modern states-system. In its early history, the dynastic principle determined membership of the system and established the rights and duties of sovereign rulers. In the following period, the idea of national self-determination revolutionised the rules of membership with the result that the political boundaries of multinational states in Europe were substantially redrawn. In a third phase, which succeeded the struggle for decolonisation, Third World regimes defended the colonial frontiers against attempts to secede from the newly-independent states.[39] Applying this approach to more recent international relations, Bull referred to a fourth phase in which the dominance of the European principles of international relations has been challenged by the Third World, as the Islamic revival and the process of ethnic renewal clearly attest.[40]

A number of important methodological points are raised by this approach to historical periodisation. The most important are captured in Wight's question of whether rationalism should unite the domains which Waltz prefers to keep apart. In his essay on legitimacy, Wight defended the need to analyse the interconnections between domestic politics and international structures: "these principles of legitimacy mark the region of approximation between international and domestic politics. They are principles that prevail (or are at least proclaimed) within a majority of the states that form international society, as well as in relations between them."[41] To illustrate this point, Wight argued that the dynastic principle of international legitimacy expressed the aims and interests of the "European ruling class".[42] One further passage reveals that Wight doubted there was much value in abstracting the states-system from the wider domain: "A historical states-system may seem a tolerably clear or distinct kind of community, or set of relations and practices, when we study its internal life and organic life. But when we examine its penumbra, look at its connections with what lies beyond it etc., it begins to lose its coherence and identity, and doubts may arise about the validity of the concept itself of a states-system."[43] "International revolutions", which indicated that the usual vertical divisions between unitary states had been replaced by a horizontal schism between competing transnational factions, reinforced these doubts.[44] The existence of connections between "a series of organised movements for revolutionising, not simply a single state, but international society as a whole" revealed that international order was vulnerable to changes in the wider society of which the states-system was part.[45]

For Wight, then, the influence of domestic structures upon world politics is most vividly expressed in the dominant principles of international legitimacy. Since these principles link states together in a particular kind of society the states-system cannot be analysed as a field of physical forces.[46] Neither the decision to abstract the international states-system from neighbouring domains nor the supposition that states are "like units"[47] can be admitted within the rationalist account of international order. And as the phenomenon of international revolution further demonstrated, it is inappropriate to analyse the states-system, and the units of which it is composed, without giving consideration to social and political changes affecting human society as a whole. On an implicit level, Wight's approach suggested that the distinction between reductionist and systemic approaches obscured more than it revealed: it implied that a more profound understanding of world politics might result from their combination.

For a more recent discussion of legitimacy it is necessary to turn to

Bull's writings on the decline of society in the modern states-system. In his analysis of this trend, Bull developed his argument that although primary goals make international order possible, a general agreement about norms and values makes it more likely that order will be reproduced. With the global expansion of the states-system, the basis for such a consensus has, in Bull's judgement, clearly declined. Most new states stand outside the "international political culture" which underpinned the "diplomatic culture" of European international relations.[48] More importantly, many new state structures in the Third World have challenged principles of international relations which they regard as serving the dominant economic and political interests in the West or as embodying the West's continuing cultural hegemony. The challenge to the Western practice of regarding order as prior to justice exemplifies the mounting problem of legitimacy in contemporary international relations.[49]

This trend raises interesting questions for a perspective which maintains that domestic and international order are dependent not only on coercion but on consent. In his analysis of the "revolt against the West" Bull argued for new principles of legitimacy to mediate between the diverse cultural traditions and competing political perspectives which compound the problem of order in the first truly global states-system. He argued that if global consensus was to be reconstituted, then the cultural bias of Western diplomatic practices would have to be removed, and a "radical redistribution" of wealth would have to occur to correct unprecedented inequalities of power and wealth.[50] Bull added that the task of restoring legitimacy has been eased by the emerging "cosmopolitan culture of modernity, to which the leading elements of all contemporary societies belong even if the masses of people often do not".[51] But its regeneration is made more difficult by the radicalisation of regimes in some parts of the Third World, and by the fact that the demand for the redistribution of wealth is also a demand for the redistribution of military power.[52]

The rise of the Third World invited the question of whether the antinomy between order and justice might be overcome with the emergence of new principles of international legitimacy. In some places, Bull seemed to suggest that this antinomy had become a basic contradiction of modern international relations. In short, the international order could not be legitimate, as far as new states were concerned, unless there was progress in the sphere of international economic justice; but, as the traditional theory and practice contended, international order might be impossible to manage if the hierarchy of military power was overturned.[53] In a later formulation, Bull maintained that some solutions to the antinomy between order and justice are already in place: "A new international political order, in which the interests of the non-Western majority of states and peoples are reflected, is already in some measure constructed".[54] Moreover, when Bull returned to the problem of order and justice in his last writings, he denied that there was any necessary contradiction between them: "The inclination of the liberal (is) to refuse to accept that order and justice in international relations are necessarily at loggerheads with one another, and to seek ways of reconciling the one with the other. The liberal prefers to believe that order in international

relations is best preserved by meeting demands for justice, and that
justice is best realised in the context of order. He seeks to show that
the requirements of order and of justice in international relations are in
practice the same: that e.g. the measures that are necessary to achieve
justice for the peoples of the Third World are the same measures that
will maximise the prospects of international order or stability, at least in
the long run."[55]

Bull argued that the conflict between North and South had the
potential to generate changes which would reduce the tension between
order and justice in international relations. However, the demand for
international social justice was, according to Bull, only one of several
dynamics which could bring this resolution about. The demand for the
international protection of human rights made it essential to qualify the
principle that sovereign states are the main bearers of international legal
rights. A series of interlocked problems including new threats to
international security, the problem of diminishing resources and threats to
the physical environment made it timely to consider whether the classical
idea of sovereignty should give way to a more internationalist perspective
in which states are perceived as "local agents of a world common
good".[56] These issues made it necessary to reconsider the answer given to
a question posed in the earlier writings: whether it had become essential
to "liberate thought and action" from "the tyranny of concepts and
normative principles" which are constitutive of the sovereign state and
international order; and whether the international theorist had an
obligation to proclaim "new concepts" which would "give shape and
direction to the trends" running counter to the existing order.[57]

These remarks invested Bull's earlier comment that "alternative forms
of universal political organisation have not received the attention that
their historical importance warrants"[58] with new meaning. For the most
part, it will be recalled, the rationalist tradition has been concerned with
analysing the preconditions of international order rather than with
defining the principles of a just world system. Bull's main writings on
this subject concluded that order was prior to justice. To some extent,
this argument rested on the empirical observation that states are able to
agree on the need for order despite their competing views of justice. But
Bull also invoked the skeptic's argument that there are no grounds for
thinking that any one version of justice is more valid than any other.[59]
When he returned to these issues in his last writings, Bull maintained
that international order was increasingly dependent on justice: for states
and for individuals. It is arguable that this was a conditional defence of
justice which presumed that order would be strengthened as a result. But
it can also be argued that the muted defence of justice which existed in
earlier writings is more strident in the later writings, and that
rationalism came nearer as a result to considering the rights and duties
which might underpin a different form of universal political
organisation.[60]

If this is so, the later version of rationalism may be regarded as a
bridge between realism and the critical theory of international relations.
The realist argument that the struggle for power is inevitable in the
context of anarchy is also stressed within the rationalist tradition. It is

incorporated, however, within a specific investigation of the bases of international order. On a related front, rationalism highlights the state's practical commitment to consensus and order without underestimating the importance of its technical interest in power and control. In this context, rationalism maintains that international order is unlikely to survive unless certain norms are regarded as universally binding and unless governments increase their commitment to developing a community of states. Traditionally, its exponents have been skeptical of the revolutionist argument that the study of international relations should be committed to realising universally valid norms. It is unclear whether Bull's later writings ought to be regarded as a retreat from the philosophical skepticism present in his earlier work. What is clear is that the commitment to the extension of community reduces the distance between rationalism and revolutionism which was present in Bull's earlier writings. This creates new theoretical possibilities which have been considered more fully by critical approaches to international relations.

REVOLUTIONISM AND CRITICAL SOCIAL THEORY

Wight argued that revolutionism was distinguished from other patterns of international thought by its commitment to the abolition of the international states-system. Revolutionists invoked the "ideal unity of international society" to condemn the passing "empirical divisions" between sovereign states.[61] What is more, they denied that conflict between nation-states was the fundamental conflict in the world system. This role belonged to the "horizontal conflict of ideology that cuts across the boundaries of states and divides human society into two camps - the trustees of the immanent community and those who stand in its way".[62] Wight and Bull, who also characterised revolutionism in these terms, accepted part of this moral critique of the states-system. However they disagreed with revolutionism on two grounds. In the first place, they argued that its moral absolutism was linked with violence and fanaticism; and secondly, they claimed that the notion of the primacy of horizontal conflict threatened to undermine the fragile diplomatic practices which made international order possible. In their view, the limited progress that is possible in international relations cannot occur unless mechanisms for limiting inter-state conflict are securely in place.[63]

Kant's revolutionist perspective recognised the force of this point. There is no doubt that Kant believed that human subjects had an obligation to remake their social world in the image of the categorical imperative. However, the experience of the French revolution persuaded Kant that a politics of human emancipation should seek to release the universal potential that was latent in existing international institutions rather than to destroy the achievements of the past. The Kantian political project took account of the way in which the struggle for power constrained the development of moral freedom. In addition, it sought to uncover any evidence that the categorical imperative might become essential for the maintenance of international order. Kant regarded the mounting economic and political crisis of the European states-system as the probable driving force behind the emergence of an international community of autonomous moral subjects which would eventually be valued in its own right.[64] For these reasons, Kant's theory of international relations embraced the themes of power, order and emancipation.

Marx's thought may seem to be a better example of revolutionism. It aimed to deepen the horizontal divisions in world society and it regarded international revolution - and violence in certain circumstances - as the means to socialism. However there are more important dimensions to Marx's political theory. Unlike the Kantian project, Marx did not argue that change was necessary so that human society would at last comply with permanently true moral propositions. The aim of social theory and political revolution was the realisation of the higher society which was already developing within the existing world.[65] It is arguable that the concept of revolutionism does more to obscure than to explain this method of inquiry. Critical theory is the appropriate term to use to describe this mode of social and political inquiry.

The nature of the approach is best explained by considering the political theory of the Frankfurt School.[66] Members of the Frankfurt School sought to recover the classical Greek idea that human reason is an instrument of enlightenment and emancipation. Their approach was deeply influenced by Marx's argument that "men make their history, but they do make it just as they please; they do not make it under circumstances chosen by themselves, but under circumstances directly encountered, given, and transmitted from the past".[67] On this basis, the Frankfurt School accepted Marx's contention that social theory is a critical activity which can help to liberate human beings from the alienating social and political institutions created by the "dead generations". They offered a "defence of subjectivity" in the face of the "objective, law-governed process of history";[68] and they called for a political project to construct a society in which the whole species would "for the first time be a conscious subject and actively determine its own way of life".[69]

The Frankfurt School argued that all human powers - including the ability to reason - have a history. It opposed the natural law perspective on the grounds that political theory can no longer presume "the natural, authentic, or essential actions and institutions of a human race constant in its essential nature; instead, theory now deals with the objective, overall complex of development of a human species which produces itself, which is as yet only destined to attain its essence: humanity".[70] Although it rejected the idea of permanent moral truths, it did not abandon the notion that the aim of social theory is the realisation of the good life. Its concept of historical development led to the conclusion that the process of realising the "rational life" is "stretched out along the vertical axis of world-history".[71]

According to the Frankfurt School, the social theorist cannot criticise social relations or suggest future possibilities by contemplating permanent moral truths. The alternative is to engage in a sociological analysis of actual or potential conflicts which may give rise to a society in which there is a higher level of autonomy. In executing this project, members of the Frankfurt School were specifically concerned with the historical possibilities foreshadowed by the dominant ideology. They argued that the tension between social relations and higher possibilities secreted within the dominant ideology enabled the critical theorist to compare "the existent in its historic context, with the claim of its conceptual principles, in order to criticise the relation between the two and thus transcend them".[72] The important point here is that "again and again in history, ideas have cast off their swaddling clothes and struck out against the social system that bore them. The cause, in large degree, is that spirit, language and all the realms of the mind necessarily stake universal claims...Thus originates the contradiction between the existent and ideology, a contradiction that spurs all historical process".[73] This formulation reiterated Marx's claim that the critical theorist does "not anticipate the world dogmatically, but rather wish(es) to find the new through criticism of the old".[74] The critical theorist therefore employed the method of immanent rather than ethical critique.

This defence of critical social theory was developed in opposition to the growing influence of positivist sociology. The Frankfurt School rejected the latter's claim that statements were either empirical and open to scientific forms of scrutiny or normative and subjective in kind. The notion of immanent social criticism was in conflict with the notion that science is the sole determinant of truth. However this was not the worst consequence of regarding the natural sciences as a model for sociology. Horkheimer maintained that the positivist's repudiation of the classical quest for the good society effectively abandoned individuals to their fate: "reason has never really directed social reality, but now reason...has finally renounced even the task of passing judgment on man's actions and way of life. Reason has turned them over for ultimate sanction to the conflicting interests to which our world seems actually abandoned".[75] Not only did positivists abandon a critical and emancipatory approach to social inquiry: by raising the level of understanding of the most economic and efficient means of realising political ends, positivism revolutionised the state's ability to administer society. Classical political philosophy had attempted to establish the possibility of a rational consensus between free and equal citizens; the positivist conception of sociology with its exclusive concern with technical rationality reduced reason to an "instrument...completely harnessed to the social process" of control and administration.[76] Positivism brought increasingly compliant individuals under the complete dominion of technical rationality.

Marxism was the target of similar criticisms because it became a quasi-science of the iron laws of historical development. Along with Lukacs, Gramsci and Korsch, the members of the Frankfurt School recovered the Hegelian emphasis upon the part that active and conscious subjects played in the unfolding of history. In this way, one of the main themes in Marx's critique of classical materialism was turned against the prevailing Marxist belief that the inexorable laws of capitalist development made the triumph of socialism inevitable.[77] The Frankfurt School emphasised the need for a revolutionary mass movement which was free from the distortions of the dominant bourgeois culture. Their analysis of the effects of technical rationality on the politics of capitalist societies was designed to highlight one such constraint upon the transition to socialism. But as the prospect of socialism receded, the Frankfurt School made the further observation that the potential for revolution had been thwarted by the embourgoisement and nationalisation of working class culture. In the 1930s, the Frankfurt School rejected the claim that Marxism provided unique insights into the nature of historical change. And in the same period, its cultural pessimism led to the conclusion that an emancipatory politics might be an impossibility.[78]

The contention that official Marxism simply developed the "latent positivism" of Marx's theory of history need not detain us here.[79] In a related criticism the Frankfurt School argued that the Marxian emancipatory project had its own potential to generate structures of oppression and domination. This criticism was directed at Marx's belief that capitalism had so revolutionised the forces of production that it was possible to construct a society in which individuals would be free to develop the powers which were unique to their species. The Frankfurt School maintained that Marx's technological optimism overlooked the possibility that the mechanisms for dominating nature could just as easily be employed by the state to crush human subjectivity. In a commentary upon the negative dialectic of politics and technology in the modern world, Adorno foresaw the realisation of the Weberian iron cage in which the "social engineers" would administer the lives of the "inmates of closed institutions."[80] As a theory of human emancipation, Marxism had failed to realise that domination was inherent in the project of modernity. A naive confidence in the emancipatory potential of science and technology had blinded Marxists to the prospect of total domination, to the possibilities which had come to light in Nazi Germany and in the Soviet Union.

In light of these arguments, it is unsurprising that at one stage the Frankfurt School argued for "a movement to a new problematic, in the tradition of Marx and his spirit, but not of his word";[81] nor is it surprising that it concluded that "Marx's social theories are phases through which thought has to pass, as it had to pass through Nietzsche and Kant".[82] To develop the implications of the argument that critical theory could no longer be "simply Marxist",[83] the Frankfurt School would have had to engage in an immanent critique of Marxism which cancelled its weaknesses while preserving its strengths. It would have had to consider the forms of oppression (sexual, racial, national etc.) which are affected by, but not reducible to, class domination. A post-Marxist critical theory would have had to construct a broader vision of the meaning and preconditions of emancipation; and it would have required an analysis of social movements which could complement the proletariat's struggle for freedom and equality in the sphere of production.[84] The Frankfurt School did not undertake this project. Having relinquished its faith in the proletariat's power of historical redemption, and having lost confidence in the emancipatory potential of modern society, the Frankfurt School turned to theoretical concerns which were tenuously linked with the project of emancipation.

The Frankfurt School's bleak interpretation of international relations was part of the explanation for this retreat from practice. Horkheimer argued that Marx's vision of the society of the future, in which history would at last be the product of a "unified, self-conscious will", totally neglected the constraining role of warfare.[85] Other thinkers had possessed a deeper insight into the conflicts which troubled the modern age. Schopenhauer had foreseen the intensity with which the "struggle between the great national power blocs" and the "ruthless competition among nations" would be conducted.[86] Adorno maintained that Spengler had identified the central logic of the modern world by predicting the "coming of the professional military corps of the embattled states...(and) the rise of war as the universal experience of the coming time, encompassing continents and beyond the will of man to control".[87] In a reference to the tarnished notion of historical progress, Adorno observed that: "No universal history leads from Savagery to Humanity, but there is certainly one leading from the stone catapult to the megabomb".[88] The absence of an historical subject with the power to arrest this course of development undoubtedly reinforced the Frankfurt School's pessimism. As Marcuse later observed, the gulf between the "ought" of critical theory and the "is" of the actual world was the product of an "unfree world" which lacked the contradictions necessary for historical development.[89] Horkheimer referred to "a universal feeling of fear and disillusionment" as the gap between theory and practice steadily widened.[90]

The Frankfurt School abandoned Marxism without establishing the basis for an alternative form of critical social theory. By contrast, the leading figure in the "second generation" of the Frankfurt School, Jurgen Habermas, has sought not only to recover critical theory but to do so within the Marxist tradition.[91] Habermas has criticised mainstream social science for its failure to theorise "ideologically frozen relations of dependence that can in principle be transformed".[92] But he has added that historical materialism must be reconstructed in order to "attain...the goal it...set for itself": the goal of universal emancipation.[93] The project of reconstruction must proceed on the understanding that contemporary social theory no longer addresses a "clearly circumscribed social group which could be singled out as the representative of a general interest that has been violated" (for example, the proletariat).[94] At a deeper level it must diminish the part that capital accumulation played in classical Marxism; and more deeply still, it must correct Marx's understanding of the nature of human development.

Marx regarded the struggle to control nature as the key to the evolution of the species. Habermas distinguishes between "labour" and "interaction" in order to draw attention to the part that language and culture have played in the formation and development of human society.[95] For Habermas, a modern philosophical history must be as interested in the moral development of the species as Marx was in its progress towards the conquest of nature. This process of moral development is frequently the main "pacemaker of social evolution".[96]

Habermas' critique of Marx may seem to revive the Hegelian contention that history is the development of more rational forms of consciousness. In fact, Habermas argues that the logic which runs through the evolution of moral thought does not explain the appearance of higher normative structures in specific societies. The institutionalisation, if not the evolution, of more advanced normative standards occurred because of their capacity to overcome "steering crises" which threaten the continued stability of social systems.[97] This formulation is designed to avoid the problems encountered in idealist and materialist interpretations of history.

Habermas argues that the critical theorist must address the species as a whole rather than the specific concerns of the international proletariat.[98] This position stems in part from Habermas' controversial argument that the possibility of a universal moral consensus is inherent in the structure of human language.[99] An additional influence is Kohlberg's analysis of the key stages in the development of the individual's moral capacities.[100] Habermas argues that a reconstructed historical materialism must explain the evolution from the earliest customary and particularistic moralities to modern ethical systems which assert the importance of the rationality and autonomy of all human subjects. The emancipatory project in this context must seek to extend the realm of social interaction which is governed by universalisable moral principles.

The important question is whether these moral principles are likely to be expressed in a new form of world political organisation. In a tentative answer to this question, Habermas restates the Marxian claim that capitalism is responsible for drawing all societies into a single stream of universal history.[101] In the modern world the great majority of human beings have become aware of the interdependence of the species. They are also aware of their inability to control the forces which have brought this condition about. In a concurrent development, modern citizens now possess a divided moral identity. On the one hand, they have rights and duties as citizens of particular sovereign states; on the other hand, they are human beings with a morality which is better "suited to the identity of world citizens" than to the "citizens of a state that has to maintain itself against other states".[102] Habermas argues that a series of interconnected global crises may ensure that the notion of membership of the species will make further inroads into the sense of loyalty to the sovereign state. Among these crises Habermas includes the problem of managing an international economic system while states continue to justify their actions by particularistic criteria, the increasing threats to the ecological system and the threat which modern instruments of violence pose to the survival of the species.[103] As a result, "for the first time a situation has come to pass which...has made the entire world a theme of political decisions".[104] In this context, "Kant's sketch of a cosmopolitan order no longer concretises the moral-philosophical postulates for improving the world; under present conditions it defines, rather, theoretically ascertainable chances of survival for the world as a whole".[105] Habermas further observes that the idea of the unity of the species - one of the major "presuppositions of the philosophy of history" - has not "become invalid" in the twentieth century; indeed, "it is only today that (it) has become true".[106]

Habermas argues that the critical theorist ought to defend the ideal of the unity of the species, although there is no guarantee that its unification will ever come about. Emerging global problems or crises may generate new historical subjects, but at present there is no single movement or organisation with the ability to promote universal moral principles in practice. Nevertheless, by identifying the conditions which may engender universalistic social movements, Habermas has shown how a contemporary critical theory can overcome the impasse which led Horkheimer and Adorno to abandon the emancipatory project.

It is interesting that Habermas' method of recovering critical theory should focus upon the same global problems and crises which Bull cited in his argument for new principles of international legitimacy. This suggests one way in which social theory and the study of international relations might be combined to produce a more comprehensive account of society and politics. It is true that different accounts of social theory underpin Bull and Habermas' belief that it has become necessary to move beyond the principle of state sovereignty. It may be equally true that the emancipatory intent of Habermas critical sociology is superior to the practical interest which underlies Bull's hermeneutic mode of inquiry. Nevertheless, they have a similar view of how the international system is changing, and a similar belief in the importance of understanding language, culture and morality. This raises the question of how far critical theory and the classical approaches to international relations can contribute to one another's development.

THE CRITICAL TURN IN INTERNATIONAL THEORY

Critical theory became increasingly important in the 1960s and 1970s as traditional forms of sociology came under attack. Its advocates called for the adoption of new rules of sociological inquiry although they did not challenge the orthodox view that the aim of sociology is to understand social interaction within the realm of the sovereign state. The contention that sociology must now deal with international relations is an important dimension of more recent arguments for critical social theory. To date, perhaps unsurprisingly, there has been little progress in deciding how a politics of universal emancipation might make inroads into the divisions between sovereign states. But an impressive start has been made towards incorporating elements of realism and Marxism within a critical perspective.

By comparison, the discovery of critical theory in the study of international relations has been quite recent. In the latter field, more so than in sociology, it has been necessary to begin by breaking down the resistance to radical, idealist or critical modes of inquiry. As a result, much of the literature has been concerned with exposing the methodological limitations of classical approaches. There has been one major attempt to show how critical theory can be used in the development of a post-realist analysis of international relations, namely Robert Cox's approach to world politics which relies on historical materialism to analyse alternative paths of historical development and to assess the prospects for a politics of universal emancipation.[107]

The recent critical turn in international theory has been profoundly influenced by the Frankfurt School's critique of mainstream sociology. Its importance is exemplified by Cox's distinction between "problem-solving" and "critical" theories of international relations. The former "takes the world as it finds it, with the prevailing social and political relations and the institutions into which they are organised, as the given framework for action. The general aim of problem-solving theory is to make these relationships and institutions work smoothly by dealing effectively with particular sources of trouble". A critical perspective "stands apart from the prevailing order of the world and asks how that order came about. Critical theory, unlike problem-solving theory, does not take institutions and social and power relations for granted but calls them into question by concerning itself with their origins and how and whether they might be in the process of changing. It is directed towards an appraisal of the very framework of action...which problem-solving theory accepts as its parameters".[108]

Whereas problem-solving theory is "a guide to tactical actions which, intended or unintended, sustain the existing order", critical theory provides "a guide to strategic actions for bringing about an alternative order".[109] Its method of immanent as opposed to ethical critique supersedes the dichotomy between realism and idealism: "Critical theory allows for a normative choice in favour of a social and political order different from the prevailing order, but it limits the range of choice to alternative orders which are feasible transformations of the existing world. A principal objective of critical theory, therefore, is to clarify this range of possible alternatives. Critical theory thus contains an element of utopianism in the sense that it can represent a coherent picture of an alternative order, but its utopianism is constrained by its comprehension of historical processes. It must reject improbable alternatives just as it rejects the permanency of the existing order".[110]

These arguments against problem-solving approaches resemble the Frankfurt School's attack on positivism. The former are also accused of betraying the classical ideals of rationality and autonomy. They are found guilty of abandoning the analysis of the higher possibilities which are immanent within the modern world. Despite their protestations of value-neutrality, the exponents of problem-solving approaches are said to be guilty of reinforcing the status quo. On the assumption that the states-system will survive indefinitely, they focus on expediency in foreign policy and on the maintenance of strategic equilibrium between the major powers. They recommend forms of political action which serve "particular national, sectional or class interests which are comfortable with the given order".[111]

Cox argues that a critical sociology of world politics must explore the possibility that actors are capable of moving beyond conventional strategies for preserving national security and international order. For this purpose, he rejects the realist decision to abstract the states-system from domestic social forces and from the process of global social and economic change more generally. Cox's argument for a "broadening of our enquiry beyond conventional international relations" theory in order to explain the linkages between domestic social forces, state structures and principles of world politics shares some of the features of Wight sociology of international legitimacy.[112] However, Cox's approach differs from Wight's study of legitimacy in two respects: by using the method of historical materialism to explain the connections between domestic and international politics, and by employing Gramsci's concept of hegemony to reveal that the central principles of international relations not only serve the most powerful economic and political interests in the dominant states but provoke, in turn, the principal forms of opposition and conflict.

Cox's main argument is that historical materialism can "correct" realism in "four important respects". In the first place, whereas conventional approaches to international relations maintain that conflict is an agent of the reproduction of the international system, historical materialism regards conflict as the stimulus to historical development. Secondly, historical materialism adds the vertical axis of dominance and dependence, encompassing states, classes, economic sectors and geographical areas, to "the horizontal dimension of rivalry among the most powerful states" which is analysed by orthodox international theorists. Thirdly, whereas realism assumes that states enjoy considerable autonomy from domestic social forces, historical materialism emphasises the impact of class structure on the state's organisation and behaviour. A materialist perspective concludes that the international system is best understood as a "combination of state/society complexes", and not as an aggregate of "like units". Finally, historical materialism begins with the production process in order to understand how the most powerful interests in the leading state/society complexes convert their power into hegemony at the international level. An analysis of the "connections between power in production, power in the state and power in international relations" can explain the main constraints upon the objectives of critical theory. By analysing "dialectical possibilities of change in the sphere of production which could affect the other spheres, such as those of the state and world order", this method also seeks to identify the possible sources of international social and political change.[113]

Cox offers two historical illustrations of this approach. The first concerns the demise of the liberal international economic system in the late nineteenth century. The constitutive principles of that order were established in the age of laissez-faire capitalism when British military supremacy was at its height and when British commercial interests reigned supreme. The dominant ideology in the period of British hegemony came under challenge as new state/society complexes emerged throughout the advanced capitalist world. In response to the demands of the organised working class, states began to assume responsibility for social welfare. They also turned to protectionism to cushion their populations from the harmful effects of international competition. These powers challenged the free trade principle on the grounds that it preserved Britain's dominance vis-a-vis the industrialising states. This marked the beginning of an intensely nationalistic phase of international relations characterised by the grab for overseas colonies, increasing economic and political rivalries and the gradual drift towards war.[114]

In a second illustration, Cox discusses the rise of nationalist and socialist forces in the Third World and their resultant challenge to the contemporary international economic system. These forces have argued that peripheral development is frustrated by international economic institutions which are biased towards the liberal ideological preferences of the core. They have maintained that transnational alliances which link "the imperial state" and multinational capital with dependent state structures and the peripheral bourgeoisie have imprisoned the periphery in an exploitative international division of labour. Many are critical of peripheral elites because they expose the labour force to the economic exploitation and social dislocation which accompanies the global expansion of capitalism. But the principal aim of some of these elites has been to articulate a rival vision of world order which demands international action to promote peripheral development. What has emerged is "a counter-hegemony based on a Third World coalition against core country dominance and aiming towards the autonomous development of peripheral countries and the termination of the core-peripheral relationship". Cox claims that the possibility of a counter-hegemonic challenge "lies very largely in the future development of state structures in the Third World".[115]

However Cox adds that success is somewhat remote.[116] The counter-hegemonic challenge which exists in the demand for a New International Economic Order "lacks a sufficiently clear view of an alternative world political economy" to pose a serious threat to the international status quo.[117] In addition, the option of unilateral as opposed to collective advancement may be so tempting, and the core's power of co-option so powerful, that anti-systemic forces may be unable to flourish. Nevertheless, it is the task of critical theory to identify "the emergence of rival structures expressing alternative possibilities of development".[118] As a result, the impact of the internationalisation of production upon peripheral state structures is as important to contemporary critical theory as conflict between states is to realism.

As previously noted, the opposition to the vertical axis of global dominance and dependence may be too weak to change the international system. Even so, there are other possible sources of the demand for reform. Cox observes that the dominance of super-power rivalry in the 1950s and 1960s favoured problem-solving theories, whereas the 1970s engendered "a sense of greater fluidity in power relationships, of a many-faceted crisis, crossing the threshold of uncertainty and opening the opportunity for a new development of critical theory directed to the problems of world order".[119] There is substantial agreement among different schools of thought as diverse as rationalism and the Frankfurt School that this "many-faceted crisis" is the result of several developments including the problem of legitimation in core-peripheral relations, the destruction of nature by the process of industrialisation and the specific threat which the modern instruments of violence pose to the survival of the species and to the physical environment.

It is instructive to compare Cox's argument that historical materialism provides the foundations on which to build a critical theory of international relations with Giddens' claim that a modern critical theory must be post-Marxist. What is interesting about this second approach is the contention that orthodox approaches to international relations correct Marxism. Giddens argues that Marxist and non-Marxist approaches to sociology are both victims of the high level of international order which existed in the middle of the nineteenth century. All of these approaches agreed that the new industrial order would produce strong international loyalties which would replace war and conflict with collaboration and harmony. Notwithstanding their internal differences, all accepted the idea of the inevitability of human progress.[120]

Giddens argues that Marxism and the classical sociological tradition relied upon an "unfolding model of social change"[121] which led to an inadequate explanation of the development of the modern world. More specifically, the failure of Marxism was its assumption that the process of capitalist development was the dominant logic in modern times. Marx and Marxism failed to distinguish between the evils of capitalism and the harmful effects of the industrial exploitation of nature. Marxism greatly underestimated the dangers inherent in the state's increasing capacity to monitor and control the lives of citizens. But most important of all, Marxism did not foresee the survival of the struggle between nation-states and the unprecedented development of the instruments of physical violence.[122]

The upshot of Giddens' argument is that Marxism can no longer justify the claim that it is a privileged guide to an emancipatory politics. The observation that the revolutionary proletariat is the historical subject which will dismantle the complete range of constraints upon human autonomy is incompatible with the notion that the modern world is governed by multiple logics. In fact, Giddens goes on to argue, each logic engenders a separate political arena with its own distinctive reformist social movement. Capitalism continues to give rise to class conflict; industrialisation generates ecological movements which contest modern attitudes to the exploitation of nature; the increase in state surveillance is the reason for the appearance of movements which are committed to the protection of civil liberties; and the danger of nuclear war has brought about a resurgence of peace movements. In this context, Giddens argues for a "post-Marxist" critical theory which breaks with the supposition that an emancipatory politics is mainly concerned with the transition from capitalism to socialism.[123]

Now Cox does not dispute the proposition that great power rivalry is a central dimension of international relations.[124] What he is especially keen to challenge is the realist's exclusive preoccupation with this realm and the attendant belief that international theory is solely concerned with the matter of problem-solving. Yet Cox proceeds to discuss the merits of historical materialism without discussing its apparent vulnerability to realism. By contrast, Giddens' argument for a post-Marxist critical theory places special emphasis on the enduring threat of violence in international relations and the continuing danger of nuclear war. Although Giddens argues that socialist planning on a global scale remains relevant in an increasingly unequal world economy, he adds that it is clearly no solution to the threat of nuclear war. Arms control and detente between the super-powers are deemed to be more realistic interim strategies for diminishing the dangers of conflict and war.[125] On one level, Giddens argues that the strengths of realism and Marxism ought to be incorporated within a sociology of the modern world. And as a consequence of this he concludes that strategies which are usually associated with realist or rationalist approaches to world order ought to be preserved within a post-Marxist critical theory which considers the realm of inter-state relations.

The proposition that the idea of a dialectical development of the three sociologies can be applied to theoretical debates in international relations is worth returning to at this point. One of the central parts of this argument stated that the achievements of positivism and hermeneutics ought to be incorporated within a critical theory of society. By implication, the attempt to construct a critical theory of international relations ought to preserve the main strengths of the realist and rationalist traditions. As a result, it should be concerned, firstly, with understanding how the struggle for power and security constrains progress in international relations; secondly, with analysing the way in which the states' competition for power and security is moderated by their commitment to international order; and, thirdly, given the continuing power of nationalism and the state, with identifying any actual or conceivable developments which may strengthen the bonds of international community.

These theoretical disagreements with Marxism generate major differences at the practical level. It is necessary to conclude that a post-Marxist critical theory of international relations must concede that technical and practical orientations to foreign policy are inescapable at least at this juncture. Such an approach must appreciate the need for classical realist methods of protecting the state under conditions of insecurity and distrust, and recognise the importance of the rationalist defence of order and legitimacy in the context of anarchy. It is important to take account of the rationalist claim that order is unlikely to survive if the major powers cannot reconcile their different national security interests. In a similar vein, a critical approach to international relations is obliged to conclude that the project of emancipation will not make significant progress if international order is in decline. One of its principal tasks would then be to understand how the community of states can be expanded so that it approximates a condition which maximises the importance of freedom and universality. In this case, a critical theory of international relations which recognises the strengths of realism and Marxism must aim for a political practice which deals concurrently with the problem of power, the need for order and the possibility of emancipation through the extension of human community.

CONCLUSION

This chapter has argued that realism, rationalism and the critical theory of world politics form a dialectical sequence of patterns of international thought. Each of these perspectives contributes to the sequence in a distinctive way. Realism provides an explanation of the reproduction of the system of states, and it accounts for the state's technically-rational orientation to foreign policy. On the more obviously normative front, realists argue that the state's resort to the politics of manipulation and control is rational in the context of international anarchy.

Rationalism supports each of these claims while concluding that realism offers no more than a partial account of international society. The former incorporates what is true in realism inside its distinctive project of understanding the legal and moral conventions which make international order possible. It differs from realism by arguing that a sociology of international legitimacy must analyse the interplay between domestic and international structures. Moreover, the rationalist interpretation of international society is distinctive because of its practical interest in strengthening the bases of international order. In contrast with earlier formulations which emphasised the tension between order and justice, the most recent statement of the rationalist perspective claims that justice in international relations is now essential for the maintenance of global stability. In this version, rationalism displays a clear normative commitment to international economic and political change.

This commitment to change is central to the critical theory of international relations. Marx's critical theory assumed that capitalism would transform the life of the species. Capitalism would first unify the species and then the triumph of socialism on a world scale would realise the promise of freedom and equality which was inherent in bourgeois society. The recent critical turn in international theory has used Marxist international political economy to argue that realism is wrong in thinking that the logic of systemic reproduction is the dominant logic in the modern world system. However this attempt to correct realism is not free of problems. In the 1930s the Frankfurt School argued that Marxism had failed to take account of nationalism, the state and war. In the 1980s this critique of Marxism has become increasingly important in sociological thought. This approach agrees that a critical theory of international relations must supersede realism. But it adds that it ought to supersede Marxist political economy too since its emphasis on class, property relations and production cannot provide an adequate explanation of the constraints upon, and prospects for, the extension of moral and political community.

2 Marx and the Logic of Universal Emancipation

Marx's political theory extended Hegel's claim that the development of the consciousness of freedom was the inner thread running throughout the whole of human history. The revisions which this doctrine underwent in Marx's writings reflected many different influences. From the Young Hegelians Marx derived the idea that philosophy was a critical and revolutionary activity with a cognitive interest in the promotion of universal freedom. Marx's shift from the atheistic attack on religion to the political economy of material alienation was inspired by Feuerbach's contention that human beings found solace by projecting their frustrated hopes and ambitions onto imaginary objects of religious worship. For Marx, the realisation of freedom and universalism, which Christianity had manifested in an alienated form, necessitated this move from the "critique of heaven" to the "critique of earth". British political economy and French socialism were the two main doctrines which shaped Marx's analysis of the reproduction and transcendence of the social and material constraints upon more autonomous and universal forms of life.

The materialist interpretation of history which assembled these multiple influences contended that the struggle with the natural environment was the principal source of economic and political constraints in human affairs. This struggle was also the force behind the development of the human understanding and control of nature. Further, it shaped the various social contexts in which human beings unfolded the powers and needs which were unique to their species. Of these the most important was the capacity to negate social structures which had become fetters upon the realisation of the more advanced human needs and capacities evolving within them. Marx maintained that this capacity had developed in the modern world to the point where it had become possible for all individuals to participate in a universal society of autonomous producers. In this condition individuals would collectively regulate their interaction with the physical environment while dismantling the social and political constraints which had become entrenched in the course of their historical formation. Accordingly, Marx's major project was the construction of a critical sociology of industrial capitalism which would uncover the prospects for greater self-determination which were latent within its social relations of production. In this project, the possibility of overcoming the tension between the possibility of freedom and universalism and the actuality of necessity and particularism was especially important. The conflict between the particularistic class constraints of the capitalist mode of production and the promise of universal freedom and equality which was secreted within its dominant ideology was a central theme in the earliest stages of Marx's intellectual development. The subsequent progress of his thought, it may be argued, was an attempt to understand the means by which this tension might be resolved in practice.

These comments on the importance of the Enlightenment themes of freedom and universalism in Marx's thought are sufficient for the purpose of noting some fundamental differences between historical materialism and conventional theories of international relations. In the first place, Marx defended the Enlightenment ideal of a universal society on the grounds that it was the only condition in which human beings could bring their social existence under their collective control.[1] Beginning with this proposition, Marx proceeded to construct a critical sociology of the evolution of universalism which reflected upon the revolutionary practice which would promote its further development in the modern world. By contrast, realism has treated universalism as a threat to the maintenance of international order and as a danger to the nation-state which underpins it. It has sought neither to defend the idea of a universal society nor to construct a sociological account of the evolution of universalism.

These themes have been treated with greater seriousness in the rationalist perspective. Although rationalists have not advanced a philosophical defence of a universal society they have argued that international order generates universal norms and they have maintained that further progress in the institutionalisation of universal principles is essential for the preservation of international order. Notwithstanding a degree of sympathy with some dimensions of the materialist interpretation of history,[2] rationalists have mainly endorsed the realist contention that Marx's investigation of the immanence of universal emancipation rested upon an analysis of modes of production and class relations which underestimated the importance of relations between states - not only their importance for the shape of human history as a whole but, more specifically, their impact upon the formation and reproduction of particularistic social identities.[3] We shall return to this theme later. It is important to begin by outlining the role which Marx's philosophical anthropology of the development of universal capacities played in his critical theory of society.

HISTORY AS AN ASCENT TO UNIVERSALITY

Marx's approach to universalism is most usefully contrasted with the natural law doctrine that universal moral principles are embedded in human nature and accessible in principle to human beings at any stage in their history. The difficulty with this perspective was first stressed in Vico's remark that human beings in the state of nature are equipped with moral categories which are clearly unique to the modern world.[4] Hegel reaffirmed the point that moral universalism is an historical product rather than a prior condition of all social life. The development of ethical universalism was for Hegel a central part of the growth of the species' consciousness of its capacity to create a free and rational form of life.[5]

Marx's claim that "history is the continuous transformation of human nature" also denied that universal moral truths were inherent in an immutable human essence.[6] Marx's emphasis on the primacy of production in the self-creation of the species nevertheless marked his disagreement with Hegel's idealist claim that history is the "product of thought concentrating itself, probing its own depths, and unfolding itself out of itself, by itself..."[7]. Even so, Hegel's conviction that the meaning of history was revealed in the development of the consciousness of freedom reappeared in the *Grundrisse*. There Marx distinguished between three stages of social development: a primitive stage in which humans were governed by "relations of personal dependence"; a succeeding phase in which they were associated in "relations of personal independence"; and a final condition, yet to be realised, in which the whole species would attain the condition of "free individuality" or "socialised humanity".[8] These stages conveyed Marx's belief that the human race had progressed from a primitive stage in which concepts of universality were unknown to a more advanced stage in which moral universals existed albeit in an alienated form. Marx distinguished these stages from the condition of socialised humanity in which universality would at last find authentic expression.

Marx argued in the *Grundrisse* that the "more deeply we go back into history, the more does the individual, and hence also the producing individual, appear as dependent, as belonging to a greater whole".[9] The whole to which Marx referred is the "family, clan, tribe etc. - which then, in a historic process of intermixture and antithesis with others" acquires its particular "shape" and identity.[10] Marx argued that estrangement from neighbouring communities and the perception of nature as an alien and mysterious force were the two phenomena imprinted on the structure of the earliest societies. The connection between these aspects of their alienation was displayed most vividly in the role which war played in the struggle to reproduce material life. Referring to the commune, Marx noted that: "The difficulties which the commune encounters can arise only from other communes, which have either previously occupied the land and soil, or which disturb the commune in its own occupation. War is therefore the great comprehensive task, the great communal labour which is required either to occupy the objective conditions of being there alive, or to protect and perpetuate the occupation. Hence the commune consisting of families initially organised in a warlike way - as a system of war and army...this is one of the conditions of its being there as proprietor."[11] The primitive nature of the forces of production revealed the extent of nature's domination of society in the earliest stages of human evolution. Intersocietal estrangement was an additional illustration of the limited development of human powers in this phase of human development. This was a stage in which neither the biological unity of the species nor the supposition that there could be universal moral ties between its individual members had any meaning. It was a condition in which the capacity to associate in more inclusive communities was one of the "slumbering powers" which had still to be discovered by the species.

In his analysis of the dissolution of these early societies Marx developed a philosophical anthropology of the formation of the capacity to participate in more inclusive social arrangements. One of the main agents of their dissolution was conquest which had various effects upon the "original forms" of community. The "conquering people" either "subjugates the conquered under its own mode of production", "leaves the old mode intact and contents itself with a tribute", "or a reciprocal interaction takes place whereby something new, a synthesis, arises". Where "human beings themselves are conquered along with the land and soil", "slavery and serfdom" arise and members of original communities are forced into relations of personal dependence. In this way conquest replaced the original condition of intersocietal estrangement with a new form of vertical estrangement in which the conquerors exercised class domination over a subject people which had become one of its "conditions of production". The possibility that a new "synthesis" could arise indicated that the rise of empire was a major reason for the development of unequal yet more inclusive social formations which destroyed the symbols of an exclusive tribal unity. These were the processes which propelled the earliest forms of society beyond the condition in which intersocietal estrangement seemed natural and unchangeable.[12]

Marx argued that the development of exchange relations first appeared "in the connection of the different communities with one another, not in the relations between the different members of a single community".[13] Their emergence was a second reason for the dissolution of the earliest forms of human society. Initially, exchange did "not so much take a grip on the life of entire communities as, rather, insert itself between" them.[14] Although the exchange of "superfluous products" began as an "accessory" to production and only slightly "modified" the "organisation of domestic production", it did not maintain its "relative indifference in respect of the inner construction of production" for long.[15] When exchange relations became entrenched within these societies their members became incorporated within an ever-expanding and deepening social division of labour: "Not only was the mode of production altered thereby" but "all the...economic relations which corresponded to it, were dissolved". As the money economy emerged, earlier "ties of personal dependence" which posited natural differences between human beings (differences of caste, etc.) simply "exploded".[16] New relations of personal independence were installed in their place.

Marx describes these relations of personal independence as "the second great form" of social life "in which a system of general social metabolism, of universal relations, of all-round needs and universal capacities (was) formed for the first time".[17] Under these conditions, the freedom of individuals seemed "to be greater" than it was when they were joined by relations of personal dependence. In fact, one set of constraints was replaced by another because individuals became subject to impersonal social forces and to domination by "abstractions".[18] In short, "private independence created complete dependence on the so-called world market", the condition of "objective dependence" in which "it is not individuals...but "capital which (has been) set free" by the rise of capitalist "competition".[19] The universal interdependence of needs which developed as a result of "the universal exchange of the products of all alien climates and lands" transformed the consciousness of individuals whose "common species-being" came to be "acknowledged by all".[20] But in circumstances in which their relations with each other were determined by the exchange of commodities and where money became the "universal equivalent" (the universal measurement of the exchange-value of commodities), human beings did not belong to a free, rational and universal community.[21] With the development of relations of personal independence, "money" had become "the real community".[22] To the extent that universality existed it was in an alienated form.

Marx believed that this second stage of social development created the material and cultural basis from which authentic universalism would evolve. Without that expansion of the relations of personal independence which had occurred during the epoch of bourgeois hegemony the human race could not have attained its virtual mastery of nature. The notion of abolishing material scarcity on a global scale would have remained purely fanciful. For Marx, these possibilities would not have arisen but for the fact that wage-labour had become a commodity which was bought and sold in the labour market for a wage significantly lower than the value created in the process of production. As a result, bourgeois society had been able to employ the surplus value which resulted from the exploitation of labour to promote the continuous transformation of productive forces.

This modern system of exchange relations was the "real basis" of "equality and freedom", of values which "presuppose relations of production as yet unrealised in the ancient world and in the Middle Ages".[23] Where the commodity is the real social nexus between individuals, there is, at the formal level at least, "absolutely no distinction between them": "Each of the subjects is an exchanger; i.e. each has the same social relation towards the other that the other has towards him. As subjects of exchange, their relationship is that of equality".[24] In the bourgeois epoch, social transactions seem to be based on consent rather than force: "Although individual A feels a need for the commodity of individual B, he does not appropriate it by force, nor vice versa, but rather they recognise one another reciprocally as proprietors, as persons whose will penetrates their commodities. Accordingly, the juridical moment of the Person enters here, as well as that of freedom, in so far as it is contained in the former. No one seizes hold of another's property by force. Each divests himself of his property voluntarily".[25] For this reason "there enters, in addition to the quality of equality, that of freedom".[26]

For Marx, freedom and equality had formal significance in bourgeois society. They were contradicted by class inequalities, by the oppressive effects of the social division of labour and by the free play of market forces. Even so, bourgeois society contributed to the formation of a socialist world order in which all individuals could enjoy true freedom and equality by mastering the natural forces which previously enslaved them and by eradicating the unequal enjoyment of the fruits of human labour. It made these possibilities available to the whole human race because it inevitably surmounted every obstacle to its progress. The capitalist world economy created the global organisational networks which the socialist system would inherit and employ for collective social advantage.

It is worth considering some of the elements of Marx's doctrine of global transformation in rather more detail. Marx observed that the "tendency to create the world market is directly given in the concept of capital itself. Every limit appears as a barrier to be overcome".[27] The subjection and destruction of societies outside Europe provided the clearest evidence of the inexorable nature of capitalist expansion. Through this process, capitalism established the "material conditions of a new world" though not without first dragging its victims "through blood and dirt, through misery and degradation".[28] Although the destruction of village communities was "sickening" to contemplate, Marx referred to their less than idyllic natural state, predicated as they were upon distinctions of caste and blood and upon the fetishism of nature.[29] No less important, in Marx's judgment, was the absence of internal social contradictions which could liberate these miserable social systems from deprivation and squalor. Their parochialism would have endured but for the intrusion of capitalism. Individuals would not have been wrenched free from closed and stagnant social relations, and the tyranny of natural forces would have survived.

As for the organisational preconditions of the development of socialism on a world scale - in his analysis of the advanced capitalist world Marx noted that the joint stock company foreshadowed an end to the contradiction between the social nature of production and the private appropriation of wealth. The organisational structure of world socialism also emerged in embryonic form within the "womb" of capitalism itself. This was so because capitalism required the technology of global surveillance in order to gather information about developments across the world as a whole. In the capitalist system, "institutions emerge whereby each individual can acquire information about the activity of all others and attempt to adjust his own accordingly, e.g. lists of current prices, rates of exchange, interconnections between those active in commerce through the mails, telegraphs etc. (the means of communication grow at the same time)".[30] On a related front, capitalism has to unify the world which it seeks to monitor: "while capital must on one side strive to tear down every spatial barrier to intercourse, i.e. to exchange, and conquer the whole earth for its market, it strives on the other side to annihilate this space with time, i.e. to reduce to a minimum the time spent in motion from one place to another".[31] Capitalism was compelled to bring this technological unification of the world into being because of the unpredictability of its own internal laws of motion which constrained the bourgeoisie and the proletariat alike. Capitalism created "world history"[32] not only in the course of searching for new markets or raw materials and a cheaper labour supply but because of a concomitant need to anticipate developments in a world economy which was increasingly susceptible to contradiction and crisis.

The capitalist mode of production created a condition of alienated universalism. And so it deserved to be condemned. But Marx enthused about the part that capitalism had played in dissolving traditional forms of community and about its role in forging the preconditions of the socialist world to come. The condition of "objective dependence" was preferable "to the lack of any connection" between societies. Individuals could not "gain mastery over their own social interconnections" until "they (had) created them". The "alien and independent character" of these interconnections simply proved that individuals "were still engaged in the creation of the conditions of their social life, and that they (had) not yet begun, on the basis of these conditions to live it."[33] Objective dependence had to have been endured. History had not begun with "the free social individual" but with "herd-animals" who experienced nature and neighbouring societies as alien and obscure.[34]

The epoch of objective dependence was therefore a long and painful but necessary stage in the journey towards that condition in which human beings would at last be at home in the world. This was the "third stage" of social evolution in which "free individuality, based on the universal development of individuals and on their subordination of their communal, social productivity as their social wealth" would finally be achieved.[35] As already noted, it was the capitalist mode of production which created the preconditions for social relations which would otherwise have seemed purely "quixotic".[36] Socialism on a world scale therefore released the possibilities immanent within the process of capitalist development, possibilities which capitalism created but which it was unable to realise: "The universality towards which it irresistibly strives encounters barriers in its own nature, which will, at a certain stage of its development, allow it to be recognised as being itself the greatest barrier to this tendency, and hence will drive towards its own suspension".[37] The crises and contradictions which intensified as capitalism matured were "the most striking form in which advice is given to it to be gone and to give room to a higher state of social production".[38]

Marx displayed nothing but contempt for romantic visions of alternative societies. He may well have been right to scorn the efforts of the utopian socialists to construct blue-prints for societies which would result from human experience and experiment. The result of this disdain was that Marx's tantalisingly brief comments about the nature of the communist system hardly equipped the Marxist Left with an adequate vision of the future. Marx's failure to explain the nature of communist universalism is an interesting case in point. It was clearly Marx's belief that the future would be shaped not by conflicting class interests or by antagonisms between "various localities, tribes, nations etc." but "by a general plan of freely combined individuals".[39] Although Marx was certain that freedom could only exist in a society which had eradicated all types of social particularism, the precise level of difference which was necessary for, or compatible with, the condition of socialised humanity was left unclear as subsequent interpretations of Marx's thoughts on the nation have only too clearly revealed. These have embraced the belief that Marx envisaged a socialist society which furthered the cosmopolitan sentiments which appeared in mature capitalism where the commodity ignored "all religious, political, national and language barriers", and where nationality was "but the guinea's stamp".[40] They have included the argument that Marx foresaw a "world of nations" rather like the socialist international commonwealth advocated by the Austro-Marxists.[41] On this point it may be sufficient to note that it is impossible to reconcile Marx's concept of freedom with the existence of any kind of particularism. But difference without division - particularity without particularism - not only seems consistent with Marx's communist vision but appears to be an essential ingredient of its success. It is far from clear, however, that Marx thought that national differences would have much of a role to play in a society of universal individuals organised not only to share the benefits of material production but to share in the development of their creative human powers.

CAPITALISM AND UNIVERSALITY

Marx's analysis of the evolution of the species stressed the relationship between the growth of international interdependence and the gradual mastery of nature. His discussion of the dissolution of the earliest forms of social relations revealed how these dimensions were interconnected. The ability to produce a surplus led some of the earliest societies to establish the first and most elementary forms of intersocietal interdependence. In turn, the larger social formations created by conquest and commerce led to a greater (but unequal) level of control of nature: a control which was appropriated by the owners of the instruments of production. Marx's analysis of the subsequent universalisation of social existence emphasised the international relations which existed between different modes of production and the nature of their individual and collective relationship with the physical environment. None of these moments could be understood in isolation. In conjunction they formed the setting in which human beings collaborated to modify and control their natural environment, and together they shaped the circumstances in which producers brought about the transformation of their own inner human nature. These were the moments of the totality which was the evolution of the species as a whole.

At a certain stage in human history the international division of labour had become the clearest embodiment of these multiple relations. In a letter to Annenkov, Marx posed this question: "Is the whole organisation of nations, and all their international relations anything else than the expression of a particular division of labour. And must not these change when the division of labour changes?".[42] *The German Ideology* answered this question in the affirmative. In that work, Marx made it clear that the concept of the social division of labour was applicable to relations between as well as to relations within societies: "the same conditions are evident with the development of intercourse, in the relations of different nations to each other".[43] The question which arises is whether the analysis of capitalism provides a complete explanation of the nature and tendencies of the modern international division of labour, or whether such an analysis is inevitably partial. To put the matter differently, the question arises of how far world history is shaped by metropolitan capitalism and how far by numerous other factors.

Marx's central project was the development of a critical sociology of industrial capitalism. This project was concerned with the possibilities which capitalism presented before the whole world - the mastery of natural processes, the eradication of the remaining vestiges of international estrangement and the establishment of many of the cultural and material preconditions of increased human autonomy. Perhaps this was the reason why Marx regarded "the whole world as one nation, and (assumed) that capitalist production is everywhere established, and has possessed itself of every branch of industry".[44] In fact, there was rather more to this assumption than the belief that capital accumulation was the propelling principle in the modern world. By assuming that the world was one nation, Marx hoped to understand how a social system would develop if it was governed by capitalism alone. Such an analysis would explicate the logic of pure capitalist development. It would cast light on the necessary as opposed to the contingent developments within actual capitalist societies. But such a method would not capture the multiplicity of factors which shaped actual capitalist societies. Nor would it reflect the complete range of forces which shaped a world economy in which capitalism was the dominant mode of production.

Several years ago French structural Marxists distinguished between the capitalist mode of production and actual capitalist societies.[45] They claimed that the former was an intellectual abstraction, and added that no society consists of capitalism alone. It can also be argued that although Marx assumed that the whole world was a capitalist nation he did not confuse the capitalist mode of production with the totality of social and economic relations. There are, in fact, many similarities between Marx's mode of deliberation and Hegel's dialectical method of inquiry. Each approach began by abstracting specific objects of investigation - whether they were social institutions or philosophical categories - from their wider context; each then reconstructed the whole from which these objects of inquiry had been isolated. Only when the whole had been understood would the analysis be complete.

The *Grundrisse* appears to presuppose just such a method, while *Capital* begins with the commodity and proceeds to construct the whole from which the commodity has been abstracted. It is not clear at what point the journey would have ended. The *Grundrisse* lists the state, international trade and the world market as parts of the whole which will be considered in the course of the analysis.[46] The important point however for any assessment of Marx's analysis of the international capitalist division of labour is that Marx did not complete the project of tracing the connections which extended from the commodity to the structure of the world economy.

Yet Marx believed the analysis was sufficiently advanced to conclude that a society based on the separation between bourgeois and proletarian could not be reproduced indefinitely. But for this relationship, the continuous transformation of the forces of production in the modern world would not have occurred. Nevertheless, as capitalism matured, this relationship became an obstacle to the further development of the productive forces and a barrier to the general satisfaction of the new powers and needs which were made possible by the transformation of technology. Spurred on by competition, capitalists mechanised labour and destroyed the source of surplus value. As the numbers of the "industrial reserve army" increased, capitalism quickly came up against the limits of its development and reached the point at which it could neither consume its product nor guarantee the reproduction of its own social relations.

Marx did not maintain that the iron laws of capitalist development made the triumph of socialism inevitable, and at no stage did he suggest that the crisis of overproduction would be sufficient to bring about the overthrow of capitalism. What Marx seemed to suggest was that the moral and political development of the industrial proletariat would be most likely to flourish under conditions of crisis. To understand why crisis should generate historical progress rather than lead to social breakdown, it is important to recall Marx's point that capitalism claimed legitimacy on the grounds that it was the only society which expressed the principle of individual consent. The dominant ideology of the capitalist system emphasised a free and equal contract between the bourgeois and the proletariat in which each gained what the other could supply: the control of labour-power in exchange for access to the means of subsistence.[47] The fact that the worker was under no legal compulsion to surrender the control of labour-power to the owner of the means of production was evidence, as far as the apologists for the bourgeois apologists were concerned, of the extent to which capitalism had succeeded in realising the principles of human freedom and equality.

Capitalism could be condemned in Marx's view for compromising the freedom and equality of individuals in numerous ways: for creating seemingly unprecedented opportunities for the expression of the full range of human powers while reducing labour to the performance of purely repetitive and mechanical tasks; and for bringing about an extraordinary increase in the level of social power over nature while placing individuals at the mercy of international market forces which they were powerless to control. Marx was not averse to discussing the apparent moral paradoxes and shortcomings of capitalist development. However the moral imperfections of capitalism were far from central to his argument that capitalism could not be indefinitely reproduced. To support the latter claim Marx sought to uncover the logic of development which would necessarily unfold in any society in which the separation of bourgeois and proletarian was the constitutive social relationship.[48]

On the positive side, this relationship had created modern subjects who were increasingly conscious of the value of freedom and equality. On the negative side, it had purchased a revolution in the forces of production by subjecting the proletariat to a process of covert exploitation in which they were deprived of a just reward for their labour. Marx argued that this negation of freedom and equality would not be permanently hidden from the victims of capitalist exploitation and oppression. Their enlightenment would increase as the process of capitalist competition led to a greater reliance on technology rather than human labour. Not only would this inevitable trend eventuate in crises which revealed that capitalism was unable to consume its own product; it would bring the proletariat to the realisation that its labour had fuelled the process of capital accumulation. At this point the language of freedom and equality would be exposed as a veil shrouding the deeper reality of class exploitation. The crisis of overproduction would not only be an economic crisis but a crisis in the social and political organisation of capitalist society which signified the destruction of its pretence of legitimacy. In this context subordinate class forces would organise to construct new social relations in which freedom and equality would no longer be compromised as they had been by the structure of capitalist society.

These conclusions were derived from an analysis which assumed that capitalism was "everywhere established".[49] They were most likely thought to correspond with the developmental tendencies of the most advanced capitalist societies. In any event, it was unlikely that they were designed to capture developments in the international system with quite the same precision. If it is true that Marx's analysis of the capitalist mode of production did not set out to explain the complete range of forces which shaped particular capitalist societies - and if it is true that this analysis sought to understand a process which would always be modified in practice by the multitudinous forces present in such societies and in their external relations - then Marx's account could have been no more than an approximate guide to the process of change in international society. Marx seemed to distinguish between the propelling principles of the capitalist mode of production and the multiple forces which governed the nature of particular capitalist societies. By the same token, the former cannot have been identical with the capitalist world economy. An analysis of pure capitalism may have provided the key to certain dominant trends in the capitalism world system, but it was also necessary to understand how these trends were affected by relations between societies at different levels of economic and political development.

Marx did not present a systematic analysis of how these various societies were organised to form a world system. In *Capital*, Marx cited Britain as "the chief illustration" of his argument. The preface to that work contains the famous remark that "the country that is more developed industrially only shows to the less developed, the image of its own future".[50] Even so, Marx did not assume that world history was European history writ large. In a letter to Mikhailovsky, Marx protested against any attempt to turn an analysis of the historical development of Western Europe into a unilinear philosophy of history which set out the sequence of stages which all societies would encounter on the route to socialism.[51] The proletarian revolution in the West might well free the East from its vegetative existence, but progress there could just as likely result, in India's case, from the efforts of the "Hindoos" to unite to expel British imperialism.[52] In the preface to the 1882 Russian edition of *The Communist Manifesto*, Marx alluded to the possibility that Russia might achieve socialism without first passing through a capitalist stage.[53] Several references to the plight of Ireland revealed a growing concern with the phenomenon of uneven development which would become so important later in Marxist and neo-Marxist theories of the world economy. The belief that Irish nationalism might be a progressive force foreshadowed subsequent attempts to accommodate nationalist movements within the process of socialist revolution.[54] The bourgeoisie had created a global civilisation in its own image. Nevertheless, it was dominant in one region of the world system, and possibly in a highly vulnerable one at that: "On the continent, the revolution is imminent and will immediately assume a socialist character. Is it not bound to be crushed in this little corner, considering that in a far greater territory the movement of bourgeois society is still in the ascendant?"[55]

There is some justification for supposing that Marx's later thought recognised that the world system consisted of very different societies with their individual historical dynamics. At no point was the nature of their international connections made especially clear. Nor did Marx spell out the political consequences that such an account of the world system might have for the international socialist movement. On the other hand, there is no reason to assume that Marx modified his early claim that the global expansion of capitalism was the single most powerful event affecting human society as a whole; that it would imprison the majority of the world's population in a coercive international division of labour, and yet equip its victims with the notion of human subjectivity which they would eventually turn against it; and that it would create the conditions in which the idea of universal emancipation would no longer be quixotic but be the basic ingredient of an indefinitely reproducible form of life.

THE PARTICULAR AND THE UNIVERSAL

We might usefully pause at this stage to consider the difference between Marx's analysis of the capitalist world economy and the realist explanation of the international system of states. As Giddens has recently noted, these two perspectives barely touch.[56] Notwithstanding this fact, they do possess a somewhat similar method of intellectual abstraction. As previously noted, Waltz's form of realism isolates the states-system in order to bring the logic of systemic reproduction clearly into view. Marx, on the other hand, proceeded by isolating the capitalist mode of production in order to understand processes of global change. It is possible that the realist might invoke the distinction between anarchic and hierarchic systems in order to explain the difference between these perspectives. On this argument, an analysis of the reproduction of the system of states need not be concerned with the process of capital accumulation or with the rise and fall of the bourgeois way of life; and perhaps an analysis of domestic social and economic change can proceed without offering an explanation of the persistence of the system of states. The process which concerns one theory can be analysed in isolation from the process which the other regards as most important. One need only recall the rationalist analysis of international legitimacy to realise that this argument will not quite do. Marx's inquiry into the role which capitalism has played in the formation of modern subjects laying claim to freedom and equality is of crucial importance for the rationalist analysis of the current problem of international legitimacy. Although Marx's analysis may deepen one area of the rationalist project, one important question remains: whether Marx's account of the universalising role of modern capitalism took sufficient account of the countervailing influence of national animosities and conflict between states.

This charge - which is a familiar theme in orthodox international theory - has acquired some prominence in recent Marxist and non-Marxist sociology. Two members of the Western Marxist tradition, Perry Anderson and Tom Nairn, have stressed the fact that Marxism has traditionally lacked a sophisticated account of nationalism and the international system of states.[57] In his defence of a post-Marxist critical sociology, Anthony Giddens has argued that these omissions belong to a larger list of "absences" in historical materialism which include sexual and racial forms of exploitation and domination.[58] Anderson and Nairn suggest the need to reconstruct historical materialism so that it deals with non-economic realms of particularism and exploitation.[59] Giddens argues that Marx's thought is nothing more than a starting point for an emancipatory politics which opposes Marxism from the left.[60] Notwithstanding these differences, each perspective would subject a contemporary critical theory to the same test of whether it reveals sufficient sensitivity to the process of universalisation and to the endurance of particularism in the sphere of world politics, to the struggle between possible causes of systemic transformation and the sources of systemic reproduction. To assess the strengths and weaknesses of Marx and Engels' thought in this regard, it is necessary to engage in a brief overview of their reflections on nationalism, the state and war.

The fact there is no detailed consideration of the national question in Marx's early writings is a convenient point of departure. One important strand of Western political thought in the aftermath of the French Revolution welcomed nationalism as an expression of the human capacity for endless cultural diversification and infinite improvisation. The French Revolution also gave birth to the concept of ideology which Marx employed in a very different characterisation of nationalism. Marx alleged that in its struggle for economic and political ascendancy the bourgeoisie had recognised that nationalism could serve a dual purpose. It was a force behind the unification of a region which was large enough for the prosecution of the bourgeois class project, and it secured the compliance of subordinate class forces by convincing them that the bourgeoisie represented a general societal interest. As capitalism developed, these ideological functions became transparent to the proletariat. Members of the proletariat were compelled to articulate an internationalist theory and practice in response to the global constraints of the international capitalist system. In an earlier stage of development, nationalism had performed a progressive role by destroying the feudal barriers to social interaction and collaboration. During the early part of the nineteenth century it had become a regressive force which was used by the bourgeoisie and its apologists as an antidote to revolutionary class consciousness and international proletarian solidarity. Nationalism had already expired amongst the more advanced ranks of the international proletariat, the class which would continue the universalising process to which nationalism had once contributed.

Marx's antipathy to nationalism is explained by a number of early statements about the privileged relationship between the proletariat and the ideal of universal emancipation. In his *Contribution to the Critique of Hegel's Philosophy of Right*, Marx described the proletariat as the first class to embody universal suffering and to promise universal emancipation.[61] One year later in the *Paris Manuscripts*, Marx reaffirmed this role by arguing "the whole of human servitude is involved in the relation of worker to production, and all the relations of servitude are only modifications and consequences of the worker's relation to production".[62] *The Communist Manifesto* gave this theme a different twist when it suggested that the last remnants of estrangement between nations would be dispelled by the establishment of the classless society: "In proportion as the exploitation of one individual by another is ended, is the exploitation of one nation by another ended too...In proportion as antagonism between classes within the nation vanishes, the hostility of one nation to another will come to an end."[63]

In the aftermath of the revolutionary events of 1848, Marx began to modify his earlier statements about the inevitability of proletarian internationalism. From this point on, Marx's references to the affinity between the interests of the proletariat and the welfare of humanity at large were far less frequent. The continuing appeal of nationalism - not least amongst the European proletariat itself - led Marx and Engels to reassess the part which national movements might play in the creation of socialism. The hostility which English workers displayed towards the Irish, whom they regarded as unwanted competition in the labour market and whom they held responsible for the depression of wages, provided clear evidence that the proletariat could generate its own forms of national antagonism, at least while the constraints of the capitalist labour market endured.[64] Still on Ireland, Engels maintained that its colonial status created two bourgeoisies in England: one bourgeois, the other proletarian, which were united by enmity towards the Irish.[65] The problem, as Engels saw it, was that no society could be free while it subjugated another. The persistence of estrangement between societies perpetuated an unholy alliance between dominant and subordinate class forces in the hegemonic nation. A similar arrangement inevitably arose in the subject nation.[66] It was for this reason that Marx and Engels supported the emancipation of the Irish which they believed would weaken the artificial bond between bourgeois and proletarian in England and promote an alliance between the working classes of both societies.[67] Anticipating Lenin's position on the place of national movements in the struggle for social equality, Marx and Engels claimed that there were two nations, the Poles and the Irish, which had not only the right but the duty to achieve national independence before promoting international proletarian solidarity.[68] Engels articulated the general principle at stake here by suggesting that an "international movement of the proletariat is in general only possible between independent nations...To get rid of national oppression is the basic condition of all free and healthy development".[69] This approach to the relationship between national movements and the class struggle was diametrically opposed to the position advanced in *The Communist Manifesto*.

Marx and Engels therefore recognised that international conflict could be solved separately from, and prior to, the struggle between classes. To that extent they recognised the autonomy of national animosities. However any shift in their attitudes towards national movements barely affected their view that nationalism was a distraction from the more serious matter of proletarian revolution. The problem of whether or not to support Polish nationalism, to cite one example, was resolved by the evidence that an independent Polish state would weaken the counter-revolutionary regime in Russia and strengthen the geopolitical position of the Western proletariat: "the Poles are a doomed nation to be used as a means until Russia itself is swept by the agrarian revolution. From that moment on, Poland has no raison d'etre any more".[70] This concern with the relationship between national independence and the prospects for proletarian revolution meant that some of the deeper questions about the place of nationalism in any critical social theory and practice were to pass unnoticed.

Marx and Engels' comments on the hostility between the English and Irish recognised, quite properly, that the struggle for material resources could give rise to ethnic differences. What they did not recognise was that material inequalities are only one of the causes of ethnic rivalry, and that the struggle for national security, or for recognition of cultural rights and independence, can be equally important reasons for nationalism. Marx and Engels offered no grounds for concluding that national antagonism was specific to class-divided societies and impossible in a society which had completely eradicated class differences. To have recognised even the relative autonomy of national antagonism would have been to suggest, albeit implicitly, that relations of production cannot be the only, or even the main, phenomena in which a theory of universal emancipation should be interested. This in turn would have raised important issues for the politics of critical social theory. The significant point here, as Marx and Engels came to realise, is that the emancipation of labour need not make any significant impression upon national or racial forms of exploitation and discrimination. More seriously still, it is in principle possible that the emancipation of the proletariat might not only fail to bring about the emancipation of other groups but actually impede their liberation. This being so, there are major problems with the view that support for national movements must depend on the existence of collateral gains for the proletarian revolution. A critical social perspective may find it necessary to support the victims of national domination even though the position of the proletariat might suffer as a result.

It has often been argued that these shortcomings are expressive of a larger failure to develop an adequate theory of the state, international relations and war. As far as the first of these is concerned, it is true that only fragments of a theory of the state exist in Marx and Engels' writings. Nevertheless, Engels' comments on the state in *The Origins of the Family, Private Property and the State* remain paradigmatic. Engels maintained that the state "is a product of society at a certain stage of development" when it "has become entangled in an insoluble contradiction with itself", when "it has split into irreconcilable antagonisms which it is powerless to dispel", and when a "power, arisen out of society but placing itself above it" has become necessary to ensure that conflict between classes does "not consume themselves and society in fruitless struggle". Whether the state arose from an internal process of class formation or "as a direct result of...conquest", "it is, as a rule, the state of the most powerful, economically dominant class, which, through the medium of the state, becomes also the politically dominant class, and thus acquires new means of holding down and exploiting the oppressed class".[71] Marx argued that the modern state "exists only for the sake of private property".[72] It invariably possesses the appearance of being "a separate entity, beside and outside civil society; but it is nothing more than the form of organisation which the bourgeois necessarily adopt both for internal and external purposes, for the mutual guarantee of their property and interests".[73] In bourgeois society, it has "assumed more and more the character of the national power of capital over labour, of a public force organised for social enslavement, of an engine of class despotism".[74]

Pointing to such formulations, Marx and Engels' opponents have subjected their writings to two interdependent lines of criticism: that the materialist interpretation of history treated the state as an epiphenomenon and, secondly, that its analysis of the state's location in civil society revealed an "excessively endogenous" method of explanation.[75] These criticisms warrant closer examination here if only because their impact upon conventional interpretations of Marx and Marxism within the field of international relations can scarcely be overestimated. We begin with Marx's alleged reductionism, proceed to the charge that Marx's method is excessively endogenous and then turn to the question of reductionism once again.

Ironically, the debate over whether or not Marx was guilty of economic reductionism was prompted by his attempt to clarify the principles which had been the "guiding thread" of his inquiry. In a famous passage Marx explained how he arrived at the conclusion that "the anatomy of civil society is to be sought in political economy". Marx then claimed that the social relations of production form "the economic structure of society, the real foundation, on which rises a legal and political superstructure and to which correspond definite forms of social consciousness". The observation that the "mode of production of material life conditions the social, political and intellectual life process in general" followed.[76] The precise meaning of Marx's statement that the relations of production condition the form of the state has been the subject of some of the keenest disputes about the meaning and validity of historical materialism. Less prominent in recent years are those interpretations which regard the base-superstructure relationship as one in which the former enjoys absolute dominance over the state apparatus.[77] A further and more attractive interpretation argues that Marx did not deny the existence of a reciprocal interaction between base and superstructure in which the latter exerted a countervailing influence upon the material base of society. It can cite Engels' letter to Bloch in support of its view.[78] Yet another approach denies that it was Marx's intention to separate the economic from the political in order to establish their relative causal importance. According to this interpretation, Marx developed a theory of the "internal relations" between dimensions of society which appeared to be separate in bourgeois society but which were in fact entangled in complex relations of interdependence and interpenetration.[79] Unsurprisingly given these differences of interpretation, a further approach has reached the conclusion that Marx operated with several different conceptions of the relationship between economics and politics which he failed to organise into a systematic and coherent whole.[80]

Any attempt to resolve these differences would go beyond the boundaries of the present work. For existing purposes it is sufficient to note that Marx and Engels specified some of the conditions in which the state could exercise considerable autonomy. Engels referred to periods in which the "warring classes balance each other so nearly that the state power, as ostensible mediator, acquires, for the moment, a certain degree of independence of both". The absolutist state in the seventeenth and eighteenth centuries, Bonapartism in the First and Second Empire and Bismarck's Prussia were cited as historical examples.[81] In *Capital*, Marx introduced the intriguing formulation that although religion was dominant in the Middle Ages, just as politics had been central in the Ancient World, it was the economic which determined the sphere of society which was dominant in any epoch. Human beings could not live on politics or religion alone.[82] Also in *Capital*, Marx argued that while the method of extracting surplus value held the key to the state in any particular society, the precise nature of the state apparatus could not be determined in an a priori manner.[83] In the light of some earlier comments in this chapter, it is tempting to argue that Marx believed that the capitalist mode of production in its pure form required a particular kind of state apparatus. Actual capitalist states, on the other hand, were shaped by a considerable range of internal and external forces. Marx was aware that the same economic base was compatible with different political superstructures, and that geographical and racial factors were often an important influence upon them.[84]

As with some of their more recent followers, however, Marx and Engels may not be entirely innocent of the charge that they advocated an economic-reductionist interpretation of the autonomy of the state apparatus. Otto Hintze was one of the first critics of historical materialism to make this point against it. Hintze maintained that Marx's class analysis of the origins of the state ignored the state's primary responsibility for the organisation and conduct of war.[85] In some passages Hintze came very close to defending the need for a completely opposite exogenous explanation of state formation in which history was regarded a continuous process of struggle for military power, rather than a procession of conflicts between classes.[86] In one particularly important passage, Hintze adopted an intermediate position in which capitalism and the states-system were regarded as different moments in modern historical development.[87] Recent references to Hintze's writings usually note that this observation that the state was located at the intersection of domestic social forces and the international system of states took account of exogenous factors which were undervalued in the major works of historical materialism.[88]

As stated earlier, the belief that Marx's thought is vulnerable to this line of criticism has been particularly influential in the study of international relations. But as Gallie maintained in an important essay on Marx and Engels, the problem was not that the founders of historical materialism neglected war and international competition but that their comments upon these phenomena were neither "developed systematically" nor "clearly enough related to the core principles of Marxist social and political theory".[89] Engels, for example, proclaimed war to be "as old as the simultaneous existence alongside each other of several groups of communities" - older, that is, than class societies.[90] Whether or not Marx and Engels regarded warfare as an exogenous force is a different matter, particularly as (albeit in a different context) Marx warned against any rigid distinction between the internal and the external determinants of societies.[91] Marx and Engels' comments on warfare invariably emphasised connections with the sphere of production whilst conceding that war was, as Gallie puts it, "a social force having an inherent dynamic of its own; a force which, whatever its causes, can produce effects which show no definite relation of dependence upon the main pattern of mankind's economic advance".[92] Their writings suggested that although "the susceptibility of different governments and peoples to the temptation of war" and the methods used in military conflict reflected the state of development of the forces and relations of production, war and strategy nevertheless left their own indelible mark on social and political development.[93] This theme became crucially important when Engels became alarmed by the accumulation of military power in the late nineteenth century and by the concomitant rise of the doctrine of total war. The significance of "the industrialisation of war",[94] as it is now called, for Engels' later writings on revolutionary socialism can scarcely be overestimated.

Whereas warfare had once seemed "a useful springboard for revolutionary action", its avoidance now became a central priority in Engels' later reflections on socialist strategy.[95] Engels was especially prescient about the effect which the potentially ruinous consequences of modern warfare would have for future efforts to realise socialism. As nationalist sentiments and national security fears grew in importance in Western Europe, Engels concluded that the socialist movement had no alternative but to accommodate itself to popular demands for the defence of the national homeland.[96] This recognition of the "intrusive and distorting effects which inter-state rivalries and wars were to play in the predicted transition from capitalism to socialism" did not lead Engels to support traditional military means of protecting national security. Engels suggested that a system of territorial defence based on the existence of popular "militia" might offset the dangers of war without postponing the struggle for socialist revolution.[97]

Notwithstanding Marx's opinion that Engels was "a little too much influenced by the military aspect of things",[98] the "logically uneasy relationship"[99] between Marx and Engels' reflections on war and their main statements of historical materialism still needs to be explained. Trotsky argued that Engels' military writings revealed a determination to approach new areas of inquiry with a freedom from the dogmatic "pseudo-Marxism from which Marx had distanced himself".[100] But this explanation raises more problems than it solves. It is hardly a solution to Gallie's important question of whether historical materialism was the adequate vessel to contain Marx and Engels' wealth of insight and analysis. The fact that warfare is barely mentioned in any of the main formulations of historical materialism seems to confirm Gouldner's point that Marxism possessed its special "anomalies and contradictions" and assorted "background assumptions" which intruded into the conduct of research without ever being formally recognised or theoretically explicated.[101] The relatively peaceful nature of international relations in the middle of the nineteenth century is now widely regarded as one of the main reasons for the anomalies which surround Marx and Engels' discussion of warfare. Gallie makes the important point that "the fundamental structure of historical materialism had been laid down in an age of military acquiescence", whereas the main reflections on inter-state violence, in Engels' case at least, were a response to the later "threat of total war".[102] Giddens' comment about the relationship between the uncommonly high level of international order in this era and the relative indifference of the classical sociologists to military organisation and war makes a similar point.[103] What makes Engel's writings particularly significant, as Gallie argues, is that they were among the first to appreciate the theoretical and practical limitations of that tradition.

In one sense at least, the creators of historical materialism shared the "the illusion of the epoch"[104] and embraced what Karl Polanyi called "the economistic fallacy"[105]. They subscribed to the idea, which can also be found in the writings of Ricardo, Saint-Simon and Cobden and Bright, that freeing modern social and economic relations from arbitrary governmental controls would internationalise human existence and end the destruction inherent in the European system of states. Marx's protest that the illusion of the epoch overlooked the significance of class struggle obscured his own acceptance of the widely-shared belief in an irreversible trend towards the unification of the human race. So deeply was this assumption held by liberals and socialists alike that Marx and Engels did not think it important "to spell it out explicitly in their earlier writings"[106], and Engels never quite broke with it in his later reflections on war.

This was the context in which Marx abstracted the capitalist mode of production from the totality of social relations in order to understand the main pattern of development in the modern era. Some of Marx's critics have argued that the inquiry which followed smacked of economic reductionism. The number of references to the autonomy of the state and to the importance of war must cast some doubt on the proposition that Marx thought that societies could be divided into their basic and derivative parts. Marx almost certainly did find it useful to separate primary class forces which generated historical progress from "secondary and tertiary" phenomena which could affect and frustrate the promise of class struggle. (In the *Grundrisse* Marx suggested that international relations should be included among them).[107] The distinction between primary and secondary factors is not the same as the distinction between basic and derivative phenomena although it is easy to confuse the two, and it is far from clear that Marx and Engels always distinguished between them with sufficient care. Reductionist Marxism which became prevalent in the early twentieth century certainly transformed the distinction between primary and secondary forces, which is a useful distinction for any critical theory of society, into a crude division between basic and derivative phenomena.

It is often suggested that Engels was responsible for the emergence of this vulgarised version of historical materialism. Whether or not this is true, Gallie's interpretation of Engels' military writings indicates that they ran counter to economic reductionism. More importantly, these writings were a serious effort to reconsider the traditional distinction between primary class forces and secondary factors such as relations between states. The obsolescent nature of this distinction has become even more evident to contemporary Marxists who have begun to stress the importance of strategic rivalries within the international system of states. Sylviu Brucan has argued that the analysis of the reproduction of the system of states, an analysis which has been undertaken by analysts who do not belong to the Marxist tradition, must be addressed by those who rely on the categories of historical materialism.[108] Theda Skocpol has criticised the classical Marxist explanation of social revolution and recent world-systems theory for their neglect of the "realist" dimension of international relations.[109] Finally, Perry Anderson's examination of the effect which international military competition had on the rise of the absolutist state and on the early stages of capitalist development also emphasises phenomena which Marx thought were of secondary or tertiary importance.[110]

Some of these formulations are similar to Hintze's claim that the rise of capitalism and the appearance of the international states-system are the two interconnected developments which have dominated modern history. They have become important in recent arguments that a contemporary critical theory requires a far more complex sociology than the kind which is available within orthodox Marxism. They are an important part of the argument that many forms of particularism (including the kind which exists in inter-state relations) cannot be reduced to the particularism of class. Furthermore, they highlight the need for a critical project which is equipped with a more extensive repertoire of ideas for promoting international economic and political change. The modern critics may argue that contemporary problems of peace and war point to the "immobilism"[111] of traditional Marxist categories, or they may present the case for constructing a post-Marxist critical social theory which addresses the need for a normative theory of violence.[112] Whether they argue for the reconstruction or the transcendence of Marxism, all of these perspectives agree on one point: that the project of critical social theory requires a more complex account of the relations between state structures, and a more sophisticated political response to the particularism which is inherent within them.

CONCLUSIONS

This chapter has sought to assess Marx's contribution to a critical theory of world politics. Particular attention has been paid to Marx's inquiry into the role which commerce and conquest played in the early history of the universalisation of economic and social life, and to the contribution which capitalism has made to its development and possible completion. We have noted that Marx and Engels recognised a conflict between the process of universalisation and the forces which renewed the particularism of nations and states. Marx and Engels nevertheless endorsed the more general theme in nineteenth century social thought that the process of human unification would overcome the forms of resistance displayed in these particularistic associations. Contemporary developments in social theory have noted that Marx and Engels seriously underestimated the extent to which the system of states was a barrier to the achievement of human unity. (In this respect, as the first chapter noted, they were pre-empted by Frankfurt School sociology.) It seems necessary to conclude that a critical theory of world politics requires a more complex understanding of the struggle between universalism and particularism. The next two chapters seek to ascertain the extent to which Marxist explanations of nationalism and imperialism contributed to this task.

3   The Nation and the Species

The liberal and Marxist branches of political economy in the nineteenth century assumed that the species would be united by the process of industrialisation. The coming of industrial society confirmed only part of their argument. As expected, the economic and social unification of the species turned out to be one of the most important tendencies in the nineteenth century, but an unanticipated concurrent increase in the level of international conflict was to prove that industrialisation was a more complex and paradoxical force than liberalism and Marxism had supposed. Neither perspective had been alert to the possibility that the process of national unification would rapidly overtake the trend towards international integration, and neither had envisaged the increase of state power in both the domestic and the international realm.

Prior to "the dawn of universal history", Raymond Aron once argued, societies were conscious of their cultural differences above all else. The age of industrialism produced a far greater sensitivity to inequalities of power and wealth. The more the world was unified, the greater was the capacity of societies to measure their economic and political differences.[1] The nationalist claim that political frontiers should correspond with cultural boundaries flourished in this environment, although some of the early statements of nationalism continued to uphold the value of internationalism. Mazzini's nationalism was one such example. The dominant strand of nationalist thought pointed in a different direction. During the nineteenth century, the "democratisation" and "socialisation" of the nation brought the "most international of modern historical epochs" to an end.[2] The "international of monarchs" and the age of "aristocratic universalism" were rapidly superseded.[3] This trend posed the first major challenge to liberal and Marxist analyses of the probable course of universal history. It was the first major threat to their conviction that the species would be united in a politics of universal emancipation.

When Marxists began to respond to these developments in the late nineteenth and early twentieth centuries they confronted many of the same problems which Marx and Engels had addressed earlier. They were faced with the question of whether historical materialism had presented an oversimplified analysis of human development in which too much weight was attached to the class struggle. Since it was clearly wrong to suppose that all forms of national conflict were simply a distorted expression of the class struggle, it became even more important to define the conditions in which the struggle for national rights might deserve the support of the socialist movement and it became essential to decide whether support for national liberation might represent a necessary detour from the expected path towards the goal of internationalism. The resilience of nationalism raised the question of whether revolutionary socialists should continue to subscribe to the cosmopolitan ideal or foreshadow a world of nations in which cultural differences would flourish and not merely survive.

One of the most original and enduring lines of argument to develop in this context regarded nationalism as a product of the uneven development of the world economy. From this perspective, progressive national movements are similar to subordinate classes in that each represents a radical challenge to social inequalities. The literature on the uneven development of the world economy has attempted to explain why capitalism failed to fulfil its promise of universality. It is far from clear that this argument goes far enough to explain either the existence of nationalism in the capitalist world economy or the nationalist antagonisms which have divided socialist states. At least since the outbreak of the First World War when the European working class was shattered into national fragments, it has been abundantly clear that nationalism is much more than a mere antidote to class divisions in capitalist societies and far more than a response to international economic inequalities. Since then the impact of war and state-building on the formation of nationalism has warranted equal emphasis. The fact that nationalism has been a divisive force in the socialist as well as in the capitalist regions of the world system has prompted the argument that Marxist sociology has failed to appreciate the interconnections between war, state-formation and the reproduction of particularistic loyalties, and that Marxism has failed to address these problems in its efforts to construct an emancipatory politics. What is more, Marxist theory has been slow to recognise that the preservation of national loyalties and antagonisms (not least in the socialist bloc) reveals the extent to which cultural differences can be valued for their intrinsic worth.

The conclusion that nationalism has been Marxism's "greatest historical failure"[4] would seem incontrovertible in light of these arguments, although it would be a mistake to conclude that Marxism is powerless to contribute to a theory of nationalism. Its apparent failure was the subject of an interview in the 1970s in which Regis Debray maintained that the frequency with which Marxism was "broken...upon the reality of the nation" led him to question Marxist social theory and political practice. Debray's central claim was that the persistence of nationalism exposed Marxism's erroneous belief in the "plasticity" of human nature. The Marxist notion of the malleability of human nature explained the belief that nationalism was a transient phenomenon whose dominance was about to pass. Debray did not take issue with the argument that nationalism was a specifically modern political doctrine. Where he differed from Marxism was in arguing that nationalism was a modern manifestation of immutable and universal "laws governing the survival of the human species". Debray cited the human need to locate societies in time (through the creation of foundations myths, for example) and the need to anchor human communities in a determinate space as the two principal social universals. Consequently, what was novel or unique about nationalism was less important than its similarities with other doctrines of social closure which were expressions of an ineradicable human desire to belong to communities which were clearly "delimit(ed) within an enclosed space". For Debray, this need for "clear delimitation of what is inside and what is outside" one's particular society is an "archaic" feature of social existence. Neither the appeal to the alleged universality of proletarian class interests nor the vision of a cosmopolitan world order can possibly compete with it.[5]

If Debray is right that natural forces bar the emergence of a cosmopolitan political community then the project of overcoming the antinomy between particularism and universalism is inevitably misconceived. The existence of this moral antinomy suggests that there is more to it. It could not have arisen but for the development of a sense of obligation to an "imagined community" which is wider than the nation, and but for the partial transcendence of more limited moral associations. The nature of this process of moral development requires explanation just as much as nationalism does. Its existence casts some doubt on the proposition that human beings are intrinsically incapable of surmounting the obstacles to the creation of a universal society - in which their cultural differences may nevertheless survive. Debray's comments are a useful reminder of the difficulties which nationalism has created for Marxism in theory and in practice. They do not nullify the latter's attempt to identify the economic causes of nationalism, and the latter's efforts to determine whether nationalism may be superseded by, and may even anticipate, a universal political community.

These last two issues have been inextricably connected in Marxist approaches to nationalism. Approaches to nationalism which regard it as a product of the uneven development of the world economy frequently conclude that the progressive qualities of subordinate class forces may also reside in peripheral national movements. The analysis of uneven economic development has often supported the conclusion that progressive national movements and revolutionary class forces are equally involved in the struggle for freedom and equality. On this basis, it has been argued that nationalism is a "detour" on the way to a socialist world community.[6] This method of argument has affinities with one larger strand of the Western theory of nationalism which denies that supporting national movements is necessarily incompatible with the commitment to internationalism. It is similar, for example, to Plamenatz's contention that nationalism "is confined to peoples who, despite their rivalries and the cultural differences between them, already belong to, or are being drawn into a family of nations which all aspire to make progress in roughly the same direction".[7] There are affinities too with Deutsch's thesis that the reduction of global inequalities would allow the species to reach an unprecedented level of political, and not only economic and technological, unification.[8]

This response is one side of the ambivalent nature of the Western intellectual response to nationalism. It is important to recall a second tradition, to which Acton and Kedourie belong, which regards nationalism as a betrayal of the principles of the Enlightenment. From this perspective, the factors which distinguish national movements from each other, and which create bitter rivalries between them, invariably prevail over such apparent similarities as their common reaction to international inequalities and their shared hostility to cultural domination and political subjugation.[9] A similar strand of Marxist thought argues that far from comprising an indirect route towards internationalism, nationalism always threatens to become "the journey" itself and to close rather than to open possibilities for the international extension of moral and political community.[10] In these disputes about whether or not there are any secure grounds for a compromise between nationalism and socialism, Marxism reveals an ambivalence towards nationalism which cuts across many of the main traditions of Western political thought.

THE AUSTRO-MARXISTS AND THEIR CRITICS

The difficulty of achieving proletarian solidarity within a multinational empire led the Austro-Marxists to recommend a revolutionary socialist party based on a federation of nationalities. At the Brunn Congress of 1899, the Austrian Social Democrats debated the best means of accommodating the rights of nations within the socialist party. In their deliberations they considered the possibility of regional organisations, which protected the "cultural autonomy" of nations, and the need for extra-territorial national organisations which took account of the way in which nationalities were intermingled throughout the empire.[11] Their endorsement of the principle of the cultural autonomy went well beyond Marx and Engels' point that there were circumstances in which the international working class could only be organised into an effective political force by first acquiescing in the demand for national secession. The Austro-Marxists envisaged a future socialist commonwealth in which nationalities would not only survive, or be tolerated, but enjoy the conditions which would enable them to flourish. Adopting the principle of cultural autonomy would ensure that the revolutionary movement already embodied these socialist ideals.

In the course of making this argument, Austro-Marxism was obliged to deal with the objection that the persistence of the "national factor" revealed one of the major weaknesses in the materialist interpretation of history. Recognising the "triumphant air" with which the critics of Marxism asserted this proposition, the Austro-Marxists maintained that differences between nationalities reflected the diverse conditions in which human beings laboured in order to reproduce their material lives.[12] Otto Bauer added that national differences would inevitably survive the transition to socialism where the social conditions of production would continue to be as diverse as they had been under capitalism.[13] The materialist element in this discussion indicated that Stalin's accusation that the Austro-Marxists had succumbed to "spiritualism" and philosophical idealism was somewhat misplaced, useful though the point may have been in the politics of trying to halt the spread of Austro-Marxist influence.[14] In one important respect Stalin's observation about the idealist core of the Austro-Marxist defence of the nation was far from misdirected. The argument that each culture perceived "identical" objects differently because of the unique conceptual framework which it brought to the world reflected the influence of neo-Kantian epistemology.[15] The belief that nations were "indestructible and undeserving of destruction" combined the observation that each culture possessed distinctive qualities - even though these had to be viewed in conjunction with social relations of production - with the judgment that further cultural differentiation would enhance human life.[16] On this score, Austro-Marxism was closer to the position associated with Herder and the historicist tradition than to orthodox Marxism with its expectation of, and enthusiasm for, moral and cultural convergence.[17]

The Austro-Marxists took Marx's statement that the working class was without a country to mean that it was excluded from the dominant culture as well as from the material wealth of the national society. The nature of social inequality was such that only "the citizens of each nation (were) clearly distinguished from each other".[18] Members of all subordinate classes tended to display the same dull uniformity. Whereas Marx's claim that the working class was without a country seemed to suggest that it had transcended national allegiances, the Austro-Marxists concluded that class struggle would "nationalise" the working class by granting it access to the dominant culture and by opening the door to participation in the educational system.[19] Socialism would not realise the universal potential which was inherent in capitalism by abolishing every trace of cultural diversity. On the contrary, it would accentuate cultural differences by removing the constraints which barred the proletariat from access to the dominant culture: "...only socialist society will bring this tendency to fruition. It will distinguish whole peoples from each other by the diversity of national education and civilisation in the same way as at present only the educated classes of the different nations are distinguished".[20] Revolution would lead to the creation of "unitary socialist nation(s)" in which "socialist education" would, in Bauer's words, "provide every individual with the cultural objects of the whole nation and indeed a good part of those of the whole human race".[21] In a passage which is reminiscent of Schiller and Hegel's idea of history as fall and regeneration, Bauer maintained that the socialist nation would reconstitute the original condition of harmony which had once existed in the primitive commune.[22]

There is the question, of course, of how these socialist nations would conduct their external relations in the future world system. It is important to note that the Austro-Marxists celebrated the prospect of national diversification but rejected the nationalist argument that cultural differences must find expression in a world of sovereign states. Like the revolutionary party, the world order envisaged by Austro-Marxism would be a federation of nationalities possessing the right of cultural autonomy but collaborating to share the material wealth of the entire world: "All of us, however many different tongues we speak, fight together for the "complete restoration of man", and we shall be reborn in the universal humanity which knows struggle and domination only with respect to nature, while among individuals and peoples there are only equal rights, and equal shares in the ideas of the spirit and the joys of the earth".[23] It was thought that a socialist international division of labour would reconcile the interests of the nation with the welfare of the species.

Small nations would be able to develop highly specialised economies secure in the knowledge that through external relations they would gain access to the products which they could not produce by themselves. Through involvement in this international specialisation of labour, each nation would retain its cultural individuality while enjoying the benefits of a "social structure of a higher order", a "great organism" of the entire species "united for the common domination of nature".[24] On the question of how this world order was to be constructed, Bauer referred to a cooperative system of nationalities free from the complications of national sovereignty. The objective was a kind of Marxist "neo-medievalism" in which associations of foreign-speaking nationals would exist inside each principal nation, bound to their own nationality for certain purposes, to the society in which they lived for others, and to the species as a whole in order to bring their interaction with nature under that "conscious regulation" which was the hallmark of socialism.[25]

Only a small part of the Austro-Marxist literature on nationalism has been translated into English. If it is representative of the whole, then the Austro-Marxists underestimated the possibility that nations might come into conflict with each other, and they neglected the prospect that the interests of the nation and the welfare of humanity might turn out to be opposed. There was insufficient analysis of the institutional arrangements and social principles which socialist nations might use to resolve their political differences. In one sense, what was important and distinctive about Austro-Marxism was its attempt to construct a political theory of socialism in which popular demands for cultural diversity were regarded as having intrinsic worth. But the fear of continuing conflict between nations was what was emphasised in subsequent Marxist arguments that the Austro-Marxists had gone too far in their search for a compromise with the national principle.

Rosa Luxembourg's hostility to any compromise with the principle of national self-determination - an opposition which was manifested in her opposition to Polish secession from Russia - may be described as the antithesis of Austro-Marxism. In his biography of Luxembourg, Nettl argued that her writings stood at "the apex of the attempt to make operational the Marxist concept of class as the primary social referent, and to break once and for all the alternative stranglehold of nation".[26] Luxembourg took the view that in "a society based on classes, the nation as a uniform social-political whole simply does not exist".[27] There is in capitalist societies no "arena...in which the possessing classes and a self-conscious proletariat would take one and the same position and figure as one undifferentiated whole".[28] Lenin made a similar point when he argued that the Austro-Marxists' desire for making national cultures accessible to the working classes overlooked the formers' predominantly bourgeois character.[29] Although he was equally opposed to the doctrine of the indestructibility of nations, Lenin did not share Luxembourg's unconditional hostility to national movements and national secession. Lenin recognised that national oppression created solidarity between the dominant and subordinate classes. For these reasons Lenin was prepared to concede that the revolutionary proletariat and progressive national movements could be allies in the struggle for social equality. What he was not prepared to concede was the idea that the nation either would be or should be the primordial human community in the future socialist world system.[30]

Lenin's need to find the middle ground between the Austro-Marxist principle of "cultural autonomy" and Luxembourg's unconditional opposition to national movements became particularly urgent when the Jewish section of the Russian Social Democratic Party, the Bund, endorsed the idea of national autonomy at the Party Congress in 1903.[31] Although Lenin believed that the principle of cultural autonomy had fragmented the socialist movement and contributed to the survival of the Austrian-Hungarian empire,[32] pragmatic considerations made it impossible for him to leave the matter there. Moreover, to have dismissed nationalism as irrelevant would have been tantamount to defending the dominant nations. It would have been to suggest that there was nothing in the phenomenon of cultural arrogance - as exemplified by Great Russian chauvinism - which justified organised national resistance. The fact that Jewish workers in Russia were doubly exploited as workers and as Jews was ample reason for concluding that the struggle for national equality had its own contribution to make to the struggle for social justice.[33] This conclusion was reinforced by the emergent anti-colonialism of the nations of Asia and Africa which had been forced into a dependent role within the international division of labour. Here too, contempt for nationalism would have undercut the appeal of revolutionary socialism but it would also have neglected the justice of the anti-colonial cause.

For the most part Lenin's perspective focused on the relationship between nationalism and the uneven development of capitalism. Lenin distinguished between three principal phases of capitalist development. The first stage occurred in Western Europe between 1789 and 1871 during the bourgeois-democratic period of revolution. From there capitalism had spread to Eastern Europe and to Russia where the bourgeois-democratic revolution erupted in 1905. This stage overlapped with a more recent third period of development in which capitalism finally penetrated the societies of Africa and Asia. The second and third stages of capitalist development were characterised by the diffusion of the modern European type of class structure and by the appearance of new national antagonisms between the economically advanced regions of the world economy and the peripheral societies which were the victims of colonial and neo-colonial oppression.[34]

In this context Lenin referred to the paradox of capitalist expansion: "Developing capitalism knows two historical tendencies in the national question. The first is the awakening of national life and national movements, the struggle against all national oppression, and the creation of national states. The second is the development and growing frequency of international intercourse in every form, the breakdown of national barriers, the creation of the international unity of capital, of economic life in general, of politics, science, etc."[35] Nationalism was the product of the internationalisation of "the entire economic, political and spiritual existence of humanity"[36] not only because it would have been unable to spread without the unifying role of capitalism, but because it represented the universalisation of the Western idea of the human subject. For this reason, Lenin was prepared to recognise the legitimacy of those movements, and only those movements, which were involved in the struggle against national oppression and capitalist exploitation. The removal of "every trace of national distrust, estrangement, suspicion and enmity" still remained the basic long-term goal.[37] Neither unequivocal support for nationalism nor an unconditional rejection of its political aspirations could promote the logic of human unification. A compromise position could make support for nationalism compatible with the long-term objective of a universal society. The point then was to recognise the emancipatory potential of nationalist movements without "adapting socialism to nationalism", as Plekhanov put it, and without dividing the proletariat into what Stalin called "separate, national rivulets".[38]

In Lenin's political theory, the proletariat was the only revolutionary force which deserved unconditional support.[39] Support for other movements depended upon the extent to which their success would advance the cause of revolutionary socialism. Stalin reiterated this theme in the essay *Marxism and the National Question*, written at Lenin's request to counter the influence of the Austro-Marxists. Marxist political organisations could not extend support to nationalist movements which would simply perpetuate cultural stagnation and economic backwardness. (Stalin regarded the movements led by the mullahs and beys of the Transcaucasian Tatars as revealing examples.)[40] Nor could they accept the Bund's use of the principle of cultural autonomy to argue for a national right to separate schools.[41] The groups which deserved support, in Stalin's view, were the "oppressed nations" which were attempting to free themselves from externally-imposed restrictions upon their economic and political development. Although these restrictions were introduced by the metropolitan bourgeoisie to retard the development of their competitors in the periphery, they created additional hardship for the working classes in the developing societies. This allowed the bourgeoisie to appeal to the unity of the "folk" in order to mobilise the proletariat behind its specific class project.[42] Stalin repeated Marx and Engels' point that the attainment of national independence would therefore increase the prospects for class conflict in the periphery.

The belief that large nation-states would undergo rapid capitalist development and create the conditions in which revolutionary class consciousness would be most likely to develop was a crucial theme in Lenin's reflections on nationalism. On the surface of things, the aim of preserving large territorial states clashed with the principle of assisting even the more progressive national movements. The appearance of numerous small states threatened to retard human development.[43] Recognising the problem here, Lenin argued that nationalist movements should be presented with a straightforward choice between complete secession from the dominant nation or continuing membership on the understanding that they would possess the same rights and duties as all other citizens. What they have would to renounce if they selected the second option was any claim to exercise special rights by virtue of their nationality.[44] By presenting the choice in this way, Lenin ruled out the Austro-Marxist option of a federation of nationalities. In opposition to the demands of the Bund, Lenin denied that any distinct nation had the right to establish separate educational facilities. All peoples had the "democratic right", on the other hand, to preserve their separate language and culture within "desegregated schools".[45] The option of total secession was intended to remove any suspicion that Marxism remained unsympathetic to the nationalists' cause. Lenin believed that in practice most national movements would opt to remain part of their existing nation-states - on the terms mentioned above - as opposed to seceding to form less viable political communities. The appeal of material progress made it unlikely that many national movements would actually choose to secede, particularly if the right to secede had already been granted. For these reasons, large political entities would survive the challenge of nationalism. They would preserve the context in which the process of capitalist development would continue to unfold.[46]

The right to secede was easier to grant if its exercise seemed likely to be limited. In addition, Lenin made it clear that like divorce, the entitlement to secede was a last resort rather than a recommended course of action: "We are opposed to particularism, and are convinced that, all other things being equal, big states can solve the problems of economic progress and of the struggle between the proletariat and the bourgeoisie far more effectively than small states can. But we value only voluntary ties, never compulsory ties. Whenever we see compulsory ties between nations we, while by no means insisting that every nation must secede, do absolutely and emphatically insist on the right of every nation to political self-determination, that is, to secession."[47] Even if the right of secession was widely exercised, Lenin was confident that internationalism would triumph over nationalism in any case. The beneficial consequences of breaking the compulsory ties between Norway and Sweden could be repeated elsewhere: "the breaking of compulsory ties strengthened voluntary economic ties, strengthened cultural intimacy, and mutual respect between these two nations which are so close to each other in language and other things. The common interests, the closeness of the Norwegian and Swedish peoples actually gained from the secession, for secession meant the rupture of compulsory ties".[48] Lenin's search for the middle ground between Luxembourg and the Austro-Marxists concluded that the internationalism of the proletariat would grow in strength whether or not national movements exercised their right of secession. In this way Lenin reaffirmed the principle that revolutionary socialists had the duty to promote internationalism, although he attempted to establish a more solid theoretical foundation for subsuming support for progressive national movements within this design.[49]

Lenin's judgment that progressive national movements could be associated with the proletariat in the struggle for universal emancipation regarded nationalism as the product of the uneven development of the capitalist world economy. As we shall observe later, there is much to be said in defence of Lenin's argument that the emergence of capitalism was crucial for the formation of modern nationalities, and real merit in his contention that its uneven diffusion was a major reason for the politicisation of cultural differences. The inequality of material progress created new possibilities for different classes to unite on the common ground of nationalism; but the expectation that the antagonisms between nations would eventually be replaced by more important struggles involving social classes (and the belief that national secession was defensible because it would contribute to this condition) has been so wide of the mark that it is necessary to move beyond Lenin's theoretical framework and political conclusions.

Borochov's materialist investigation of nationalism is instructive in this regard.[50] This approach followed traditional class analysis by pointing to the particular reasons which led each class to support nationalism. It was distinguished also by a more complex realisation of the way in which common interests shaped national allegiances. On the first point, Borochov argued that the bourgeoisie supported nationalism in order to restrict foreign competition in the domestic market and to mobilise the masses in support of its class aims in the world economy. For the aristocracy, nationalism was mainly linked to a traditional attachment to territory and land.[51] Nationalism enjoyed the support of the proletariat for the simple reason that "as long as the national work-place is not secure, the national problem overshadows the labour problem".[52] On the second point, Borochov's distinction between the relations of production and the conditions of production sought to explain commonalities of interest which made nationalism possible. The conditions of production in any society included the conditions which were "imposed by...neighbouring social groups".[53] In an important passage Borochov added that "the most vital" of the "conditions of production" is the control of "territory".[54]

Borochov's position was similar to Bauer's insofar as it regarded the various circumstances in which societies reproduced their material lives as the most obvious reason for the "division of humanity".[55] Although this perspective was not inconsistent with Lenin's argument about the connection between nationalism and uneven economic development, there was far less confidence that the transition from capitalism to socialism would lead to the demise of the national question. Borochov made this clear when he suggested that it was "far-fetched and hazardous" to suppose that "national differences will be eradicated simultaneously with the eradication of class differences".[56] In fact, his argument about the importance of controlling territory in the face of external threats - an argument which is reminiscent of Marx's position in the *Grundrisse* - suggested that the elimination of the inequalities of development would not be sufficient to bring national antagonisms to an end.[57] This emphasis on territorial conflict raises the question of whether geopolitical rivalries were treated with sufficient seriousness in Marxist accounts of the origins and reproduction of national differences.

Nationalism developed more recently than geopolitical rivalry and it cannot be reduced to it. On the other hand, it is improbable that uneven economic development would have produced nationalism unless humanity had already been divided into separate sovereign states. Capitalism generated a level of social and economic integration which made it possible for states to mobilise their populations, while strategic competition provided states with a powerful incentive to create politically unified nations. For these reasons, it is not surprising that nationalism made its appearance in Western Europe where the emergence of capitalism and the formation of the states-system more or less went hand in hand.

Nor is it surprising that demands for national autonomy and secession were activated inside and outside the European state not only by the homogenising effects of capitalism and industrialisation but by the role which state-building played in the process of cultural unification. Lenin's account of nationalism overlooked the importance of state-formation and conflict within the international states-system. It underestimated the extent to which a socialist response to the challenge of nationalism required strategies for ending uneven economic development, methods of reconciling the demand for recognition of cultural differences with the process of state-building and techniques for reducing strategic rivalries between nation-states. By themselves, state formation and geopolitical rivalries could not have caused nationalism but in the context of industrialisation they possessed the capacity to manufacture social support for nationalism and to ensure its reproduction. The failure to recognise the extent to which the state was crucial to the whole process of national integration, and the cause of further ethnic rivalries within its own borders, was one of the most important oversights of Lenin's account of nationalism. It meant that the critical sociology which accompanied Lenin's universalistic aspirations contained an inadequate understanding of what was involved in undertaking the passage from particularism to universalism.

One dimension of the problem of eliminating national antagonisms had appeared in Engels' military writings, as noted earlier.[58] It was only when Marxists were forced back on the policy of building socialism in one country that the relationship between state security and nationalism was more widely recognised, and even then not so much in theory as in practice. Marx and Engels had claimed that each national proletariat would first settle the score with its own bourgeoisie, but they were confident that once revolution had erupted it would spread quickly across the more industrialised capitalist societies.[59] Engels' remark that Europe was split between two powers - "Russia with is philosophy of Absolutism, and Revolution with its philosophy of Democracy" - illustrated the extent to which Marxism was ill-prepared for the question of how socialist universality was to be realised in a world divided into sovereign states.[60] When Trotsky's "few revolutionary proclamations" failed to have the desired effect of undermining the supposedly crumbling foundations of the international states-system, Marxists were compelled to rethink the received position on the transition from capitalism to socialism. The upshot of this development was that it began to make its own compromise not only with nationalism but with the traditional methods of conducting relations between states.

The nature of this metamorphosis was revealed most clearly in the evolution of Bukharin's thought. In his earliest reflections on the transition from capitalism to socialism, Bukharin declared that the "Russian revolution will either be saved by the international proletariat or...perish under the blows of international capital". It was for this reason that Bukarin urged that each national proletariat should regard itself as a subordinate "detachment" of the international socialist movement. When international revolution failed to occur, Bukharin advocated the doctrine of socialism in one country, although his continuing commitment to internationalism led him to warn of the danger of "national narrow-mindedness" and an exclusively "national Bolshevism".[61] It is interesting that Bukharin contemplated the possibility that a socialist state might ally with a capitalist power in order to crush a neighbouring bourgeois state.[62] This strategy may not have involved the "national messianism" which Trotsky regarded as an inevitable product of the notion of socialism in one country, but it was symptomatic of the trend towards elevating a Marxist "realism" above earlier strategies of revolutionary change.[63] It was an expression of the constraints which were to lead the Soviet Union to subordinate the putative universal interests of the international socialist movement to the exigencies of Soviet national power. We need not dwell here on later developments in which the spread of socialism - with or without Soviet support - to other countries intensified the trend whereby nationalism and realism appeared to extract their revenge for the disdain with which Marxism had previously regarded them.

Marxism was absorbed within the international states-system without so much as denting the "pre-existing patterns of violence and its threat among nation-states".[64] Whether this process was inevitable is less easy to determine. When realists have addressed this question, they have often concluded that Soviet submission to the conventions of power politics was more or less inevitable once it had adopted the policy of national survival. From this perspective, the intellectual resources which Marxists used to interpret the world entirely failed to understand the ease with which "nonconformist states" are "socialised" into the states-system.[65] A lack of understanding of the systemic qualities of international political life was mirrored in a practice which failed to appreciate how little could be achieved at the international level by the politics of domestic social and economic transformation.

Since the Bolshevik revolution occurred in a peripheral or semi-peripheral region of the international system, it is not surprising that the Soviet Union responded like other revolutionary states by increasing military power as quickly as circumstances would allow; and it is no less surprising that its revolutionary agenda was distorted by the urgency of coping with a hostile international environment as much as by any internal process of degeneration and decay. That aside, there is absolutely no guarantee that Marxism would have realised its universalistic aspirations had it taken control of state power in areas which were not as economically and politically disadvantaged. Other factors such as disputes about the means of realising socialism and differences over the nature of the socialist ideal itself might have arisen anyway, particularly in the context of differences of culture and dissimilar geopolitical positions.[66] Nevertheless, in practice, the task of resolving these differences has been complicated by inequalities of economic and military power between socialist states themselves, and by their initially weak position within the international economic and political system.

There is no reason to assume that a number of concurrent processes of social and political reconstruction which aimed to create a sense of obligation to a community wider than the nation-state must be powerless to modify what realists regard as the dominant logic in world politics.[67] Suffice to say that powerful systemic forces were been able to thwart the national path to international socialism undertaken earlier this century. Lenin's reflections on nationalism failed to explain how an alternative to the logic of systemic reproduction might be introduced in these circumstances. Lenin was too inclined to regard progressive nationalist movements as expressions of the dominant logic of systemic transformation. On this assumption Lenin concluded that internationalism had more to gain than to lose from recognising the national right of secession. To a certain extent, Lenin's recognition of the legitimacy of the struggle against specifically national forms of domination, and his resistance to efforts to entrench national differences in the socialist party and future world system, was an astute compromise between Luxembourg and the Austro-Marxists. What it failed to recognise was that the aim of creating voluntary ties between nations might be frustrated by international military competition. And it failed to take account of international anarchy in its consideration of the means of transcending the tension between the nation and the species in the socialist (and not only in the capitalist) world order.

NATION, STATE AND UNEVEN DEVELOPMENT

The idea that the expansion of capitalism has brought about the economic and technological unification of the species only to fragment it along national lines remains a dominant theme in more recent theories of nationalism. As the writings of Deutsch, Aron and Gellner reveal, non-Marxist sociologists have found this approach equally appealing although it is the uneven development of industrialisation rather than of capitalism which they generally regard as the proper object of analysis.[68] Despite this shift, important parallels with Marxist sociology exist. Each of the writers mentioned above dismisses the idea that nationalism is the stirring of "dark atavistic forces" which make human beings crave for social enclosure, and each emphasises the essential modernity of nationalism.[69] In the belief that nationalism is largely a reaction against the phenomenon of global economic and political inequalities, these authors have argued that the satisfaction of demands for international social justice would ease, if not entirely eradicate, antagonisms between nations. As this section illustrates, this approach has made a major contribution to the theory of nationalism by explaining how cultures became national with the emergence of industrial societies and by revealing how the idea of national culture was politicised by the unequal development of industrialisation. The claim that nationalism is the result of the industrialisation of national economies and the unequal economic development of the world nevertheless fails to consider the relationship between nationalism and the system of states. This failure to analyse the relationships between the structures and processes which constitute these three levels - the mode of production, the world economy and the system of states - is a weakness which extends beyond recent theories of nationalism. Some of the implications for the critical theory of world politics will be considered at a later stage.

Nairn's *The Break-Up of Britain* is one of the most recent Marxist works to consider the relationship between nationalism and the unequal development of the capitalist world economy. In this book, Nairn maintains that the Enlightenment belief in the equal diffusion of progress led Marx and Engels to assume that capitalism would divide the human race between "two cosmopolitan classes...locked in the same battle from Birmingham to Shanghai".[70] In fact, the capitalist world system created international inequalities which served as the material foundation for "the most notoriously subjective and ideal of historical phenomena" in modern history.[71] In this context, world history came to be shaped by unanticipated forms of national conflict which "enveloped and repressed the antagonism upon which Marxism laid such stress".[72] When socialist revolution did occur it was invariably in the periphery, and inevitably as part of the struggle for national independence.

Leaving aside Third World Marxism, Nairn's sympathy with nationalism is a departure from the norm within the Marxist tradition. This sympathetic reception of nationalism stems from the belief that the more advanced stages of capitalist development made it essential that the classical position on class and nation should be overturned. In the context of uneven capitalist development, nationalism rather than the ideology of international proletarian solidarity became the dominant ideology of the oppressed. More specifically, the idea of the nation was the single most important resource available to the periphery in its efforts to free itself from dependence within the "world political economy" and the key to its attempt to work out its own solution to the alien concept of progress which the West had imposed upon it. In Nairn's view, an analysis of the structure of global inequality makes it possible for Marxism to develop a materialist account of nationalism; and it forces it to recognise that nationalism is an agent of social progress which deserves more than the begrudging support which is all that most Marxists have been prepared to lend it.[73]

In short, the traditionalism and irrationalism which Marxists have often imputed to nationalism has been more apparent than real. The leadership of the periphery had to exploit the mythical qualities of the people in order to mobilise society for the forthcoming "ordeal of development": "All that there *was* was the people and peculiarities of the region: its inherited ethos, speech, folklore, skin colour and so forth".[74] Although the mythology of the nation frequently invoked romanticised notions of the past, and accentuated traditional and often irrational forces, it did so to prepare society for the passage to modernity: "...nationalism can in this sense be pictured as like the old Roman god, Janus, who stood above gateways with one face looking forward and one backwards. Thus does nationalism stand over the passage to modernity for human society. As human kind is forced through its strait doorway it must look desperately back into the past, to gather strength wherever it can be found for the ordeal of development".[75] The uneven development of the global economy removed any possibility of international working class solidarity. Peripheral societies were compelled accordingly to resort to nationalism in order to challenge the structure of the world system. Nairn argues that the political consequences for Marxism are obvious: it has become inevitable that Marxists should choose a different path towards socialism, one that regards national movements as the crucial agents of international social and political change.[76]

It should be pointed out that Nairn describes his own perspective as preliminary and qualifies it in some important respects which will be mentioned later in this chapter. Some critics of Nairn's argument have maintained that it contains more than a grain of truth although they have suggested that there are several omissions and limitations which restrict the explanation. There is, for instance, surprisingly little analysis of the fact that nationalism appeared in the core long before it spread throughout the periphery.[77] By contrast, Gellner's approach begins with nationalism in the core. It suggests that industrialisation was essential for the formation of nationalities, although it regards the uneven development of industrialisation as the reason for the subsequent politicisation of national differences across the world. Gellner evidently aims to reveal his disagreement with the Marxist tradition by shifting the discussion from capitalism to industrialisation and by emphasising the extent to which national conflict has largely superseded class conflict in the modern world.[78] The shift to industrialisation is a plausible move. However it is not as different from Marxism as it seems for the simple reason that it considers the process of industrialisation in isolation from the process of state-building and from the realm of strategic interaction between nation-states.

The contrast between agrarian and industrial society is fundamental to Gellner's explanation. Gellner argues that nationalism is impossible in agrarian societies. The attempt "to impose on all levels of society a universalised clerisy and a homogenized culture with centrally imposed norms, fortified by writing, would be an idle dream. Even if such a programme is contained in some theological doctrines, it cannot be, and is not, implemented. It simply cannot be done. The resources are lacking".[79] What is more, in agrarian social orders the "power-holders" are invariably "loyal to a stratum which is much more interested in differentiating itself from those below than in diffusing its own culture to them, and which quite often extends its own limits beyond the bounds of the local polity, and is trans-political and in competition with the state".[80] Feudal society is one system in which order is possible without the existence of a single language and a common culture. As far as the customary exchanges between lord and peasant are concerned, "it matters very little whether they both speak (in the literal sense) the same language".[81] General compliance with the rights and duties which are attached to their respective social roles is more important than the sense of belonging to a shared culture.

Prior to industrialisation, the absence of correspondence between cultural and political boundaries did not create social friction. Neither the alien character of government nor the desire of the ruling class to separate itself from the governed by identifying with an international "high culture" was thought to violate a right of national self-determination.[82] Nationalist movements did not emerge for the purpose of remedying an obvious wrong. In industrial societies, on the other hand, such a clear discrepancy instantly triggers nationalist grievances and fuels demands for political autonomy. A theory of nationalism must therefore explain why industrial societies are unique in that they alone generate national allegiances and trigger national conflict when cultural and political boundaries do not correspond.

In his answer to this question Gellner maintains that the process of industrialisation breaks down the difference between "high" and "low" culture. An industrial society demands that all citizens must recognise "a fairly large anonymous unit defined by shared language or culture" as "the natural object" of their "loyalty".[83] All citizens must possess a "minimal clerical competence" before they can enact their allotted roles,[84] and all must have a basic literacy in a common language to comply with the need for mobility, whether social, functional or geographical. Without this linguistic competence individuals would be unable to take part in the routine exchanges between strangers which are intrinsic to any industrial society. For these reasons, the individual members of an industrial society derive their identity from the particular linguistic and cultural medium which regulates everyday social interaction. They come to regard themselves as members of a nation-state since the modern state is the only association which possesses the administrative power and economic resources to support the sophisticated educational system which is required for the maintenance of an industrial society.[85]

Modern cultures are defined by, and are coterminous with, nation-states. In principle, however, industrialisation would appear to be compatible with a universal society which is "sustained by a single political authority and a single educational system".[86] Gellner adds that what seemed imminent to the main traditions of social theory in the nineteenth century "may yet come to pass".[87] The vision of human unity failed to come about because the process of industrialisation was and still is uneven: "There was no reason why they should all suddenly fuse into a single (culture), and there were good reasons why they should *not*: industrialism, in other words the type of production or of the division of labour which makes these homogeneous breathing tanks imperative, did not arrive simultaneously in all parts of the world, nor in the same manner. The differential timing of its arrival divided humanity into rival groups very effectively. These differences in arrival-time of industrialism in various communities became acute if they could utilise some cultural, genetic or similar differentiae, left behind by the agrarian world...Internationalism was often predicted by the prophets and commentators of the industrial age, both on the left and the right, but the very opposite came to pass: the age of nationalism".[88] Uneven development foiled the liberal expectation of universal harmony, while the "difficulty of maintaining real solidarity between societies at differing stages of industrialisation" demonstrated that the Marxist idea of the international "solidarity" of the working class was a "myth".[89]

The effects of industrialisation vary with the level of cultural homogeneity or difference which exists in each of the regions which it has affected. In relatively homogeneous societies, the underprivileged groups could assume that their share of material progress would increase. If the potential leaders of the less-developed areas could assume that their own upward mobility was assured, it would be improbable that they would seek to mobilise the masses behind the objective of improving their economic fortunes through secession from the larger system. However, where inequalities of progress have converged with racial, ethnic and related communal differences, national conflict has been the inevitable result.[90] These differentiae have become a source of conflict in industrial orders where there is an expectation that the distribution of economic and political power and resources in society will be determined by meritocratic criteria rather than by differences of "ascribed status".[91] Consequently, although differences of ascribed status may not threaten the stability of pre-industrial societies, they become a "septic sore" in every society which has embarked on the process of industrialisation.[92] Where the intelligentsia has found that its social and political advancement has been closed because of racial or ethnic considerations, it has invariably politicised the most obvious marks of "identification" to rally the masses behind the goal of secession from the larger social order.[93] Success has provided the intelligentsia with a "virtual monopoly" of privileged positions in an independent political system.[94]

This approach has several uses. Gellner argues that the process of decolonisation can be understood as a consequence of the uneven development of the world economy. The colonial empire was "a global version of an open field system: each political unit was a kind of strip, starting at the centre of the global village (i.e. in developed areas) and stretching out towards the badlands. As a consequence of nationalism, political boundaries now run at right angles to the previous ones; roughly speaking, they are rather like a system of locks, separating areas with diverse levels of economic development".[95] In addition to accounting for the failure of internationalism in the late nineteenth and early twentieth centuries, the study of uneven economic development therefore casts light on one of the most important dimensions of the modern states-system, namely its expanded reproduction across the world as a whole. What is more, the very existence of uneven development has been a major reason for the debate about the relative importance of order and justice which has arisen in the dialogue between the representatives of the North and South. The question of whether the global expansion of the states-system is likely to be followed by a corresponding "expansion of international society" immediately raises the issue of whether it is likely that states will agree on measures for redressing inequalities of development in the modern world system.[96] Whereas liberal and socialist internationalism in the nineteenth century assumed that industrialisation would erode nationalism and the state, the uneven development literature invites the conclusion that the expansion of moral and political community in international relations depends most of all on the actions of states themselves.

In this connection, it is important to recall Gellner's point that nationalism is an instrument for fostering peripheral economic development and for promoting state-formation in an unequal international system. Its internal uses include the construction of a wider national community from the diverse ethnic groups which were drawn within the same political unit by the colonial power. These domestic uses reveal that nationalism is compatible with the existence of profound internal economic and political inequalities, and that in order to achieve "rapid development" nationalist elites often impose "hardships" on their populations which are at least as severe as those that existed under colonialism.[97] On this much at least Marxist and non-Marxist analyses of uneven economic development tend to agree. Moreover, as Krasner has noted, the nationalist protest against the injustices of unequal economic and political power is often an attempt to create international conditions which will make it easier for peripheral elites to build more powerful states.[98] Where nationalist elites turn out to be as tolerant of continuing international inequalities as they have been of domestic inequalities, they obstruct rather than strengthen the bonds of international community.

Gellner's analysis of the uneven development of industrialisation is not confined, as Nairn's was, to explaining the existence of nationalism in the capitalist regions of the world economy. In addition, its consideration of the origins of modern national identities gives rise to a specific prediction about what the future has in store. Nairn's explanation seems to imply that nationalism and national antagonisms will decline with the reduction of international inequalities, although there is no explicit discussion of whether this eventuality might produce a decline in the significance of the nation, and no statement on whether or not any possible decline in the sense of national differences should be actively desired. Gellner's position is that the emergence of a cosmopolitan culture of modernity and the possible reduction of international inequalities of development will bring about a mellowing of nationalist antagonisms. But so central are language and culture in modern communities that the sense of national identity is certain to survive.

Were Gellner to be concerned with alternative world orders he would seem likely to insist that the sense of national community should be respected from the outset - as the Austro-Marxists argued at the turn of this century. This conclusion will not be disputed here. What cannot pass without comment, however, is the fact that consideration of the state and international relations is missing from the analysis. A close relationship between the uneven development of the world economy, nationalism and the process of decolonisation undoubtedly exists, as Gellner has insisted. Whether this relationship is any stronger than the connection between the demand for national independence and the desire for an independent voice in the international system of states, the analysis fails to discuss. It is worth noting that the logic of strategic interaction, the process of state-building and the formation of national identities have long been connected, and it seems inevitable that nationalism will survive as long as "cultural identities and historic communities seek to insert themselves into a relatively fixed and inelastic state system".[99] The literature on uneven economic development has failed to take account of this dimension of the struggle for national rights. Accordingly, it not only underestimates the extent to which the struggle for national rights will survive even in a world which has eradicated uneven economic development but fails to identify the need for a practice for dealing with non-economic sources of national conflict and antagonism.

NATIONALISM AND CRITICAL INTERNATIONAL THEORY

The conviction that nationalism is a positive response to international inequality has received widespread support from Third World Marxists. One example is Arrighi Emmanuel who has noted that nationalism became the dominant ideology in contemporary politics when the "problems (of inequality) that confronted the industrial nation at the end of the eighteenth century and the beginning of the nineteenth" began to "stand before the world as a whole".[100] The extent to which the working classes of the "privileged" nations have preferred to enjoy the benefits of the exploitation of Third World labour has compelled socialists in peripheral regions to reach their own compromise with nationalism.[101] On this basis Emmanuel concluded that "the antagonism between rich and poor nations is likely to prevail over that between classes" in the struggle to create a more just world economic and political system.[102]

It is undoubtedly the case that nationalism has been a powerful weapon which the weak have used to redress racial, cultural, economic and political inequalities in the modern world system. The above-mentioned criticisms of the attempt to explain nationalism in terms of the uneven development of the world economy point towards the conclusion that there is another face to nationalism which is in conflict with the emancipatory objective of critical social theory. The way in which some dominant nations have behaved towards national minorities in the aftermath of independence, and the methods which some have employed in their relations with neighbouring states, reveal this other side. With these phenomena in mind, Hobsbawm has argued that Marxists should only extend their support to those political movements which are prepared to place the welfare of other societies ahead of their own. Otherwise, according to Hobsbawm, the decision to "welcome nationalism as ideology and programme" contains the risk that the nationalist route to socialism will end up being the "journey" itself.[103] Some of these concerns about the dangers of flirting with nationalism find expression in the writings of more sympathetic observers such as Nairn who recognises that nationalism has often received support from privileged groups which are fearful that their margin of advantage may decline.[104] His remarks about the "Janus-faced" character of nationalism recognise the danger of future degeneration of the kind that occurred in Europe in the inter-war years.[105] Furthermore, when Nairn suggests that "competing national socialisms could be as bad as, or worse than, competing bourgeois nationalisms", and when he argues for the need to unravel the complex "inter-relationships and order of priorities" between class and national movements, he comes close to Lenin's position that conditional support for nationalism is as much as Marxists should be prepared to concede.[106]

The belief that nationalism is mainly a reaction against international economic inequality has led some within the Marxist tradition to concede rather more. On this argument, nationalism is a manifestation of the desire for self-determination which characterises the modern political subject, while the spread of nationalism to the periphery is evidence of the universalisation of the modern European concept of freedom. To a certain extent this is true, but other forces can explain the trend towards formulating political claims in the language of self-determination: "...we have to remember that when these demands for justice were first put forward, the leaders of Third World peoples spoke as supplicants in a world in which the Western powers were still in a dominant position. The demands that were put forward had necessarily to be justified in terms of...conventions of which the Western powers were the principal authors; the moral appeal had to be cast in the terms that would have most resonance in Western societies. But as...non-Western peoples have become stronger..and as the Westernised leaders of the early years of independence have been replaced in many countries by new leaders more representative of local or indigenous forces, Third World spokesmen have become freer to adopt a different rhetoric that sets Western values aside, or at least places different interpretations upon them. Today, there is legitimate doubt as to how far the demands emanating from the Third World coalition are compatible with the moral ideas of the West".[107] In other words, there is nothing in the demand for national rights to justify the belief that there is an emerging "family of nations which all aspire to make progress in roughly the same direction". It is useful to consider this observation in conjunction with the argument - which is now advanced as frequently on the left as on the right - that meeting the demand for a New International Economic Order may reduce inequalities between states only to increase inequalities between individuals within developing societies and within the world economy at large.[108] According to this line of argument, at least some peripheral states have hijacked the moral ideas of the West for the purpose of promoting conventional political and economic ends. They have exploited a potent theme among various groups in the West that contemporary global economic relations no longer command - and do not deserve to command - international legitimacy.

These points are connected with a broader discussion which concludes that a general theory of nationalism cannot be built upon the limited foundations provided by the concept of uneven economic development. Put differently, Marxism has been guilty of assuming that nationalism is really "something else" which turns out to be "the world economy". Moreover, "the sheer weight of the economistic tradition" has prevented Marxism from making "further progress" in understanding the sources and political significance of the national question.[109] The contention that nationalism has been a potent force in regions where marked inequalities of development are absent (in the British West Indies, for example), and the observation that it has failed to appear in regions where this approach would lead one to expect it (in Northern England, for instance) are further points made in criticism of the economism which is inherent in the literature on uneven development.[110] A parallel line of argument which notes that societies have often been prepared to incur substantial economic costs in order to realise their national aspirations points towards the conclusion that threats to cultural identity and national survival or security have often been more important than issues of economic inequality in the politics of nationalist movements. A more advanced discussion of these dimensions of nationalism would be obliged to recognise that the state and international relations are levels of analysis which are at least as important as the capitalist or industrial modes of production and the international economy.

CONCLUSIONS

It has been argued that critical perspectives have often reached an assessment of nationalism which takes insufficient account of state-formation, international rivalry and war. For this reason a general theory of nationalism will have to recognise the strengths of statecentric realism without assuming that nationalism could have been caused by international conflict alone. The pre-industrial societies which formed the early modern European states-system lacked the resources with which to construct national identities. It was the process of capitalist industrialisation that introduced the necessary resources. The Marxist tradition was the first to recognise the link between capitalism, uneven economic development and nationalism. What it did not recognise, and what more recent Marxist analyses have failed to realise, is that the state possessed the resources to harness national sentiments in support of its own geopolitical ends. If these observations are correct, then nationalism was the natural accompaniment to a three-tiered social and political revolution which began in Europe from which it spread to all parts of the world. This was the transition from pre-industrial to industrial systems of production, the rise of sovereign states and the development of an international economy which divided the world between core and periphery.

Because the logic of capitalist industrialisation was the privileged realm in historical materialism, Marxist approaches to nationalism inevitably focused upon its relationship with bourgeois society and its specific product, the world economy. Often they highlighted those dimensions of the national struggle which most resembled the struggle between classes - those dimensions which indicated that there was a serious problem of legitimation in the world system, a contradiction between the universal expectation of freedom and equality and the actual system of international inequality. Then the issue was just how far the national solution was a genuine approach to the problem of international inequality and a means of strengthening rather than eroding the bonds of international community. When it wrestled with this theme, Marxism mirrored one of the paradoxes of the modern world, that it was (and in many ways still is) sufficiently united so that political movements have to employ the same nationalist discourse in order to have their claims taken seriously, but not so united that the main challenges to global constraints on human freedom and equality emanate from transnational social and political movements. Marxist analyses of nationalism understandably wished to avoid the conclusion, which the theory of imperialism would subsequently confirm, that the prospects for an international alliance of the working classes were increasingly remote, yet they were unable to point to any other means of overcoming the antinomy between the nation and the species.

4 Class, State and Nation in the Theory of Capitalist Imperialism

A systematic attempt to understand the connections between domestic social change, state structures and foreign policy, and the uneven development of the world economy was presented in the theory of capitalist imperialism. This analysis was prompted by the failure of the European working classes to respond to the call for international revolution at the beginning of the First World War. At the theoretical level, Marxist theories of imperialism broke with earlier accounts of the transition between capitalism and socialism in two main respects. In the first place, they attached far greater importance to the way in which the symbols of national power and prestige had contributed to the reproduction of capitalist societies; and secondly, they stressed the inadequacy of any discussion of the transition between capitalism and socialism which failed to take account of the fact of war. These shifts of emphases embodied a recognition that the power of nation-states had been greatly enhanced by the process of industrialisation. In this context these approaches raised serious problems for earlier Marxist attempts to construct a critical sociology of world politics.

To some extent the founders of the theory of imperialism were among the first to recognise the emerging crisis of the classical sociological tradition. The main theorists of imperialism contended that the liberal belief in the inevitability of "peace through free trade" was no longer tenable.[1] They also recognised that the dominant version of historical materialism had absorbed a similarly naive faith in the progressive effects of industrialisation. To set this right, the Marxist analyses of imperialism sought to reclaim the nation-state and war for modern social and political theory. In so doing they posed the crucial question of how the world-system was shaped by the interaction between the process of industrialisation and the realm of inter-state relations. That is not to say that the theories of imperialism freed themselves from the traditional emphasis on the primacy of capitalist development or that they accorded strategic interaction equal status within their revised systems of explanation. The main line of argument contended that between the end of the nineteenth century and the outbreak of the First World War, European - indeed world - history had been shaped by the process of monopolisation. The renowned conclusion of this approach was that monopolisation provided the link between the structure of modern capitalism and the influence which militarism had come to exert over all social classes. The rise of monopoly capitalism explained the growth of state power over civil society and the collapse of the liberal international order as capitalist states edged ever closer towards war.

Lenin maintained that the essence of the "new" capitalism could be captured in five basic principles. First of all, there was the trend in which "the concentration of production and capital has developed to such a high stage that it has created monopolies which play a decisive role in economic life". In the second place, Lenin pointed to "the merging of bank capital with industrial capital" and to the rise of the modern "financial oligarchy" which exercised control of "finance capital". In the third place, Lenin argued that "the export of capital as distinguished from the export of commodities (has acquired) exceptional importance" in the modern epoch of capitalist development. The "formation of international monopolist capitalist associations which share the world among themselves" was the fourth principle in Lenin's schema. This theme was the bridge towards Lenin's last and most basic proposition that when "the territorial division of the whole world among the biggest capitalist powers (was) completed", the major powers employed force in order to eliminate their greatest rivals.[2]

The first three of these propositions were an extension of Marx's analysis of late capitalist development. In *Capital*, Marx regarded monopoly as the inevitable outcome of the unhindered operation of the free market. Marx's references to the concentration and centralisation of the ownership and control of capital pointed to the fact that market forces replaced small economic enterprises with powerful economic organisations such as modern joint stock corporations. The latter's part in substituting technology for human labour, and their parallel responsibility for increasing economic output while lowering the cost of production, were the main reasons for the suspension of free market liberalism.[3] These were the developments which led Marx to the conclusion that the most advanced capitalist societies could neither consume their own product nor stem the tide of revolutionary opposition.

Lenin and Bukharin believed that Marx had been right to argue that monopolisation was a necessary rather than a contingent feature of capitalist development. Even so, the categories which Marx had employed in *Capital* required thorough revision. Neither the actual process of monopolisation nor its effect on class relations had conformed exactly with Marx's analysis. More specifically, it was essential to recast Marx's political economy in light of the most recent trends in capitalist societies which Hilferding had examined in his study of finance capital. In Hilferding's judgment, the most important trend was the emergence of a small number of banks which controlled the capital reserves which were necessary in order to finance the modern process of production. These banks comprised the new "finance oligarchy" which advanced capital to the managers of the corporations and participated in corporate decision-making by virtue of their direct representation on modern boards of management.[4] The growing power of the new finance oligarchy was both cause and effect of the inexorable law of monopolisation. The placement of capital in those enterprises which were able to deliver the highest return accelerated the demise of family capitalism. It also triggered a similar process of monopolisation amongst the banks.

Lenin's third proposition identified the main reason for the basic crises and contradictions of modern capitalism. Monopoly had not led to the overproduction of commodities, as Marx had anticipated, but to the exhaustion of domestic outlets for the absorption of surplus capital. For Hilferding this development had made it urgent for the state to gain control of additional "economic territory" so that surplus capital reserves could be suitably placed.[5] Lenin observed that Hobson had also drawn attention to the oversupply of capital in his writings on the expansionist tendencies inherent in the modern British capitalist state. But Lenin proceeded to dismiss Hobson's reformist solution to the predicament of modern capitalism which suggested that new domestic openings for the placement of surplus capital would be created by redistributing wealth to alleviate the poverty of the working classes. Lenin's conviction that any society which initiated these reforms would not be "capitalism at all" led him to conclude that national capitalist monopolies had no alternative but to search beyond their own borders for outlets for their surplus capital reserves.[6] Moreover, these monopolies' own recognition that this was the only means of dealing with a threat to the survival of capitalism explained the centrality of the state in modern societies. Their growing power and importance was the reason for the state's greater involvement in the management of the national economy and for its increasing interference in the commercial relations which tied capitalist societies to one another.

Lenin and Bukharin maintained that the distinction between domestic and international politics had been broken down by the dominant logic of monopolisation. This was the single thread which brought domestic capitalist systems, state structures and the realm of international relations within a single process of historical development. The struggle for monopoly power became the propelling principle in international relations once the trend towards monopolisation within each nation-state had been completed. Its first appearance within the realm of world politics was evident from the formation of international cartels which partitioned the world market among themselves as a means of eliminating other sources of competition. These international cartels reflected the approximate equality of power of their constituent parts, an equality which would be disrupted in the longer term by the uneven development of capitalism. This being so, Lenin repudiated Kautsky's notion of "ultra-imperialism" which alleged that the evolution of capitalism would culminate in the "joint exploitation of the world by an internationally united financial capital".[7] International cartels lasted only as long as equality between their constituent parts. When the condition of equality no longer existed, the latter turned to their primary objective of attaining monopoly power within the world system with the consequence that each of the surviving national monopolies called upon the state to support its struggle for the control of the world economy. The ensuing transition from the minimal state of classical liberalism to the neo-mercantilist state of the advanced capitalist societies signified the development of the final stage of capitalism.

Of the two classical Marxist texts devoted to these themes, Bukharin's *Imperialism and the World Economy* presented the more detailed examination of this metamorphosis of the capitalist state. To some extent, Bukharin's essay was an obituary for the liberal notion that the state is a nightwatchman standing aside from civil society and the management of international economic affairs. The laissez-faire state had only existed because of the "unorganised" nature of the class which had been dominant in civil society in earlier stages of capitalist development.[8] By contrast, the modern finance oligarchy involved the state in national economic planning and implicated it in the process of economic and military competition with the dominant classes of other societies. When free market capitalism was superseded by the monopolistic stage, so was the laissez-faire state replaced by "state monopoly capitalism" - that condition in which the "entire national economy" became "one gigantic combined enterprise under the tutelage of the financial kings" who were closely allied with the holders of state power.[9] The demise of the dichotomy between state and society was accompanied by the destruction of an independent realm of international economic relations which had been regulated by the principles of the free market. State monopoly capitalism transformed state structures into agencies which were responsible for establishing protectionist barriers to foreign competition, which used their power to compel weaker states to allow the entry of foreign commodities into their markets and which forced them to accept unfavourable terms of trade.

According to Bukharin, the emergence of tariff wars was a prelude to the inevitable resort to military force for the purpose of maximising economic power. Annexation of colonial territory represented a further extension of the shift from economic competition to military conflict in the world economy. Competition for "free land" in the non-European world, for the "redivision of colonies", and finally for control of the territories of the metropolitan capitalist societies themselves formed successive stages in the inevitable demise of the liberal idea of a natural harmony of interests between capitalist states.[10] State monopoly capitalism destroyed the condition in which societies were primarily linked together by commodity exchange. It created cohesive national states which were locked in a military struggle for economic dominance in the international system. Contrary to orthodox liberalism, the highest stage of capitalism did not bring the human race closer to the ideal of universal harmony but plunged the states of Europe into a war for the final "division of the world".[11]

The analysis of imperialism located the traditional point that the universalisation of economic and social life was the dominant process in the nineteenth century within a novel examination of the rise of increasingly particularistic nation-states. In his consideration of the modern conflict between particularism and universalism, Bukharin wrote that "the growth of the system of production relations on a world-wide scale is of two kinds. International connections may grow in scope, spreading over territories not yet drawn into the vortex of capitalist life. In that case we speak of...the extensive growth of the world economy. On the other hand, they may assume greater depth, become more frequent, forming, as it were, a thicker network. In that case we have an...intensive growth of the world economy".[12] In this context the world economy was more than "an arithmetical total of national economies", just as the national economy was no longer "an arithmetical total of individual economies within the boundaries of the state territory".[13] Furthermore, relations between states no longer took place within a kind of "vacuum".[14] Their behaviour was now "conditioned by the special medium in which the national economic organisms live and grow" - the medium of the world economy.[15] Bukharin's perspective clearly denied the possibility of abstracting the states-system from other domains, particularly from the world economy which was the totality which social theorists now had to understand.[16]

The observation that the nation-state was the main beneficiary of this process of internationalisation - and the main agency through which its contradictions would be revealed - was central to Bukharin's analysis of conflict within the world economy. Marx had argued that the contradiction between the social nature of production and the individual appropriation of wealth was the basic contradiction of capitalism. It was this contradiction which would generate the movement to socialism through the agency of class conflict. Bukharin argued that the contradiction between the internationalisation of production and the national appropriation of wealth had become the fundamental contradiction in a capitalist world system in which the processes of intensive and extensive growth were developing hand in hand. The state's responsibility for extracting as large a share of world product as possible created the condition in which interstate conflicts eclipsed, albeit temporarily, the opposition between the two major social classes.[17] These rivalries between particularistic states provided the key to the transition from the alienating internationalisation of economic and social life which existed under capitalism to an authentic socialist universalism.

For Bukharin, as for Lenin, the intensive and extensive growth of the world economy enhanced the state's capacity to act as a national actor. Accordingly, references to the nationalisation of important elements of the European proletariat abound in their writings on imperialism. Bukharin expressed his agreement with Hilferding's remark that class conflict had been "annihilated" and "absorbed" in the ideology of "national grandeur".[18] In response to the increase of interstate rivalries, the bourgeoisie and the proletariat in each state developed "a relative solidarity of interests that are opposed in substance".[19] Consequently, at the beginning of the First World War the working classes, which had become "chained to the chariot of...bourgeois state power", immediately rallied to the call to defend the national homeland.[20] In a famous argument, Lenin introduced the concept of the labour aristocracy to explain how a major element within each national proletariat had been won over by the nationalism and militarism of the bourgeois state. Bribed by sharing the profits of colonial exploitation, the labour aristocracy had become the voice "of the bourgeoisie in the working class movement".[21] Its existence blurred the traditional division between the two major class antagonists. Lenin's observation that no "Chinese wall separates (the working class) from the other classes" reflected the new relationship between class, nation and state which existed in the epoch of monopoly capitalism.[22]

Lenin and Bukharin did not believe that the Marxist idea of the centrality of the class struggle would have to be renounced simply because inter-state conflict had become the dominant feature of the monopoly stage of capitalism. Their analysis sought to demonstrate that the success which the national bourgeoisie had enjoyed by shifting the "centre of gravity" from class conflict to inter-state warfare would not last indefinitely. For this purpose they argued that the experience of modern war would give rise to a new set of revolutionary circumstances. The horrors of war would demonstrate to the working class that its "share in the imperialist policy is nothing compared with the wounds inflicted by the war".[23] War would sever the "last chain that binds the workers to the masters" and destroy the formers' "slavish submission to the imperialist state".[24] Instead of "clinging to the narrowness of the national state" and continuing to succumb to patriotic ideals of "defending or extending the boundaries of the bourgeois state", the proletariat would reaffirm its mission of destroying class differences and of "abolishing state boundaries and merging all the peoples into one Socialist family".[25] Bukharin believed that the experience of total war would ensure that the centre of gravity of social conflict would return to the axis of class conflict once again. It is worth noting that Bukharin's analysis of the probable effects of war displayed a confidence which Engels' later remarks on the relationship between war and human progress seemed to lack.

THE QUESTION OF INTERPRETATION

The point which is most often made against Marxist approaches to imperialism is that the economic causes of colonialism were far less important than the exponents of these perspectives would have us believe. To support this line of criticism, it has been argued that of all the colonial powers only two powers, Germany and the United States, displayed any of the features of monopoly capitalism. Evidence that Italy and Russia imported capital in the period when colonial expansion was at its height has been cited against the Marxist theory of imperialism. So has the point that the main colonial powers invested in each other's economies during the period of colonial expansion while Britain continued to invest heavily in the United States and the dominions rather than in the newly-acquired colonial territories. Most of the literature devoted to assessing the Marxist theory of imperialism has concluded that there are no empirical grounds for arguing that colonialism was caused by the overproduction of capital.[26]

In a dissenting approach, Eric Stokes claimed that such criticisms are entirely "wide of the mark".[27] Stokes maintained that the main responses to the Marxist theory of imperialism have taken issue with a "caricature" of the original perspective.[28] As a result, the conventional critique of Marxism has failed to deal with its most important propositions. What is more, it has overlooked the extent to which Marxist and non-Marxist interpretations of colonialism possess relatively similar explanations of its fundamental causes.[29]

This dissenting approach points out that there is a distinction between colonialism and imperialism in Lenin's work which the critics usually conflate. In particular, Lenin stated that colonialism not only preceded imperialism but was one of the factors which made imperialism (the monopoly stage of capitalism) possible. According to this interpretation, Lenin clearly stated that "the era of monopoly finance capitalism did not coincide with the scramble for colonies between 1870-1900 but came after it".[30] Moreover, it was only towards the end of this period of colonial expansion, according to Lenin's own account, that the "export of capital" started to reach "enormous dimensions".[31] For these reasons the dissenting voice in the literature states that conventional interpretations and criticisms of the Marxist theory of imperialism are irrelevant. The analysis of imperialism could not have aimed to establish a causal connection between the production of surplus capital and nineteenth century colonial expansion if, by its own admission, the epoch of monopoly capitalism did not begin until the early part of the twentieth century.

We shall return to the question of colonialism in a later section. Although it may have presented a false interpretation of the Marxist theory of imperialism, the literature which deals with the causes of overseas expansion nevertheless raises important issues for an inquiry into realism, Marxism and the critical sociology of international relations. At this stage, it is necessary to turn to the revisionist claim that the Marxist theory of imperialism was not an analysis of colonialism, but an investigation into the causes of the First World War.

Norman Etherington has argued that the period between 1895 and 1920 is "the primary testing ground for all the classic theories of imperialism".[32] Etherington adds that "this was the period when financiers and economists recommended that nation states should make the expansion of capitalism a matter of conscious planning...(and) in which adventurous politicians argued that unless they employed the full force of the armed state to maintain avenues for future expansion their nations would perish in war or revolution".[33] Etherington cites Fritz Fischer's writings as the most important attempt to develop an account of the origins of the First World War which reflects the spirit of early twentieth century Marxism.[34] Furthermore, the critical literature provoked by Fischer's explanation of how "the full force of the armed capitalist state" was "employed to secure the outlets for investment capital" and to appropriate the "raw materials which were thought to be necessary for survival in the twentieth century" is for Etherington the sole exception to the "pattern of neglect" which has surrounded the central arguments of the Marxist theories of imperialism.[35]

Fischer's primary contention was that Germany's drive for world power was the main reason for the outbreak of the First World War. In part, Germany's world ambitions stemmed from the belief that industrial powers such as Britain owed much of their economic success to the material resources which they derived from their military presence overseas. A second motive was the need for external distractions to combat the domestic instabilities which modernisation caused in Germany's archaic social and political structure.[36] To that extent there are parallels between Lenin's discussion of the relationship between capitalist development and the metamorphosis of state structures and Fischer's explanation of the particular case of German foreign policy. Even so, Fischer's inquiry into

Germany's responsibility for the outbreak of the First World War did not conclude that the need to find overseas outlets for surplus capital was a major cause of increased international rivalry. In short, Germany did not experience a crisis of the overproduction of capital for the simple reason that rapid industrial growth had exhausted its capital reserves.[37] Although it may be the case that Fischer's explanation of the causes of the First World War is "basically..a Marxist approach",[38] it nevertheless fails to validate the core of Lenin's argument. Even if one allows for the fact that Lenin's hastily-improvised sketch of the nature of imperialism barely touched on the "non-economic aspects of the question" - and Lenin admitted as much - his perspective clearly concluded that monopoly capitalism was the "fundamental" cause of the First World War.[39]

It may be true that the Marxist "insistence that the real or imagined need for the armed state to promote economic well-being was the most basic cause of the war is still a hypothesis worth testing against the historical record".[40] There is no reason to suppose that the record will offer any new grounds for endorsing Lenin's argument that the dominant logic of monopolisation was the principal force at work in this period of European history. This would appear to confirm, albeit on different grounds, the conventional argument that the Marxist theory of imperialism was guilty of economic reductionism. No further comment might have been required had the proponents of this critique been content to leave the matter there. Too often, however, those who have advanced this argument - particularly those who subscribe to the more conventional forms of international theory - have drawn the inference that the reductionist character of Lenin's theory of capitalist imperialism threw the basic weaknesses of all economic approaches to international politics into bold relief; and too often the theory of capitalist imperialism has served as a foil for realists as they advanced their opposing argument that the systemic forces which dominate international relations were the real cause of colonial expansion.[41] By adopting this approach, realists overlooked the main contribution of Lenin's analysis of international relations which was its attempt to understand the relationship between the process of capitalist development, the contraction of the sense of international community (as a result of the nationalisation of sections of the working classes) and the increased propensity for violence between nation-states. The nature of this relationship was the puzzle which the theory of the superabundance of capital endeavoured to solve.

In this regard, what was interesting about Lenin's study of imperialism was its attempt to reveal the weakness of the classical liberal position that peace will reign supreme as long as extraneous factors do not disturb the equilibrium of the capitalist world economy. Lenin extended Marx's criticism that the bourgeois political economists assumed that capitalism was a natural and self-regulating economic order which greatly reduced the level of coercion in human affairs. To have thought as much was to have overlooked the extent to which the original preconditions of capitalist development had been established by force, as Marx argued in his comments on the "secret of primitive accumulation".[42] Lenin argued that the increase of military rivalry in the late nineteenth century occurred not because extra-economic factors disturbed the peaceful equilibrium of international capitalist relations but because the coercive potential of capitalism had returned with renewed vigour. By contrast, exponents of realism have argued that the liberal vision was defeated by the recurrent struggle for national power and security. The issue may not be whether strategic factors were more important than economic factors, or vice versa, but how these phenomena interacted so as to produce the international conflict which Lenin attempted to describe.

Many historical works have outlined the nature of the link between the problems of capitalist development and the decline of international order in the late nineteenth and early twentieth century. James Joll's discussion of the sweeping cultural changes which occurred during the world economic recession between 1873 and 1896 sheds a good deal of light on the period which Etherington regards as the "primary testing ground" for the Marxist theory of imperialism. Global recession undermined the liberal belief in the inevitability of human progress and created the context in which "crude evolutionary theories" such as Social Darwinism began to appear. Rapid population growth and escalating industrial militancy forced the state to assume greater responsibility for managing the national economy. In this changing environment the state began to employ the symbols of national unity as a means of holding centrifugal social forces in check. The state's resort to protectionism, which was one of the main illustrations of the changing relationship between the state and economy in the late nineteenth century, intensified international suspicions and rivalries. These in turn encouraged the process of colonial expansion which was one of the hallmarks of the period. In short, a general process of economic and political change produced corresponding changes in the international political culture and in the diplomatic culture which existed between nation-states. As a result, nation-states and their populations acquired new levels of tolerance for the use of force in international relations.[43]

Two parallel approaches to this period warrant brief consideration. One is Choucri and North's study of the sharp increase in the level of "lateral pressure" ("the process of foreign expansion of any activity") which occurred towards the end of the nineteenth century. They argue that in this period states extended their global reach in order to achieve a rate of economic growth which would keep pace with the rising expectations of their respective populations, and in order to finance the level of military expenditure which international economic competition now entailed. The ensuing dialectic between the struggle for global influence and wealth greatly expanded the possibilities for conflict between the major powers. Contrary to earlier perceptions that industrialisation would promote peace, the resultant pattern of development demonstrated that "growth can be a lethal process".[44]

George Lichtheim explored similar themes in his argument that "industrialisation promoted intra-European tensions which in the end wrecked Europe's predominance in the world scene". There is a parallel here between the "Fischer thesis" and the importance which Lichtheim attached to the domestic bloc of "industrialisers and landowners" which committed the German state to the pursuit of world power. This development gave rise to the "dynamic factor in European politics during the three decades terminating with the collapse of 1918". More specifically, there was a close relationship between the dialectic of power and wealth and the growing autonomy of the state. The state "was the only political instrument available for the attainment of supra-national aims", the only agency with the capacity to mobilise the whole nation in support of the global policies and ambitions which flowed from the state's new responsibilities for promoting "the logic of economic development". In this context the "military and diplomatic professionals" were given "a free hand" in the realm of foreign policy-making. The result was the destruction of the Concert system which had preserved international order for the greater part of the century.[45]

These approaches argue that these changes in the nature of the state and international relations can only be understood by taking account of the relationship between human society and the material environment. None of these approaches proposes an economic theory of the origins of war, but each seeks to show how international social and economic change made war increasingly likely. In particular, they begin to reveal how the sense of international community was eroded at the level of state structures.

Furthermore, although there is little explicit consideration of questions of method in these approaches, they display some similarities with recent arguments about the need for a new methodology for the study of international relations, and they overlap with current ideas about the possible composition of a post-realist theory of international relations. For example, each approach offers implicit support for Pettman's claim that the conventional study of international relations invariably begins in the wrong place by considering the strategic realm in isolation from the interaction between society and nature.[46] There are similarities between the above-mentioned approaches and Cox's argument for a more synoptic examination of the development of international society which considers domestic social forces, state structures and the principles of world order concurrently.[47] These approaches also lend their implicit support to Cox's defence of Gramsci's non-reductionist interpretation of the relationship between the material base of international society and the superstructure of interstate relations.[48] Furthermore, each approach indicates how a post-realist method for the understanding of international relations might consider the state's relationship with the three domains mentioned earlier in connection with nationalism - with civil society, the world economy and the international states-system. Finally, these approaches indicate what a critical application of this method might attempt to achieve, namely an understanding of how the state's location in these different but interconnected domains have influenced the sense of international obligation and community. They shed light on the way in which principles of international legitimacy - the region of approximation between domestic and international politics, as Wight put it - gradually changed in the late nineteenth century as the fabric of international order was torn apart by the resurgence of particularistic loyalties. The significance of these themes becomes clearer by turning to the literature on nineteenth century colonialism.

THE QUESTION OF COLONIALISM

Many of the critics of Marxist theories of capitalist imperialism may have been "wide of the mark" when they argued that colonialism was not caused by the overproduction of capital in the core regions of the world economy. Even so, this misunderstanding has had its positive side. The attempt to assess what was assumed to be an economic explanation of colonialism produced a range of competing explanations of colonialism which raise several important issues for a discussion of realist and Marxist approaches to international relations.

For present purposes the greater part of this section will concentrate on the following three approaches to the explanation of colonialism. There is, first of all, the dominant approach in international relations which holds that colonialism was the outcome of competition between the great powers, a manifestation of the strategic rivalries which are inevitable under conditions of anarchy. Waltz's analysis of colonialism belongs to this category of explanation, as does Cohen's revised formulation that the changing configuration of power within Europe was the principal cause of colonial expansion.[49] A second type of explanation locates the causes of colonialism in the domestic structure of particular societies. Schumpeter developed this approach in his thesis that colonialism was a manifestation of the atavistic qualities which had been inherited from pre-capitalist societies.[50] The idea of social imperialism, which maintains that colonialism was a means of promoting social integration in the colonising societies, also relies upon an endogenous mode of explanation.[51] A third method maintains that the differences between these approaches are ultimately less important than their shared Eurocentrism. All assume that the non-European societies were passive observers of a policy of expansion ignited by developments in Europe. In opposition to the Eurocentrism of these accounts, this third approach regards the crisis which appeared along the frontier between Europe and the non-European worlds as the key to colonialism. This crisis was the effect of peripheral resistance to European intrusion and the cause of the shift from informal to formal methods of controlling non-European societies.[52] The question of how these disputes might be resolved, or at least be narrowed, remains an intriguing problem raised by this proliferation of approaches to colonialism. This section has the less ambitious task of suggesting that there is an important element of complementarity between these approaches and a plausible case for combining elements of realism and Marxism within a more complete and convincing explanation of colonialism.[53]

Given this purpose, Lenin's comments on colonialism are an appropriate place to begin. As Stokes argued, Lenin's remarks about the causes of colonialism are sparse relative to his discussion of the international ramifications of the development of monopoly capitalism. Moreover, they are remarkably consistent with many of the mainstream explanations of colonialism which have been constructed in response to the alleged economism of Lenin's approach. This approach along with many of the critical reactions to it recognised that the colonial epoch was connected with the rise of new "independent capitalist states" in the latter part of the nineteenth century.[54] Lenin argued that the more even distribution of military power which succeeded the era of British hegemony led to a sharp increase in the level of international rivalry and insecurity.[55] This was the context in which European expansion occurred. A more recent example of this approach to colonialism is offered by world-systems theory and the literature on long cycles which both claim that the transition from unicentric to multicentric configurations of power generates a greater tolerance of the use of force in the conduct of external relations.[56]

In Lenin's thought, colonialism was one manifestation of the changing distribution of military power in Europe, a change which was deeply affected by the uneven development of the capitalist world economy. The colonial epoch marked the beginning of the resort to more violent means of appropriating the largest possible share of global product. On one level, then, the colonial powers embarked upon more aggressive forms of competition for control of raw materials and cheap labour supplies. Even so, colonialism was more than a struggle for the resources which clearly existed in the peripheral societies. Territory was often annexed without any real evidence that the colonial power would enjoy significant material benefits immediately or in the longer term. The desire to deprive competitors of any resources that these regions might be found to possess - however minimal the rewards might be - was often a more significant motive for territorial expansion. States became increasingly conscious of the long term danger of allowing free territory to fall into the hands of their rivals. As a result, they were often engaged in "the conquest of territory not so much directly for themselves as to weaken the adversary and undermine his hegemony".[57] At no stage, however, did Lenin argue that colonies were annexed because they could absorb the surplus capital of the core.

Lenin did not suggest that this discussion of uneven capitalist development, interstate rivalries and colonial expansion was in any way complete. He argued that a more comprehensive analysis would have to take account of the additional role of the "domestic" roots of colonialism.[58] In this context, Lenin cited Cecil Rhodes' famous remark that colonial expansion would help to prevent the social and political unrest which would almost certainly eventuate unless the state attempted to alleviate the poverty of members of the working classes.[59] Lenin's remarks on colonialism implied that it was important to consider the colonial state in its three principal locations - in the domestic mode of production and internal system of class relations, in the unevenly-developing world economy and in the international states-system where the process of uneven development generated the rivalries which were the immediate cause of overseas expansion. Of course, Lenin did not assume that the process of capital accumulation was one of several equally important forces which generated colonial annexation. The logic of capitalist development was the dominant logic which explained the state's role in each of the above-mentioned locations. Nonetheless, Lenin's *Imperialism* is significant because it suggests that an account of European colonialism might begin by analysing the interplay between these domains. Few of Lenin's critics have recognised that his essay - notwithstanding its commitment to the notion of the class-state - could be instructive in this regard. Ironically, the traditional reading of Lenin's essay has often replaced Lenin's imputed economism with a similarly "one logic" explanation of the colonial epoch.

Kenneth Waltz's *Theory of International Politics* is a case in point. Waltz accepts the traditional argument that Lenin was wrong to believe that the superabundance of capital compelled the great powers to annex additional overseas territory. A more accurate analysis of the causes of colonialism in Waltz's view would begin by recognising the primacy of strategic rivalry. Waltz's expression that "weakness invites control" summarises his alternative systemic mode of explanation. In short, "the imperialism of great power" will occur, in Waltz's view, as long as the major powers compete for power and security - as long, that is, as the condition of international anarchy continues to exist. Since colonialism is inevitable wherever military power is distributed unevenly, it is the "absence of imperialism in the face of unbalanced power" rather than colonialism itself which will always "sorely require explanation". As an exercise in reductionist explanation, Lenin's *Imperialism* engaged in a superfluous analysis of the way in which the internal composition of capitalist states led to the policy of colonial expansion. The process of capitalist development, or industrialisation, was significant insofar as it explained how the European powers came to surpass the non-European societies in the realm of military technology, so acquiring the capacity to wield political power over them. The incontrovertible fact that different types of society engaged in colonial expansion reveals that there was no need for Lenin to attach any significance to capitalism in order to understand the establishment of the overseas empires. The errors which lie at the centre of the Marxist explanation gave rise to equally profound misunderstandings about the prospects for international reform. Lenin reached the conclusion that socialism would eliminate colonialism from future relations between great and small powers because he failed to recognise that there are "good international-political reasons" why imperial domination will always exist.[60]

There is no reason to dispute Waltz's claim that Lenin underestimated the degree to which the system of states was independent from either domestic or international capitalist structures. It is worth noting, though, that Lenin did not assume that colonialism would be abolished simply by reconstituting capitalist states. While the project of building socialism certainly began by restructuring the capitalist mode of production within existing territorial states, its realisation also required strategies for unifying the species and for superseding international inequalities of economic and political development. In their response to the Marxist theories of imperialism, realists have rightly argued that the project of building socialism on a world scale will not progress very far if it fails to address the question of how strategic conflicts in international relations might be reduced or resolved. What should be resisted, nonetheless, is the more sweeping contention that the Marxist theory of imperialism fails to contribute to the study of international relations.

A brief excursus which considers the cognitive interests which underlie the realist and Marxist approaches to colonialism may reveal why this judgment does not hold. It may also reveal why these perspectives have different notions of what it is to explain colonialism, and why they possess seemingly irreconcilable analyses of its conditions of existence.

In the first place, it should be noted that Waltz is not concerned with the particular events and episodes which produced colonialism in the late nineteenth century but with the similarities between this historical period and the colonial epochs which went before and which may come after it. To put the matter differently, Waltz's analysis does not set out to explain the origins of colonialism in any particular era but to explain how colonialism can exist at all. It is an analysis of its necessary conditions of existence.

Such an approach may be all that it is necessary in order to explain the recurrence of colonialism. Like the analysis of systemic reproduction of which it is part, it sets out the minimal conditions for the existence of colonial expansion. This minimalist explanation is connected, moreover, with the apparently fatalistic observation that colonialism can be contained but never wholly eliminated. An approach with a cognitive interest in emancipation is no less obliged to take account of the conditions which make colonialism possible. However its interest in combatting any increase in the tolerance of force in any particular historical epoch requires a more comprehensive form of explanation. It has a more obvious need to understand not only the conditions which make colonialism possible but the complete range of necessary and sufficient factors which generate colonialism at a particular historical moment. The fact that the distinction between great and small powers is a constant feature of the system of states, whereas the incidence of colonialism is not, indicates that a systemic explanation omits a range of causal factors which must be considered by any critical response to the greater acceptance of violence in international affairs.[61]

It was for this very reason that Lenin advanced an account of the specific reasons for the occurrence of colonialism in the late nineteenth century; and it was for this reason that he endeavoured to understand how the modern colonial epoch differed from earlier periods of expansionism.[62] In order to assess the prospects for the restoration of socialist internationalism it was essential for Lenin to explain precisely how an earlier promise of universality had been broken by the resurgence of particularistic state structures. As a result, the Marxist theory of imperialism began to wrestle with the way in which the transition between capitalism and socialism had been distorted by relations between states. It is true that its explanation of the increased particularism of nation-states and its observations about how the trend towards the closure of political community might be reversed were far from convincing. Nevertheless, it addressed a question which is immensely important for any critical project in the field of international relations, namely how the sense of obligation or community in international relations expands and contracts from one historical epoch to another. By analysing the historical forces which transformed state structures and modified the dominant principles of international legitimacy in the late nineteenth century, the Marxist theory of imperialism embarked upon a project which was more intricate and profound than the attempt to explain the eternal recurrence of colonial expansion. What is most intriguing about it is its suggestion that the conflict between particularising and universalising processes can best be understood by analysing the state's locations in the three arenas mentioned above (in the national economy, in the world economic system and in the international system of states).

It is possible to construct a modified version of realism which is more sensitive to the way in which the interaction between domestic and international economic developments and relations between states generated colonialism in the latter part of the nineteenth century. Benjamin Cohen has argued that Waltz's third-image approach to war needs to be modified to bring the forces which led to a more even distribution of military power in Europe in the late nineteenth century into sharper relief. Cohen advanced the additional observation that colonialism was prompted by the realisation that the state's power in Europe was increasingly dependent on its ability to extend its economic and military influence beyond the continent itself.[63] It is worth noting that this approach has affinities with those perspectives (Lenin's approach belongs among them) which regard colonialism as a consequence of the interplay between changes in the "balance of production" and changes in the more conventional balance of military power.[64] Cohen's approach therefore enlarges Waltz's systemic explanation by including the specific historical processes and economic and strategic calculations which led the European powers to engage in overseas expansion precisely when they did. What Cohen's approach reveals, although this was not one of its major concerns, was that the traditional preoccupation with the differences between Marxism and realism has obscured real possibilities for theoretical convergence or synthesis.

Lenin and Bukharin included international systemic factors in their explanation of the trend towards national particularism among modern capitalist states. They did not isolate this dimension from developments in the class structure of colonial powers. As previously noted, Lenin thought it unwise to neglect many of the official justifications for colonialism which stressed how it might ease the strain on domestic social integration.[65] Indeed, this claim was advanced with such frequency by, for example, Chamberlain in Britain and by von Bulow and Bismarck in Germany that the literature on social imperialism has concluded that these motives were the principal reasons for colonial expansion. Hans Uhlrich Wehler has adopted this approach to analyse the relationship between class structure, state apparatus and foreign policy in the case of German colonialism. Although this approach indicates how an analysis of the transformation of principles of international relations should focus upon the impact of class forces on the state and foreign policy, it does not entirely neglect economic and international-political reasons for colonialism as we shall see below.

Wehler rephrases the argument that growth can be a lethal process. It is, Wehler argues, "a dangerous legend that rapid economic growth promotes social and political stability, thereby inhibiting radical and irresponsible policies".[66] Modernisation in Germany engendered a crisis of political authority in which new social forces challenged a distribution of power and wealth which served dominant aristocratic interests. In the context of the delegitimation of the old social order, the state was able to obtain "a remarkable degree of political independence" from "various social groups and economic interests".[67] It was able to make use of its autonomy to construct a new domestic political settlement in which "the pre-industrial elites of the aristocracy" made sufficient concessions to emergent forces to retain their customary privileges.[68] In short, the state eased the pressure on the traditional order "by guaranteeing the bourgeoisie protection from the worker's demands for political and social emancipation in exchange for its own political abdication, (and) by placating the landowning aristocracy suffering under the impact of the agrarian crisis and the industrialists complaining about depression and foreign competition with a fast-increasing tariff".[69] Bismarck abandoned his earlier hostility to colonial expansion when the forces pressing for radical social and political change threatened internal order and stability. By employing the ideology of national expansion and expounding the merits of "formal colonial rule" rather than "informal empire", the regime diverted "attention away from the question of emancipation at home towards compensatory successes abroad".[70]

Wehler's claim that "German imperialism is to be seen primarily as the result of endogenous socio-economic and political forces, and not as a reaction to exogenous pressures, nor as a means of defending traditional foreign interests" clearly downgrades the international systemic factors which are stressed in realist and Marxist accounts of colonialism.[71] Some sections of Wehler's argument suggest that interstate rivalries within the context of a depressed world economy worked in tandem with the domestic sources of colonialism. In the period under consideration national economic development became "bound up with a bitter economic competition on a worldwide scale between a number of industrial states, each grappling with similar problems and effects of growth".[72] In large part, Bismarck's renounced his earlier opposition to colonialism because rival powers had already resorted to "preclusive" imperialism from which they hoped to derive major commercial and political advantages.[73] Wehler contends that Bismarck "gradually yielded to the pincer movement from without and within, to the threatening dangers of overseas competition and to the mounting desire to cope with the crisis caused by an explosive and unstable industrialisation".[74] For this reason, Wehler's argument is closer than it might seem at first to the position that an analysis of colonialism should investigate the state's multiple relations with civil society, the world economy and the international states-system. What it does is place the emphasis upon the internal class forces which conditioned the exercise of state power though not at the cost of neglecting the extent to which developments in the national economy and in the international economic and political system made their own contribution to colonialism.

The perspectives which have been considered thus far agree on one important point which is that events in Europe were the main cause of colonial expansion. Little or no attention is paid to events within non-European societies or to their response to European intrusion. Robinson's remark that "more often than not it was (the) non-European component of European expansion that necessitated the extension of colonial empires" is one illustration of a very different mode of investigation which challenges the alleged "Eurocentric" bias of so much of the literature on colonialism.[75] This perspective, which Robinson describes as the "excentric" approach and which Fieldhouse calls the "peripheral" approach, contends that it was peripheral resistance to the European presence which triggered the establishment of the overseas empires.[76]

An important distinction between the reasons for European penetration of Africa, Asia and the Pacific and its subsequent policy of territorial annexation is central to both approaches.[77] Fieldhouse has argued that European intrusion was often caused by commercial and strategic ambitions, by a curiosity about the exotic and, not least, by a paternalistic desire to enlighten uncivilised peoples. None of these factors is, in Fieldhouse's judgment, sufficient to explain the transition from informal to formal methods of exercising control over peripheral societies.[78] In the early stages, the Europeans exhibited a clear preference for the informal control of the inhabitants of peripheral areas. The economic burden of establishing and maintaining empire seemed to outweigh any likely material benefits. Robinson argues that for this reason the Europeans attempted to realise their objectives by forming alliances with indigenous elites: "Without the voluntary or enforced cooperation of their governing elites, economic resources could not be transferred, strategic interests protected or xenophobic reaction and traditional resistance to change contained. Nor without indigenous collaboration, when the time came for it, could Europeans have conquered and ruled their non-European empires".[79] What needs to be explained then is the process whereby arrangements with local collaborators were supplanted by the very apparatus of colonial domination which the European powers had previously been reluctant to establish.

For Fieldhouse, the emergence of a widespread challenge to the presence of Europeans compelled the European states to establish bureaucratic methods of control. Far from passively observing the consequences of decisions taken in Europe, non-European societies initiated the events which brought about their incorporation within the colonial empires.[80] Robinson maintains that annexation occurred because the informal arrangements between the Europeans and local collaborators finally collapsed: "When mediators were not given enough cards to play, their authority with their own people waned, crisis followed, and the expanding powers had to choose between scrapping their interests or intervening to promote them directly".[81] Fieldhouse maintains that the decision to annex peripheral societies was a hastily-contrived response to the mounting challenge to the European presence rather than a measured and premeditated policy of colonising select areas. For the most part, the colonial powers were drawn into "an inevitable but random process" which quickly began to "(recede) out of control". They were victims of the "magnetic attraction of the periphery".[82] More recently, Robinson has reaffirmed the claim that "imperialism was not simply something that Europe did to other countries, but also something (imperialists) were persuaded or compelled to do to themselves".[83]

One of the chief merits of this approach is that it reveals that many explanations of colonialism have explained the fact but not the form of European expansion, not the reason that is for the policy of territorial annexation. Waltz's proposition, for instance, that "weakness invites control" overlooks the important distinction between the extension of influence and the particular method by which power is exercised. The peripheral or excentric approach has been criticised, however, for underestimating the impact of developments within Europe upon the process of colonisation. According to Brewer, the shift from informal to formal methods of exercising control cannot be explained by concentrating simply on the traditionally neglected phenomenon of peripheral resistance: "Excentric theory cannot stand alone, since it is an explanation of forms of political control, and these cannot be divorced from the development of economic, political and social structures in both centre and periphery."[84] And Doyle argues that peripheral explanations "neglect the metropolitan motive forces of imperialism which are needed to explain all but the most exceptional cases of active peripheral surrender."[85]

If, as Robinson maintains, colonial powers faced the choice between "scrapping their interests" and "intervening to promote them directly", then peripheral revolt was not enough to provoke colonialism.[86] It is also necessary to explain why it was that a logically possible choice was politically unattractive in the period in question. One conceivable answer is that the logical possibility of European withdrawal was unrealistic in practice because the European states were involved in what they regarded as a zero-sum struggle for military power and economic development. In fact, this struggle between the European powers is central to Robinson and Gallagher's explanation of colonialism, as their comments on Tropical Africa clearly show: "The quickening occupation of Tropical Africa in the 1890s...was the double climax of two closely connected conflicts: on the one hand, the struggle between France and Britain for control of the Nile; on the other, the struggle between European, African, Christian and Muslim expansions for control of north and Central Africa."[87] Fieldhouse also offers support for this thesis by observing that colonisation occurred in the context of "growing international rivalries" between the European powers. For this reason the idea of "defensive or pre-emptive colonialism" is a "credible hypothesis".[88]

By taking international rivalries into account, the advocates of the peripheral approach do not bring important changes in peripheral societies out of their former obscurity only to commit the error of regarding Europe as a homogeneous region which simply reacted to events in the periphery. The analysis of the crisis along the frontier between Europe and the periphery acknowledges the significance of the rivalries which were developing within an expanding European system of states. If the peripheral challenge provoked annexation because of state concerns about the impact of inaction upon national economic development and the distribution of military power in Europe, then the peripheral approach would seem to complement rather than contradict alternative explanations.

The main explanations of colonialism analysed above emphasise either the centrality of systemic factors, the problem of social integration in class-divided societies, or the crisis along the frontier between Europe and the non-European world. Each of these approaches assumes that colonialism was a response to a dominant logic of development operating inside the individual European states, in their international politics, or in their relationship with the outside world.[89] Although these perspectives often argue that colonialism was caused by a range of factors, some come very close to offering the kind of one-logic explanation attributed to Lenin. A more productive interpretation of Lenin's *Imperialism* would have recognised that it attempted to argue that political and economic factors interacted to increase the level of international conflict in the late nineteenth century, and it might have distinguished this task from Lenin's belief that war in Europe was the result of the rise of monopoly capitalism. That aside, the relationship between the logics of industrialisation and military competition - not that there is any sharp dividing line between them - is a plausible place to begin in order to explain colonialism and interstate rivalries in the period in question. One might conclude that none of the factors surveyed above "clearly dominated" and that "the impact of the one without the other would probably have been markedly different".[90] Or, one might suggest that the forces that gave rise to imperialism "are to be found in a fourfold interaction among metropoles, peripheries, transnational forces, and international systemic incentives".[91] In any event, the traditional assumption that realist and Marxist explanations of colonialism are fundamentally opposed does more to obscure than to explain the process of overseas expansion.

CONCLUSION

The realist claim that Marxist approaches to colonialism, militarism and war underestimated the independent role of strategic interaction has recently gained new advocates in the field of sociology. In an essay on the sociology of war, Michael Mann has taken issue with historical materialism on the grounds that militarism stems "from aspects of our social structure which are far older than capitalism", that is from competition and conflict between separate political associations which belong to a "multi-state system".[92] Contemporary militarism is to be explained not by analysing the unique qualities of modern social and economic structures but rather by considering the "geopolitical pretensions of the superpowers - the same pretensions as Greece and Persia, Rome and Carthage, possessed".[93] The sociology of war can therefore discount the argument that capitalism caused militarism in its own right. What it must focus upon instead is the way in which capitalism promoted the unification of nation-states and made possible the dissemination of militarist ideology across entire communities. The main weakness of historical materialism as an account of militarism was the lack of recognition that capitalism appeared within a "mould" which was already "firmly set" and that it contributed to militarism by enhancing the state's capacity to mobilise the masses in support of its political and military ambitions.[94]

Like Waltz's approach to imperialism, Mann's essay is an explanation of what it is that makes militarism possible: what it does not do is provide a complete account of how the incidence of militarism has fluctuated historically or of how different societies and their constituent groups respond differently to appeals to support militarism. Mann offers a single logic explanation of militarism which notes its relationship with the propensity for violence in international affairs and overlooks the particular episodes and developments which would explain these historical fluctuations and varying levels of social support. Consequently, in answer to the critics who have argued that the Marxist theory of imperialism may have been insufficiently sensitive to the systemic causes of militarism, it might be argued that its attempt to establish a direct relationship between capitalism and militarism did contribute to an understanding of the greater likelihood of war towards the end of the nineteenth century. There is an interesting affinity between Choucri and North's emphasis on the increase of lateral pressure in this period and the Marxist theme that the increased economic and political unification of the world which occurred because of capitalism (as opposed to the increase of national integration which Mann emphasises) enlarged the opportunities for interstate rivalry and conflict. It is certain that capitalism or any approach to industrialisation would not have had this consequence but for the prior existence of interstate conflict; but if it is also the case that the appeals of militarism would not have increased so sharply in the period in question but for the international consequences of capitalist development then there are good grounds for arguing that the strengths of realism and Marxism should be incorporated within an historical sociology of international relations in the period in question.

The same theme can be explored at a different level. Lenin and Bukharin's writings on imperialism developed Marx's point that human beings had first to create alienating universal social connections before they could either understand or control them. Bukharin's observation that the contradiction between the national appropriation of wealth and the internationalisation of production had become the fundamental contradiction in modern politics introduced the novel observation that these connections were now largely controlled or mediated by particularistic nation-states. As far as Lenin and Bukharin were concerned, there was no need to abandon Marx's ideal of a society which preserved the universal qualities of modern social and economic existence while removing the obstacles to human freedom which stemmed from the nature of class particularism. Indeed, Mill's comment that "the social problem of the future...(was) how to unite the greatest individual liberty of action with a common ownership in the raw material of the globe, and an equal participation of all in the benefits of combined labour" suggested that this political aspiration had, if anything, widened its appeal.[95] No less emphatically, Hobson maintained in conjunction with his analysis of the taproot of imperialism that the modern crisis made it necessary "to substitute struggle with the natural and moral environment for the internecine struggle of living individuals and species", and he went on to argue for a "growing solidarity of sentiment and sympathy" across the whole of humanity.[96] But, in practice, liberalism lacked more detailed solutions, while in the case of Marxism the ritual adherence to the panacea of international class revolution began to sound increasingly hollow as class conflict gave way to the new politics dominated by the nation-state.

To repeat Lichtheim's formulation, the crisis in the strategies of transition which had been favoured by these universalistic political perspectives occurred because "the nation-state was the only political mechanism available for the attainment of supra-national aims" in this historical epoch.[97] It became necessary at this point to note that the agenda of the critical theory of society was now far more complex than it had been for Marx and, indeed, for the first generation of Marxist writers. For at this point, its agenda needed to add the problem of overcoming national forms of appropriating the world's wealth to the classical aim of eliminating the phenomenon of the class-based appropriation of the fruits of production. Furthermore, it had to contend with the additional question of how to contain the worst effects of national approaches to physical as well as economic security - and it had to deal with all of these problems simultaneously.

These were important reasons for recognising the need to move to a "new problematic", as Horkheimer called it, which brought together political themes which had been developed separately in largely unrelated strands of radical political thought.[98] One strand which counts Rousseau and Kant among its members was concerned with the tension between the existence of the states-system and the possibility of moral and political autonomy. A second strand of radical analysis in which Marx's thought was dominant transformed the political project into an assault on the antinomy between material inequalities and social and political freedom. In light of the developments in economic and political affairs to which Marxist theories of imperialism reacted, it became essential to locate these considerations within a more broadly constructed radical project. The failure to undertake this project was the real failure of Marxist theories of imperialism. As the next chapter will try to show, this failure continues to afflict Marxist and neo-Marxist international political economy.

5 Marxist and Neo-Marxist Theor Inequality and Development

The events which led to the First World War made it necessary for Marxists to rework the conventional argument that capitalism would be destroyed by an international revolution of the industrial proletariat. In passing, the principal works on imperialism also commented on the extent to which international inequalities had increased in the modern era. Lenin argued that modern capitalism had "grown into a world system of colonial oppression and of the financial strangulation of the overwhelming majority of the population of the world by a handful of advanced countries".[1] In a similar vein, Bukharin referred to the effect of the uneven diffusion of the forces of production on the international division of labour. The "cleavage between town and country" - so typical of capitalist societies in general - now extended across the world as a whole in the shape of a division between the "industrial countries" and the "agrarian territories" which surrounded them.[2]

This distinction between core and peripheral regions of the world economy was not yet as significant as it would be in later theories of imperialism. Marxists in the classical mould recognised the destruction which capitalism brought about in the periphery as new territories were subjected to international relations of exploitation. But they did not break with Marx's belief that these societies would eventually enjoy social and material progress through contact with the West. This contention was disputed much later by the exponents of neo-Marxist accounts of world inequalities and development. These approaches established new categories for explaining the absence of material progress in the periphery. At the level of practice, they argued for the revision of orthodox Marxist strategies of transition so that national struggle rather than class revolution came to be regarded as the main instrument of domestic and global economic and political transformation.

Trotsky's principle of "combined and uneven development" was one of the first attempts to rework the analysis of the prospects for capitalist industrialisation in the periphery. And his claim that the revolution might erupt in the weakest link in the chain of capitalist international relations was one of the first major reassessments of the likely path to world socialism.[3] A more fundamental break with orthodox accounts of peripheral industrialisation occurred in the aftermath of decolonisation. In this context, neo-Marxist perspectives maintained that the gap between centre and periphery would not only survive but become even larger if peripheral societies remained within the capitalist world economy. This critique of the established Marxist account of capitalist expansion raised both theoretical and practical issues for socialism. It meant that the classical objects of analysis - modes of production, property relations, class antagonisms etc. - were replaced by a new conceptual framework in which the world economy was represented as a system of unequal exchange relations. In addition, it meant that the industrial proletariat could no longer be depicted as the representative of a universal interest. This class was regarded as one of the principal beneficiaries of the global system of dominance and dependence in which peripheral societies were imprisoned. Whereas classical Marxism had concentrated upon the struggle between antagonistic classes within specific national modes of production, neo-Marxists shifted the analysis to the struggle which existed between national movements and state structures as they endeavoured to appropriate the largest possible share of the world's wealth. While the former continued to believe that contact with the West would eventually bring about peripheral development, the latter argued that withdrawal from the global system of exchange relations was unavoidable if the periphery was to enjoy autonomous national development.

These approaches to international economic inequalities had a profound effect upon developments within the study of international relations. The emergence of North-South diplomacy and the South's demand for a New International Economic Order helped to create an intellectual environment in which theories of dominance and dependence became a major element in the critique of orthodox international theory. Marxist theories of economic exploitation and oppression became increasingly significant in international relations because they highlighted the normative omissions and biases inherent in classical approaches to the field. The reconstruction of international theory was defended on the grounds that the traditional preoccupation with power and security had helped to mask the international dimensions of poverty and inequality. For this reason, the analysis of dominance and dependence assisted the development of more critical orientations to international relations. By contrast with classical perspectives which focused upon strategic relations between monolithic national actors, the emergent structuralist approaches examined the relationship between the state, its constituent social classes and the stratified world economic system. Certain locations, it was observed, corresponded with high levels of economic development. Societies in these core areas of the world enjoyed a high level of domestic social integration, and they also possessed the resources with which to resist external penetration. Other locations generated economic stagnation or underdevelopment. These peripheral locations were distinguished by national fragmentation and by considerable vulnerability to external economic pressures and direct political interference. In addition, the transnational linkages which existed between dominant classes in the world economy determined the way in which life-chances were distributed unequally within the modern world system. These considerations became important in the study of international relations as a direct consequence of the growing influence of neo-Marxist theories of development and underdevelopment.

These approaches acted as a bridge which linked the study of international relations with the emancipatory project which is specific to critical social theory. The emergent structuralist approaches in international relations presupposed an emancipatory cognitive interest in altering the distribution of power and wealth in favour of the poorer regions of the world system.[4] Some proponents of these approaches within the field of international relations raised the further question of whether Marxist and neo-Marxist political economy had paid enough attention to the realm of strategic competition between nation-states.[5] The same point has been made in other branches of the literature. In a discussion of the methodological debates which have accompanied the development of various Marxist approaches to imperialism, Anthony Brewer noted that the "question of the appropriate level of analysis - world-system, nation state, unit of production or whatever...is a non-problem. There can be no question of choosing to analyse at one of these levels, and ignoring the others; any adequate account of the world system must incorporate all of them, and their interrelations".[6] With this point in mind, it is useful to consider the realist and Marxist accounts of the origins and persistence of international inequality. It is important not only to establish their main differences but to determine whether or not they are in fact amenable to synthesis.

POWER, ORDER AND INEQUALITY

The observation that anarchy breeds oligarchy is a recurrent theme in the classical theory of international relations. Inequality is regarded as inevitable as long as states are responsible for the maintenance of their own security.[7] In addition, inequality contributes to international order since it reduces the number of significant strategic actors in the international system and limits the range of fundamental national interests which have to be accommodated at any given time. Furthermore, the historical evidence does not provide any support for the proposition that "tranquility will prevail in a world of many states, all of them approximate equals in power".[8] For this reason, the inequality of states is not only unalterable but highly desirable. The benefits of inequality clearly outweigh any apparent costs as far as international order and stability are concerned.

This being so, members of the classical tradition have often been quick to sound the alarm when they have detected a serious challenge to the doctrine of the inequality of states. An important example is Robert Tucker's critique of the "new political sensibility" in which it is claimed that the West has been asked to satisfy Third World demands for a redistribution of the world's wealth in order to comply with its own moral convictions.[9] Aware that some groups in the West support this perspective, many new states have been assiduous in arguing for a major redistribution of wealth and power from the North to the South. They have argued that a transfer of wealth must occur in order to compensate the former colonies for the exploitation suffered during the colonial era. In Tucker's view, any considered response to the demand for international social justice must recognise that such demands are advanced "by states...on behalf of states".[10] It must also realise that "the growth of equality among states may prove quite compatible with a continuing, even perhaps a deepening, inequality among individuals within states".[11] A redistribution of military power in the system of states rather than the supersession of "the essence of power" would result from the decision to comply with the new sensitivity to international social injustice.[12] The emergence of a "new hierarchy" of power might make the preservation of international order more difficult to achieve in the long term: "For those who are able to pursue it, the logic of the challenge to inequality is inevitably the logic of nuclear proliferation. In turn, the logic of nuclear proliferation is one of decreasing control over the international system by those who are its present guardians".[13] In Tucker's view, the attempt to achieve equality between states would only compound the problem of preserving order in the context of anarchy.

Tucker's argument is a useful reminder that the new political sensibility can be hijacked by regimes whose commitment to social justice - in the domestic and in the international arena - can be entirely disingenuous. It does point to an important question, which has been virtually neglected by the Left, of how equalities between different societies and their inhabitants can be significantly reduced in a world in which there is distrust and competition between sovereign states. That aside, it is instructive that Tucker's analysis should concentrate exclusively on the dangers of, and constraints upon, the reduction of international inequalities. There is no attempt to refute any moral and philosophical basis for disputing the current level of inequality, and there is no investigation of the extent to which there may be more to the demand for the reduction of inequalities than sheer diplomatic deceit. By contrast, Marxist and neo-Marxist approaches observe that the demand for global equality is largely the outcome of the diffusion of the Western principle of self-determination in a world in which there are massive inequalities of power and wealth. The issue, on this account, is how this tension might give rise to movements whose commitment to the realisation of international social justice is absolutely authentic. Moreover, the argument that the demand for equality may pose a threat to international order overlooks the extent to which current levels of inequality in international relations now pose a threat to order in their own right. By neglecting this dimension of international inequality, realism is unable to defend its claim to superiority in the sphere of problem-solving. Its resistance to attempts to redress international inequalities suggests that, in this domain, realism has abandoned analysis for ideology.[14]

By contrast, the rationalist approach to international inequality argues that the principles of international order will have to be modified to overcome the harmful international effects of the uneven diffusion of modernisation. As noted in chapter one, rationalists claim that the decline of international consensus is the most serious of these effects.[15] Unlike realism, rationalism has interpreted the diplomatic objectives of new states as evidence of how the problems of inequality between states and inequality between individuals have come to be connected in modern international relations. As a result, international order will be more difficult to maintain without initiatives to reduce disparities of wealth at the national and at the international level. The rationalist argument agrees that some of the scenarios which Tucker regards as the probable result of satisfying the demand for international equality may well come about.[16] However the rationalist contention that there is indeed more to the modern doctrine of international egalitarianism than diplomatic manoeuvering, and its argument for striving to harmonise the traditionally conflicting goals of order and justice, recognise the validity of Third World claims for the reform of international economic relations. Its advocacy of practical efforts to extend the realm of society in the system of states, and its recognition of the need to expand moral and political community so that it embraces the weaker members of the human race, reinforce an earlier claim that rationalism should be placed above realism on a scale of approaches to international relations.[17]

Rationalism accepts the realist point that international anarchy is one of the main reasons for the existence of the inequality of states and one of the main constraints upon its supersession. On the subject of constraints on change, it adds that the principle of state sovereignty, which Third World states are often understandably reluctant to qualify in exchange for economic aid and assistance, inhibits a major transfer of wealth.[18] Important though this is, the emphasis upon the part that anarchy plays in generating inequality ignores the connections between international relations of production, global relations of exchange and unequal economic and political development. Here again, the realist or rationalist and the Marxist perspectives focus on dimensions of inequality which have tended to fall outside the other's purview. The Marxist tradition offers an account of the origins of international inequality in which the dynamics of modes of production and the world economy are allotted a privileged place. It analyses the political and ideological developments within the world economy which explain increasing resistance to the existing distribution of power and wealth. The realist tradition highlights one of the respects in which Marxist analyses are most obviously wanting - which is that their critical orientation towards the reduction of international inequalities may not progress very far unless they can discover means of weakening the traditional connection between the possession of superior economic and military power and the protection of national security, and unless they can identify means of increasing the level of society and solidarity between nation-states. For its part, the rationalist tradition indicates that the aim of maintaining international order requires the redress of some of the inequalities which exist in the contemporary international system. But it has not taken sufficient account of class-based constraints upon international economic and political change in the course of developing this argument. The shortcomings of realism, rationalism and Marxism reveal that no perspective analyses the way in which the relationship between the states-system, modes of production and the world economy determine the current distribution of power and wealth and shape the prospects for the extension of international moral and political community.

THE CONCEPT OF DEPENDENCY

An extraordinary proliferation of approaches to the world system which claim to be derived from, or affiliated with, the Marxist tradition has occurred during the past twenty-five years. These perspectives share Marx's observation that social stratification explains the structure of society and the nature of social change. They reiterate Marx's theme that the system of stratification generates the forms of conflict from which the main advances in human history ultimately stem. Marx's claim that social change occurs when a society fails to satisfy the new needs and wants which its own development has created - so that movements which are committed to social transformation inevitably spring into existence - also resonates throughout these approaches to the world system. Each of them advances the argument that the classical problem of social equality, which Marx analysed in the context of nineteenth century capitalism, "now stands before the world as a whole",[19] and each contends that the solution which envisaged the common ownership and management of wealth and resources must be implemented on a global scale. Beyond this point the paths of these various perspectives begin to diverge. The classical Marxist branch of this literature analyses the international relations of production through which the dominant classes in the world economy exploit the labour of others. It endorses the traditional view that class struggle remains the key to social and political emancipation at the domestic and at the international level. What is normally designated the neo-Marxist branch of radical political economy shifts the emphasis to the global web of exchange relations through which dominant nations, rather than classes, extract wealth from others. Exponents of this second group of perspectives generally conclude that oppressed national movements and state structures are the serious agents of progressive change. The group which was the privileged agent of change in classical Marxism - the international proletariat - no longer warrants this characterisation: its various parts are but the sub-divisions of the dominant and oppressor nations.

Neo-Marxist theories of development and underdevelopment emerged in response to the claims advanced by liberal modernisation theorists in the 1950s and 1960s. These claims were grounded on the basic premise that the world consists of "relatively autonomous societies developing in relation to one another along roughly the same path although with differing starting times and at different speeds".[20] From this perspective there seemed no reason to doubt that the developing world would eventually enjoy the same benefits of political modernisation and economic growth which accrued earlier to the majority of peoples in the West. In fact, the developing countries possessed significant "advantages of backwardness" including the capacity to import many of the economic and technological prerequisites of development.[21] On a different plane, they could more easily identify the components of their cultural traditions which they would have to shed in order to emulate the achievements of the West. These were important reasons for the considerable optimism with which the liberal-modernisation theorists viewed the prospects for development in the newly-independent nations in the 1950s and 1960s.

The first major critics of liberal modernisation theory - the Latin American school of dependency theorists - argued that an analysis of the particular histories of supposedly self-contained societies could not explain the different levels of development throughout the world. To discover the reasons for these inequalities it was necessary to analyse the formation of the capitalist world system, and it was essential to understand how the locations which different "societies" possessed within this system determined their prospects for economic and political development. The economic growth of the West would not have occurred but for overseas expansion which created, from the fifteenth and sixteenth centuries onwards, a periphery which was assigned the task of specialising in the production of the raw materials which were required by the core regions of Western Europe. The first regions to develop had not found it necessary to extricate themselves from colonial and neo-colonial forms of oppression and exploitation. They had not been obliged to free themselves from colonial structures which frustrated their economic development and dislocated their social and political organisations and relationships. The myth of the autonomous society invented by the modernisation theorists concealed the historical relationship between development in the core and underdevelopment in the periphery. It was the survival of these ties which continued to obstruct peripheral industrialisation and political autonomy in the latter part of the twentieth century. The supposition that economic and political modernisation would occur if the periphery emulated societies in the West failed to recognise the main reasons for peripheral backwardness. Peripheral societies would only recover past opportunities for enjoying autonomous economic development by freeing themselves from their dependent status within the world capitalist economy.[22]

These criticisms of modernisation theory were extended to cover a similar line of argument within the Marxist tradition. Marxists also assumed that the overseas expansion of capitalism would enable the periphery to repeat the journey undertaken by the first modernisers. In his critique of traditional Marxist analyses of the periphery, Andre Gunder Frank denied that the latter possessed dual economies in which an archaic feudal sector was opposed by a modernising urban bourgeoisie which would employ the benefits derived from alliances with foreign capital to promote the industrialisation of the periphery. Frank argued that all sectors and regions of the periphery - whether archaic or modern by Marxist terminology - conspired to preserve the periphery's dependent status within the global system of exchange relations. Accordingly, Frank disputed the Marxist argument that peripheral economic development would begin to occur when the national bourgeoisie acquired political hegemony. The historical evidence indicated that earlier patterns of dependency and exploitation continued despite the ascendancy of the bourgeoisie. Instead of promoting economic and political autonomy by revolutionising the forces and relations of production, the bourgeoisie perpetuated the classical pattern of trade in which the periphery exported primary commodities to the core and imported the luxury items which were desired by members of the locally dominant class. As a result, major sectors of the peripheral economy were organised to serve metropolitan interests rather than to meet the needs of the local population. From a different angle, these sectors were the foreign enclaves or outposts of the core, while the locally dominant classes were the overseas representatives of metropolitan economic and political interests.[23]

Frank's principal methodological innovation was to replace the myth of the autonomous society with the proposition that the world-system was a pyramid of exchange relations stretching from the most deprived areas of the periphery to the most highly developed metropolitan regions in the core. Frank relied on Baran's concept of monopoly power to describe this global chain of metropolitan-satellite relations and to explain the mechanisms by which surplus was extracted from the periphery and channelled upwards to the dominant interests in the core. At each link in the global chain, a metropolis exercised monopoly power over satellites which had to sell their products to its dominant interests - and every metropolis (apart from those at the pinnacle of the world economy) was the satellite of a new centre which wielded an equivalent level of monopoly power over its products. Frank argued that although each metropolis appropriated some portion of the surplus acquired from below, its main function was to serve as a transmission belt which moved surplus upwards towards the dominant regions in the core. At one end of this chain were peripheral regions suffering not only terrible poverty but an absolute decline of their income and wealth; at the other end was the developed core which was the main beneficiary of the global web of exchange relations.[24] In addition, Frank argued that this explanation of international inequality was confirmed by the evidence that economic development in Latin America had occurred only when its ties with the core had been weakened, as in periods of major war. The main political conclusion was that any serious attempt to achieve autonomous national development would have to begin by severing the bonds which tied the periphery to the capitalist world economy.[25]

Frank's decision to concentrate on the evolution of the capitalist world economy, and his analysis of the transnational linkages between core and peripheral elites, revolutionised the sociology of the Third World. The nature of the break with the classical view that national societies constituted the primary level of analysis provoked a series of debates, particularly on the Left. For the Marxist critics, dependency theory failed to construct an adequate conceptual framework for understanding core-peripheral relations. Its practical recommendations were considered naive and potentially harmful. Empirical support for the belief that economic development was impossible as long as the periphery remained part of the capitalist world economy was held to be in short supply. Consequently, although much of the general emphasis of dependency theory was absorbed within international political economy in the past two decades, there is now little dispute that dependency theory failed in its attempt to explain and to solve inequalities of development.[26]

Arguably, the most basic theoretical difference between Frank and his Marxist critics - between circulationists and productionists as they have come to be called - revolved around their contrasting views of the nature of capitalism.[27] Whereas Frank regarded capitalism as an international system of exchange relations, classical Marxists defined it as a mode of production in which the proletariat entered into a contract to receive wages in exchange for alienating the control of its labour power to the bourgeoisie. Whereas Frank maintained that exploitation occurred in the sphere of exchange, his Marxist critics argued that it occurred within the sphere of production. For Frank, a world-wide system of capitalist exchange relations had been established in the sixteenth century during the first wave of European overseas expansion. For the latter, capitalist relations of production had become dominant in core societies during the nineteenth century. In opposition to dependency theory, Marxists argued that capitalism was only one of several modes of production - the dominant one nonetheless - which were articulated to form the world economy. In fact, the existence of the world economy was itself the result of the expansion of the capitalist mode of production.[28]

One of the major issues in these debates was whether international inequalities were more likely to be explained by overturning Frank's thesis that the part (the mode of production, the national economy etc.) was subordinate to the whole (the capitalist world economic system). The Marxist argument claimed that it was essential to begin by analysing the dynamics of individual modes of production. From there one could proceed to analyse the way in which various modes of production were connected at the local, national and international levels. Such an analysis would explain the nature of the exploitation of labour. It would also reaffirm the central importance of the class basis of exploitation and recover the idea that class conflict was the principal mechanism for bringing the oppression of labour to an end. These arguments were the key to the contention that the idea of a chain of metropolitan-satellite relations conceptualised exploitation in spatial terms, as a relationship between regions rather than as a relationship between dominant and subordinate classes. In turn, Frank's argument that surplus was extracted from the periphery through the medium of exchange relations with the core was accused of presenting a static interpretation of core-peripheral relations. The significance of fundamental changes in the international organisation of labour was missing from the account. What was overlooked most of all was the more recent trend towards the internationalisation of capitalist relations of production which enabled dominant classes to appropriate wealth through the direct exploitation of peripheral labour forces.[29]

The argument that the underdevelopment of the periphery was explained by its entanglement in the global structure of metropolitan-satellite relations led Frank to the conclusion that total withdrawal from the world economy was a sine qua non of peripheral development. The Marxist analysis of the internationalisation of capitalist relations of production produced the opposing conclusion that the strategy of national secession would have disastrous results for the majority of peripheral societies. As Kay put it, the problem was not that "capital created underdevelopment...because it exploited the underdeveloped world, but (that) it did not exploit it enough".[30] Leaving aside a few underdeveloped regions which were richly endowed with natural resources, most peripheral societies could not achieve significant economic growth in isolation from the most highly-developed regions of the world economy. Without the capital, technology and expertise which the latter possessed, and which they alone could supply, most societies in the periphery would face the prospect of continued economic stagnation and prolonged social and political backwardness. The problem which confronted most peripheral

societies was how to increase the proportion of wealth which could be
created through arrangements with the managers of foreign capital. This
possibility could only be grasped if new state structures reflecting a
different configuration of domestic class forces came into existence in the
periphery. The fact that newly-independent states had exercised their
sovereign power to increase their proportion of the world's wealth
revealed that Frank's analysis of core-periphery relations was
fundamentally mistaken. It was indeed the case, as Frank had argued, that
the location of the periphery within the world economy could be a major
constraint upon autonomous national development, although that alone did
not make it impossible for the periphery to improve its position within
the capitalist world economy. To assume that economic progress could not
occur was to fail to understand how new configurations of political power
in the periphery could bring about significant material development.[31]

This mode of analysis reaffirmed the traditional Marxian argument that
capitalism is "a process of development...transforming the world" rather
than an "essentially static system of redistribution" retarding peripheral
development, as the dependency theorists had argued.[32] The Marxist
literature concluded that dependency theory was inadequate on
theoretical, empirical and practical dimensions. In the first place, the
observation that capitalism necessarily underdeveloped the periphery was
open to one major theoretical objection. By the terms of the original
argument, the core seemed to have more to gain than to lose from
promoting the industrialisation of areas where there was a plentiful
supply of cheap labour power and raw materials.[33] For certain writers,
Warren among them, the empirical evidence clearly demonstrated that
capitalism had generated peripheral industrialisation while promoting a
qualitative improvement in the economic and social conditions of Third
World populations.[34] No less important, capitalism was still the main
agent of social and political enlightenment in the periphery. It "was the
first great civilisation to create *mankind* as distinct from individual
relatively distinct communities and civilisations...As such it created the
material basis for a further advance of that morality based on a
conception of human unity".[35] In this account, capitalism retains its
special relationship with the goals of the Enlightenment: it is one of the
principal historical forces creating the possibility of emancipation for the
whole species.

When discussing the material and moral benefits of capitalist expansion,
Warren did not take issue with the approaches which have contended that
capitalist expansion integrates particular sectors of the peripheral
economy within a world market which subordinate classes are clearly
powerless to control. His approach did not deny that in many instances
the repatriation of profit from the periphery to the core had restricted
Third World development; nor did Warren disagree with the contention
that the relationship between core and periphery was characterised by
uneven development. What Warren's approach chose to emphasise in
reaction to the romantic nationalism which he imputed to the dependency
theorists was the extent to which capitalism had been a force for
economic and political progress throughout the world. Warren maintained
that the relationship between core and periphery had already been

modified by the international transfer of power and wealth which had taken place since the end of the Second World War. In this period, most peripheral societies had achieved their objective of national sovereignty, and many had used their increased bargaining power to ensure that a greater proportion of the wealth produced through arrangements with multinational capital was used to promote autonomous national economic growth. For these reasons, dependency theory had been wrong to urge the periphery to sever its links with the capitalist world economy. The central priority for radical movements in the periphery was the transformation of domestic social and political structures. Only in this way could they hope to increase the benefits which could result from international economic ties and relations.[36]

Warren's progressivist interpretation of the expansion of capitalism has come under criticism, although none of the critics denies the existence of peripheral industrialisation and the increasing power of peripheral state structures.[37] The more fundamental point is that the evidence of significant development in various sectors and regions in the periphery should be considered in conjunction with a number of countervailing trends. One trend is the continually widening gap between rich and poor in the world system. In addition, poverty and malnourishment remain prevalent in many parts of the Third World, especially in rural areas. Current levels of Third World debt seem almost certain to continue to rise. Given these indicators of the plight of the periphery, much of the recent literature suggests that any fundamental structural change in centre-periphery relations is highly unlikely. Although this literature is not as pessimistic as dependency theory in the 1960s, it frequently observes that where development has occurred it has invariably been dependent and almost always uneven. This theme typifies the more cautious tone which is present in the recent literature on core-periphery relations.[38]

Moreover, contemporary writings on international inequality often support the Marxist argument that autocentric development in the periphery ultimately depends on the appearance of state structures which reflect new configurations of class power. It is generally agreed that a large number of peripheral societies will continue to experience economic stagnation unless there is a simultaneous restructuring of international economic institutions and relations. As a result, the idea that location in the world economy is a major determinant of the nature and extent of development has not lost any of the importance which the dependency theorists attached to it. Nevertheless, it is generally agreed that dependency theory has now been superseded. It is acclaimed as the perspective which radicalised thinking about the developing world at a time when modernisation theory was supreme. But none of the existing currents of literature argues that the idea of a global chain of metropolitan-satellite relations explains the system of global dominance and dependence.

THE WORLD-SYSTEMS APPROACH TO INEQUALITY

A fuller account of world-systems theory - the most influential of the perspectives which may said to have inherited the mantle of dependency theory - will be presented in the following chapter. This section restricts the discussion to those dimensions of world-systems analysis which are specifically concerned with the origins, reproduction and possible reduction of international inequalities. Wallerstein, and other exponents of the world-systems perspective, argue that some peripheral societies have enjoyed significant industrial development without seceding from the capitalist world economy. But the simultaneous development of all peripheral societies, and the supersession of unequal development must await, as they see it, the establishment of a socialist world order. The world-systems theorists have argued that the radicalisation of the semi-periphery - a process which has occurred because of the limited prospects for development within the capitalist world system - indicates that the long term reproduction of the capitalist world economy is far from assured. On the same grounds they have argued that it is no longer utopian to envisage the establishment of a socialist world order. A socialist world economy is already developing within the current world capitalist system.[39]

There is a clear parallel between Wallerstein's argument that the world system comprises a series of "commodity chains" and Frank's contention that the world economy consists of a system of exchange relations.[40] To this common premise Wallerstein appends the additional observation that classes, national movements and state structures are concerned first and foremost with manipulating the world market so that it operates to their economic and political advantage.[41] The shape of the world economy is determined for the most part by territorial states which participate in a constant, zero-sum competition in order to capture "a greater or at least not a diminishing proportion of world surplus within (their) national boundaries".[42] Wallerstein's analysis of international inequality is distinguished from Frank's theory by the special importance it attaches to conflict between states: not only to the conflict between core and peripheral states but to the equally, if not more, important rivalries which exist between the core powers themselves.

In Wallerstein's account, all states are "like units" - to use Waltz's expression - because they are involved in an endless struggle to appropriate the largest possible share of the world's surplus. Their unequal capacity to achieve this, their principal end, is the most obvious indicator of the differences which exist between them. Wallerstein argues that it is necessary to analyse the historical development of the capitalist world economy from the sixteenth century in order to understand the origins and development of international inequality. It was in this period that the emergent core states of Western Europe solved the crisis in their economic and political organisation by integrating Eastern European societies and the non-European regions of the world within a new and exploitative international division of labour.[43] For this reason states did not come into existence as "like units duplicating one another's activities" but as differentiated units occupying quite different locations and performing diverse functions within the capitalist world economy. Wallerstein's renowned system of classification identifies three separate locations in this world economy: the polar opposites of core and periphery, and an intermediate position consisting of semi-peripheral societies which have traditionally lent an element of stability to the world system.[44] Wallerstein's account of the origins, reproduction and possible transformation of world inequality is specifically concerned with the chief characteristics of these regions and the means by which they are connected to the world economy.

The most "highly-mechanised, high-profit, high-wage, highly-skilled labour activities" have been monopolised by core societies since the establishment of the capitalist world economy.[45] These societies have dominated the production of manufactured commodities which are sold for profit in the world market. It was the wealth which resulted from this virtual monopoly of high-income earning commodity production which allowed the dominant classes in the core to establish the most powerful state structures in the world economy. By virtue of their economic and military power, core states had the capacity to overcome internal threats and the ability to ensure the pacification of their respective populations. They were able to achieve a high level of domestic social integration and to inculcate a strong sense of national identity later in their evolution. For these reasons, core states had the power to incorporate new territories and involve new populations in the international division of labour. The existence of powerful state structures enabled the dominant classes in the core to impose their will on weaker societies which were adjacent to, and which subsequently became part of, the capitalist world economy.

The peripheral regions have been distinguished from core regions by their specialisation in low-income generating "agricultural and mining activities".[46] The core imposed these forms of production on peripheral societies so that it could free itself for the task of specialising in high-profit commodity production. As a result of their allotted role as primary producers, these peripheral societies have always been highly vulnerable to changes in the world economy. States in the periphery usually lack the capacity to cushion themselves from the effects of economic downturn and recession in the world economy. Their income-earning power, which is significantly less than that of the core, prevents them from constructing powerful state structures which could counteract these global trends and alter the traditional location of the periphery within the international division of labour. Moreover, in the domestic sphere these societies have been especially vulnerable to external political interference and intervention. In part, this is a function of the external orientation of their major economic activities; but it also expresses their lack of national integration and the fact that locally dominant classes have an interest in perpetuating the periphery's dependent status.

The semi-peripheral societies combine many of the features of the core and the periphery. Their hybrid character is the result of their transitional state of development. In most instances, a society in the semi-periphery is either ascending from its peripheral location in the international division of labour or descending from membership of the core. In either event, the societies which form the semi-periphery exploit the periphery, and are in turn exploited by the core. For the most part, the semi-periphery has contributed to the reproduction of the capitalist world economy by revealing that development is possible within the existing form of world economic organisation.[47]

By virtue of their economic and military power, core states have been able to protect their domestic markets from the effects of foreign competition. They have also possessed the ability to limit the amount of repatriated foreign capital which is channelled away from the goal of continuing national development. In addition, according to Wallerstein, they have had the capacity to ensure that peripheral and semi-peripheral societies grant core commodities access to their markets. They have compelled weaker societies to accept unfavourable terms of trade. However, the economic development of the core has been furthered not only by the overt exercise of state power but by the covert operation of unequal exchange in international commodity relations. Wallerstein relies upon Emmanuel's thesis that "prices and profit rates are equalised internationally by competition (whereas)...wages are not" in order to establish the link between unequal exchange and inequalities of power and wealth in the world system.[48] According to this argument, the core imports commodities which are produced in peripheral areas where labour rates are low and, in exchange, it exports commodities whose cost reflects the significantly higher labour rates which exist in the core. The exploitation of peripheral labour through the medium of unequal exchange is the key to the process of capital accumulation in the core. Labour exploitation does not occur then in the sphere of production, as Marx's analysis of the extraction of surplus value had suggested, but in the sphere of international exchange.[49]

The main positions, into which all states are segregated as members of the capitalist world economy, have been the same for over four hundred years. On the other hand, the occupants of each of the three principal locations have changed considerably during the period in which the capitalist world economy has been in existence. The decline of core states is the clearest illustration of this dimension of the world system. The loss of competitive advantage in the world market is one of the main reasons for their decline. In particular, increasing wage rates in core societies drive capital overseas in search of the higher profits which can be obtained from investing in the less developed regions where labour costs are significantly lower. The impact of capital movements on the erosion of the core is intensified as semi-peripheral competitors erect trade barriers to protect their vulnerable infant industries. The ability to duplicate technological innovations which occurred in the core, and the capacity to purchase more sophisticated forms of technology without absorbing high research and development costs, further illustrate the advantages of backwardness.[50] For these reasons, the competitive advantage of the core is never so complete that it can regard itself as certain to escape decline.

Other strategies are available to the semi-periphery in its quest for advancement. These include adopting the strategy of self-reliance as a means of ending the status of dependency within the world economy.

During periods of intense core competition when a fall in world prices results, the semi-periphery may "seize the initiative" to acquire technology which had previously been beyond its reach. Economic development may result should one or more core states regard the co-option of a semi-peripheral society as a means of promoting their vital interests. In any event, upward mobility decreases the share of world surplus which other states can appropriate and confronts other states with the prospect of irreversible decline.[51]

Wallerstein's references to the inevitability of the de-industrialisation of the core and the industrialisation of the periphery might seem to lend some support to the Warren thesis. The main work to deal with the de-industrialisation of the core argues that the closure of the textile industry in West Germany and the relocation of textile production in South East Asia may well foreshadow a more profound restructuring of the world economy. Frobel, Heinrichs and Kreye emphasise the way in which the current revolution in technology and communications accelerates the process of major industrial relocation. Recent technological developments have made it possible to locate each of the main stages in the production of a commodity in an entirely different society. The assembly of the parts that make up the commodity may then be assembled in another society prior to sale in the world market. The various societies which take part in this process belong to what Frobel and his colleagues call the "new international division of labour".[52]

As the authors see it, the recent "transnational reorganisation of production" has already begun to dissolve the traditional dichotomy between the periphery and the core.[53] They suggest that the relocation of industrial production may be the beginning of the most important transformation of the world economy since the crisis of the seventeenth century.[54] Even so, they are far from confident that the blurring of the distinction between Western industrial societies and Third World primary producers means that the differences between core and periphery are about to come to an end. The dependent development of specialised, export-oriented enclaves in the periphery may be the principal effect of the modern internationalisation of production. It is improbable that this trend will lead to a generalised process of development of the peripheral economy as a whole. Increased vulnerability to world economic forces may create a condition in which the periphery acquires limited and dependent development in exchange for the "virtual abandonment of part of (its) national sovereignty".[55] Far from reducing current levels of international inequality, the new international division of labour may only "worsen conditions in the developing world" in the long run.[56]

Wallerstein argues that the fate of the capitalist world economy will be profoundly affected by recent trends in semi-peripheral societies. The radicalisation of the semi-periphery in the twentieth century is the main development which Wallerstein emphasises. In the past, the semi-peripheral regions lent stability to the capitalist world economy, but now the appeal of nationalism and socialism throughout the Third World has brought this function to an end. As a result, an increasing number of semi-peripheral societies in the twentieth century maintain that the capitalist world economy is the most fundamental obstacle to their social and political progress.[57]

Core states are losing the struggle to legitimate international inequalities. The options which are available to them are, moreover, severely restricted. The core cannot take measures to promote the semi-periphery as a whole without undermining its own hegemony. If it decides to procrastinate, it runs the risk of intensifying the opposition to the capitalist world economy. Wallerstein maintains that the attempt to co-opt a small number of the more powerful semi-peripheral societies will prove to be little more than a temporary solution. Other semi-peripheral states will quickly occupy any vacant positions in the queue which has formed in conjunction with the demand for economic and political mobility.[58] For these reasons, Wallerstein concludes that the capitalist world economy now faces the prospect of inevitable demise. The present stage in world development is a transitional one which will culminate in the establishment of a socialist world system.

Wallerstein's supposition that the present phase in the development of the capitalist world economy is transitional can be criticised on several grounds. As Cox and Warren have suggested, state formation and economic development in the peripheral and semi-peripheral world can be achieved by adopting strategies of individual advancement within the existing world system. The former need neither be linked with, nor need it give rise to, policies oriented towards the transformation of the international economic and political order. Secondly, the transition which Wallerstein envisages is improbable if the literature on the new international division of labour is substantially correct. The industrial decline of various core regions and the parallel industrialisation of sectors and regions in the periphery may generate new global power structures which ensure that the contemporary world order continues to be reproduced. The notion of transnational class formation points to one of the by-products of the new international division of labour in which fractions of the dominant classes in core and peripheral societies forge closer ties while opposition to the capitalist world economy continues to fragment.[59] Thirdly, Wallerstein's notion of transition can be criticised on the grounds that it wholly neglects the realm of national security politics. It fails to take account of the relationship between state-formation in peripheral and semi-peripheral regions (whether capitalist or socialist) and the continued reproduction of the logic of strategic conflict and rivalry. Paradoxically, Wallerstein's account of the capitalist world economy and its crises emphasises the state's location in the global economic system only to ignore the state's additional involvement in the diplomatic and strategic domain. The world-systems perspective overlooks the fact that in the past five hundred years strategic interaction as well as capital accumulation has developed on a world scale. What is more, it has tended to neglect the argument that the trend towards the restoration of traditional cultures in the periphery and semi-periphery may far outweigh any global convergence on the need to reorganise the world in accordance with the ideals of European socialism.[60]

MODE OF PRODUCTION, CLASS AND STATE

The issue of whether capitalism is a system of exchange relations or a mode of production might appear at first sight to be little more than a semantic dispute. In fact, it is the conceptual side of a substantive disagreement about the relationship between class and the state. According to Wallerstein, a class arises because its members have common interests vis-a-vis the capitalist world economy. The state is an instrument which the dominant class employs in its struggle with its competitors in the world market. For classical Marxists, classes form because their members have common interests vis-a-vis a particular mode of production and system of property relations. The state is an instrument which each class endeavours to control in order to achieve dominance over others. This question of how class and state are related is connected with a dispute about how to characterise the relationship between the world economy and the various forms of labour organisation which exist in its constituent regions.[61]

According to the world-systems theorists, the dominant class determines the mode of production which will prevail in its region. It is motivated by the aim of maximising profit from the sale of commodities in the world market. The classical Marxist tradition recognises that world market forces exert considerable influence upon modes of production. But it suggests that conflict between the owners of the means of production and the members of subordinate classes is a far more powerful influence. As far as this latter approach is concerned, world-systems theory underestimates the extent to which the various "parts of the world economy...have their own tendencies that derive from the modes of production installed there. This does not mean that they evolve independently of each other, but that analysis should start from the workings of distinct modes of production, and then go on to analyse how they interact with each another".[62] Put differently, to privilege the world economy is to misunderstand the real relationship between the structure of the part and the organisation of the whole.

The foregoing quotation indicates that modes of production are the appropriate point of departure for those working within the Marxist tradition. One strand of argument within this tradition maintains that a mode of production is an intellectual construct or abstraction rather than an actual historical phenomenon. In most instances actual societies comprise several modes of production. The crucial points is that the key to any society is to be found in the way in which these modes of production are articulated to form the whole - the social formation as it is called within the Marxist tradition.[63]

What applies to particular societies also applies to the world economy as a whole. It is also the product of the articulation of different modes of production. Consequently, an analysis of the way in which modes of production are combined to form national societies would be the starting point for the study of international inequalities. Such an analysis would then proceed to consider the means by which these societies and their constituent modes of production are articulated to form the world economy. Although this form of inquiry recognises the need to analyse relations between states in order to complete its analysis of the international articulation of modes of production, it has not considered the extent to which strategic rivalries within the multi-state system generate inequalities in their own right. The move from the study of exchange relations to the study of modes of production has not brought about any greater understanding of the relationship between development, inequality and the international system of states.

Those who favour the modes of production approach to inequalities of development argue that the economic development of Western Europe occurred because of a revolution in its property relations. The introduction of new forms of labour exploitation, rather than the creation of a world market which enabled the ruling classes to siphon off the wealth of peripheral and semi-peripheral regions, was the foundation of its economic success.[64] In more recent times, Soviet economic development has been regarded as the result of the transformation of its mode of production rather than as the outcome of strategies to increase its share of world surplus.[65] The opposing approach which "displaces relations of exploitation between classes in a national arena, and inserts at the centre of its analysis the problematic of the distribution of world surplus as between national units" is said to fail to explain the real origins of inequalities of development.[66] In addition, this shift from class to national forms of exploitation is also opposed because of its allegedly damaging economic and political consequences.

Of course, Marxist interpretations of the developmental opportunities available to the periphery do not assume that class conflict takes place in insulated national arenas. They have always been acutely aware of the international dimensions of economic development and class struggle. With the possible exception of Warren's critique of dependency theory, these approaches have found it necessary to reconsider the traditional belief that peripheral industrialisation would occur because of its ties with the capitalist core. Trotsky's argument that the process of combined and uneven development created peripheral social formations which were unlike any in the West stands at the beginning of this alternative line of inquiry.[67] One subsequent strand of this literature has endeavoured to show that the articulation of the capitalist and pre-capitalist worlds invariably restricts or distorts peripheral development. Amin's writings, which incorporated elements of dependency theory within historical materialism, sought to demonstrate that the articulation of these two worlds ruled out the possibility of the "autocentric" development of the periphery.[68] The latter's role as primary producer in the international division of labour largely precluded significant development. It also entrenched pre-capitalist social relations which barred the way to economic and political progress.[69] In a different approach to the articulation of modes of production, Rey argued that the structure of peripheral societies was responsible for counteracting the modernising potential which would otherwise accompany the expansion of capitalism. Many peripheral societies were articulated with the capitalist world in such a way as "to reinforce the hold of the pre-capitalist ruling class and reinforce the resistance of these societies to the implantation of capitalist relations of production".[70]

The Marxist literature has not produced a general theory of the articulation of modes of production which finally resolves these differences. Nor has it developed a satisfactory answer to the question of how the periphery could act to change its mode of articulation with the world economic system so that autocentric development would be more likely to result. To pursue this further, one must turn to a different strand of the literature which considers the nature of peripheral states and the strategies which they can adopt in their struggle for autocentric development.

One representative of this approach, James Petras, has claimed that the: "post independence national regime can choose among at least three strategies or types of class alliances for capital accumulation. In the first instance, it can join with imperial firms and regimes in intensifying surplus extraction from the labour force through a variety of post-independence working relationships outlined under the...rubric of "dependent neo-colonialism". An alternative strategy for the national regime involves extracting the surplus from the labour force and limiting or eliminating the share going to the imperial firm, thus concentrating it in the hands of state and/or private national entrepreneurs. This approach, which can be referred to as national developmentalism without redistribution leads to concentration of income at the top of the national class hierarchy. A third alternative is for the national regime to ally itself with the labouring population, extend the areas of national control (through nationalisation) reinvest the surplus of the national economy or promote a redistribution of income within the national class structure."[71]

Commenting on these approaches and their historical performance to date, Petras adds it has been "precisely the least national and most exploitative model" of development which has proved to be "the most effective instrument of capital accumulation or growth" in the periphery.[72] Those regimes which opted for radical-populist strategies of development have usually failed to generate high levels of economic growth and to survive internal or external challenges to their legitimacy.[73] Their problems have been compounded by the fact that the proponents of dependent neo-colonialism have often received decisive external support ranging from economic aid and covert political assistance to the direct use of military force. As a result, what one must attempt to understand is the internal and external factors which determine how far Third World states can combine economic growth with income redistribution.

Traditionally, observers within the Marxist tradition have emphasised two factors which are relevant to this question. They have argued that the character of the peripheral state is most deeply influenced by the nature of the domestic class structure and/or by the interests of the externally dominant class. In an attempt to develop class analysis, Petras and Cox have argued that the reproduction of domestic and international inequalities is a function not only of the articulation of modes of production but of the interpenetration or articulation of different state structures.

In his approach to this theme, Petras refers to the "imperial state" which maintains its preferred vision of world order by "integrating the commanding heights of the peripheral state into (its) overall politico-economic project".[74] In a similar argument, Cox refers to the "internationalisation of the state" to explain the role that core penetration of peripheral state structures now plays in the maintenance of inequalities of power and wealth.[75] In the modern context, Cox argues, it has become necessary to move "beyond international relations theory" with its archaic preoccupation with military order between allegedly sovereign states: "hegemony at the international level is thus not merely an order among states. It is an order within a world economy with a dominant mode of production which penetrates into all countries and links into other subordinate modes of production. It is also a complex of international social relationships which connect the social classes of the different countries. World hegemony is describable as a social structure, an economic structure, and a political structure; and it cannot be simply one of these things but must be all three. World hegemony, furthermore, is expressed in universal norms, institutions and mechanisms which lay down general rules of behaviour for states and for those forces of civil society that act across national boundaries - rules which support the dominant mode of production".[76] Cox adds that there may be enough "decentralisation of manufacturing into the Third World" to satisfy some of the "demands for industrialisation".[77] Should this occur, it will reduce the likelihood of collective action to promote structural change in the international economy in the future. As far as the forces of resistance are concerned, the internationalisation of the state and production allows the centre to marginalise radical peripheral movements and regimes. Where oppositional forces have come together "in a particular country, precipitating a change of regime, then that country might be dealt with in isolation by the world structure"; therefore, "where hegemony failed within a particular country, it could reassert itself through the world structure".[78]

This analysis of the transnational economic and political networks of influence which extend outwards from the core is a significant step beyond earlier forms of Marxist analysis. Although it might also be a significant step beyond the realist notion of an anarchic world of states, one cannot escape the question of whether it takes sufficient account of the fact that each peripheral state is located not only in a domestic and international class structure but in an international system of states. The very notion of peripheral state-formation, as opposed to peripheral industrialisation, raises the issue of how far peripheral states possess autonomy from the (internally or externally) dominant class and how far the realm of national security politics is irreducible to the international politics of class relations. This in turn invites a discussion of the relationship between the strategic domain and inequalities of economic and political development.

The realist approach to this question is that international inequality is inevitable where sovereign units are responsible for their own power and security. The recurrent problem of maintaining order provides the more powerful states with an additional reason for acting to reproduce international inequality. This being so, one should note that strategic considerations frequently underlie a core state's decision to ensure that a neighbouring power remains weak or to make sure that a sympathetic regime (which may be "dependent neo-colonial" in Petras's terms) remains in power. On the other hand, there may be strategic reasons for promoting the economic and military development of another power, or for endeavouring to bring about a more equitable distribution of power and wealth within that society. Furthermore, as rationalists observe, the problem of maintaining international order in the modern world may require a greater effort to reduce inequalities of power and wealth more generally. The upshot of these points is that since power, order and the prospects for development are connected in numerous ways, it is essential not only to analyse the internal and external class locations of the peripheral state but to analyse its location in the world of strategic interaction. An analysis of the articulation of modes of production which brings the interpenetration of state structures within the scope of the argument only to underplay the strategic dimensions of state behaviour will provide an incomplete account of international inequalities. In this context, one might conclude that geopolitical explanations of international inequality and recent Marxist or neo-Marxist economic histories of the modern world have failed to analyse the multi-dimensional nature of development prospects: that is, the way in which the constraints and the opportunities inherent in the internal mode of production, in the world economy and in the international system of states interact to shape each state's prospects for development.

CONCLUSIONS

To the extent that there is a Marxist theory of international relations it is present in the literature on the political economy of international stratification. As critical analyses of international inequality, the different branches of this literature have set out to explain the origins and reproduction of the modern world system and to understand the potential for conflict and transformation which is inherent within it. They have not reached any significant level of agreement about the processes which governed the formation and subsequent development of the world economy; and although these approaches have usually proceeded from the common assumption that the initial diffusion of Western principles of freedom and justice throughout the modern world system has opened up the possibility of new paths of historical development, they have disagreed about the probable dynamics of change and about the movements and organisations which should be central to the politics of transformation.

Most of the Marxist and neo-Marxist approaches to international inequality surveyed above have failed to develop a coherent account of the nation-state and strategic interaction. Conversely, the dominant approaches in international relations which have emphasised the link between anarchy and inequality have failed to discuss the connections between class structure and international stratification. An adequate approach to international inequality would be one that analysed the interplay between the state and class forces.[79] Furthermore, contra dependency theory, such an approach would dispute the proposition that the world is developing towards a condition in which the "high-level decision-making occupations" will be confined to "a few key cities in the advanced countries" and to "a number of regional sub-capitals" while "the rest of the world" will be nothing more than "towns and villages in a New Imperial System".[80] It would contend that the importance of state-formation and economic development in the periphery and semi-periphery is underestimated in this account. But it would also contend that while the process of peripheral state-formation is one important reason for bringing realism within the account, the analysis would not be complete unless it considered the way in which the interplay between state structures and domestic or transnational class forces shapes the distribution of the world's wealth.

Finally, although Marxist and neo-Marxist perspectives have argued that the development of the world economy has generated various demands for the realisation of universal principles, they have not attempted to organise counter-hegemonic political principles (such as the idea of the common heritage of mankind, or the concept of basic human needs) into a coherent vision of an alternative world order. Compared with the effort devoted to constructing accounts of the nature and development of the modern world system, the enterprise of specifying binding international economic obligations has clearly been a low priority. Perhaps the widespread pessimism with which the prospects for fundamental change in the world economy have been viewed is part of the explanation for this omission. Perhaps this neglect should be regarded instead as further illustration of Perry Anderson's point that Marxism has travelled "incognito" on the subject of alternative social worlds for far too long.[81] Recently, however, world systems theorists have argued that the gap between theoretical aspirations and possibilities and currently dominant practices will not be bridged without the emergence of a "transnational ideology" of change and development.[82] This observation sugges s that the political economy of international stratification may have been correct that the economic is determining in the final instance, insofar as it has created the context in which a universal consensus may eventually develop. Perhaps this is the real "meaning of interdependence".[83] Even it is, the possibilities contained within it will not be realised until a combination of analysis and vision reveals how the gap between the "is" and the "ought" can be bridged not just in a stratified world economy but in a world system which will remain divided between increasingly powerful territorial states.

6 The States-System and the World-System

We noted in the previous chapter that a large number of Marxist and neo-Marxist approaches to inequality and development have failed to theorise the international system of states. In this respect, these approaches to international inequality display one of the main weaknesses of the classical tradition of sociology. It is perfectly clear that in an earlier period the founders of critical social theorising did not regard the system of states as an insurmountable obstacle to the realisation of human emancipation. They assumed that industrialisation would dissolve nationalism and dismantle the coercive apparatus of the modern state. While contemporary Marxist and neo-Marxist analyses of inequality and development do not share this assumption, most fail to construct theoretical perspectives which take the state and its strategic relations into account.

In the last few years a number of social theorists have called for a critical perspective which is free from these outmoded ideas about the necessary demise of international relations and the withering away of the territorial state. There is growing agreement amongst sociologists that the system of states has been at least as important as capitalism and industrialisation in the development of the modern world. Some of the most important writings in contemporary social and political theory now argue for an historical sociology which will explain exactly how the modern world has been shaped by the interaction between capitalist development, industrialisation and the international system of states.

The world-systems perspective is one perspective which does set out to recover the state, international relations and war for modern social theory. The founder of world-systems theory, Immanuel Wallerstein, and subsequent exponents of the approach have argued that the state and international relations are central to the explanation of the economic achievements of the West and to a broader understanding of the origins and development of international inequality across the world as a whole. But as we saw in the last chapter, this reassessment of the role of the state is limited by the fact that world-systems theory regards state structures and their external relations as the political organisation of the capitalist world economy.[1] This decision to place the capitalist world economy at the centre of the analysis has been the subject of most subsequent critiques of the world-systems perspective.

The Marxist critique of world-systems theory shifts the burden of explanation from the capitalist world economy to modes of production and their domestic and international articulation.[2] This form of analysis is said to provide the key to inequalities of development and to the internal and external behaviour of states. According to a second line of criticism, the world-systems approach is guilty of a rather different form of reductionism. These critics take issue with Wallerstein's claim that the state is, above all else, an instrument of class rule. They dispute the proposition that states are primarily concerned with manipulating the costs and benefits of international exchange relations for the benefit of locally dominant classes, and they reject the supposition that the states-system is nothing more than the political superstructure of the capitalist world economy. Although these observations are central to the realist critique of world-systems theory,[3] they are also an increasingly important part of critical responses to world-systems theory in the sociological literature. In a sociological essay which recognises the strengths of realism but which also endeavours to steer clear of its weaknesses, Theda Skocpol has argued that the states-system is interdependent with the capitalist world economy though not reducible to it.[4]

Although there is general agreement about the need to understand the role that the state and the states-system have played in shaping the modern world, none of the main strands of contemporary social and political theory appears to have the necessary resources with which to complete this project. To repeat an earlier point, the dominant approaches to the state confine their analyses to the state's location in only one of its many domains. The states-system, of course, is the privileged domain in the classical realist theories of the state. The rationalist approach analyses the state's location in the legal and moral order which is constitutive of international society. The state's location in the class structure which is specific to its mode of production is the principal object of analysis for those working within the Marxist tradition. The capitalist world economy, which was accorded primacy by Frank and the dependency theorists, continues to occupy this position in Wallerstein's analysis of the modern world-system. One of the most important points to emerge from the critical responses to world-systems theory is that a more sophisticated approach to the modern world might begin by endeavouring to understand how states are located within all of these domains simultaneously.

The argument that the world-systems approach is limited because it chooses to analyse the state in only one of its locations - the capitalist world economy - is substantially right. What follows from this point is that the world-systems perspective fails as a critical theory in addition to failing in the realm of explanation. The realist critique of the world-systems approach is relevant here as it draws attention to the extent to which Wallerstein, despite protestations to the contrary, still relies on the classical sociological proposition that "society" and its inner dynamics of change comprise the real object of analysis. In other words, the notion of a social system governed by an internal logic of change is extended to the world as a whole. Although the state and its external relations are brought within the realm of the inquiry, they are not regarded as sufficiently independent of the capitalist world economy to pose any kind of threat to the form of global change which the theory advocates: that is, to the transition from world capitalism to world socialism. The realist strand of thought in contemporary sociology comes far closer to Rousseau and Kant's position that the project of advancing the emancipation of the species must also confront the state and war.

One might ask how a critical sociology which absorbs elements of realism can distinguish itself from conventional realism in the theory of international relations. Here it is important to note how world-systems theory develops one theme which is of major importance for a critical approach to international relations. Wallerstein emphasises the need to divide the modern international system into its principal stages. To this end, Wallerstein analyses the reasons for the rise and fall of core states and for the shift from unicentric to multicentric configurations of power.[5] Two aspects of this discussion are worth noting. First of all, Wallerstein stresses the importance of analysing the origins, evolution and decline of the state structures which have been dominant in each of the epochs into which the history of the modern world system can be divided. In the second place, his approach contains the foundations for a materialist analysis of the evolution of different combinations of states and principles of international legitimacy in the modern world system. Leaving the materialist nature of the analysis to one side, world-systems theory and rationalism have a number of important themes in common.

These points will be considered in greater detail once some of the disputes surrounding world-systems theory have been discussed more fully. Let us simply note the growing realisation that no serious sociology of the modern world can neglect the role of the state. Let it also be noted that there is an increasing awareness of the need to rework the foundations of modern social and political theory in order to take account of the international system of states which has been one of the major omissions from the classical tradition of sociology. These developments emphasise the artificial nature of the gap which has separated sociology and economic history from the study of international relations. They suggest that further explorations of the connections between the system of states and the phenomenon of social and economic change can bring about significant advances in sociological and historical explanation. Moreover, these explorations also promise to contribute to the development of a critical theory of international relations. An understanding of the forces which shaped the boundaries of moral and political community in previous combinations of states is essential for understanding the prospects for an extension of community in the contemporary world. These dimensions of the controversies surrounding the world-systems approach raise themes which have not been explored in depth by the proponents of critical theory either in sociology or in the study of international relations.

THE IDEA OF THE CAPITALIST WORLD ECONOMY

Wallerstein's account of the capitalist world economy builds on the critique of modernisation theory advanced by the dependency theorists in the 1960s. It also takes issue with the approach to development which holds that the Third World can industrialise and modernise if it replicates the structures and attitudes which are prevalent in the more advanced regions of the West. Similarly, it rejects the proposition that the world consists of national economies which are moving at different rates along a single path of historical development. In the first volume of *The Modern World System*, Wallerstein argued that the persistence of unequal development first led him to break with the idea that "the sovereign state or...national society" is the indisputable "unit of analysis". Wallerstein adopted the view that the capitalist world economy is the only social unit which is totally unaffected by external forces - the only social system which is entirely governed by nothing other than its "own internal dynamic". None of the traditional objects of sociological inquiry - classes, ethnic groups, states and so forth - has been "self-contained". The behaviour of each of these actors has been governed by its relationship with the whole, the capitalist world economy. This observation applies specifically to the main units of analysis in the classical theory of international relations. That is to say, the "changes" which affect "sovereign states" can also be explained by "the evolution...of the world system".[6]

The ruling classes of Western Europe devised the capitalist world economy as a solution to the crisis of feudalism. When the "optimal degree of productivity had been passed...and the economic squeeze was leading to a generalised seignior-peasant class war, as well as ruinous fights within the seigniorial classes...the only solution that would extract Western Europe from decimation and stagnation would be one that would expand the economic pie to be shared, a solution which required given the technology of the time, an expansion of the land area and population base to exploit. This is what in fact took place in the fifteenth and sixteenth centuries".[7] It was "a creative leap of imagination on the part of the ruling strata" in Western Europe to use the power of the state to force other regions - Eastern Europe and the Americas initially - to produce the raw materials and foodstuffs required by the Western core economies.[8] Although this world economy included empires, such as the overseas empires of Spain and Portugal, its principal innovation was the use of world market forces to expand global output and to regulate its distribution. The uniqueness of the world economy was the division of core regions between sovereign states which employed their economic and military power to ensure that the market worked to their advantage. With this technique the ruling strata of Western Europe ensured a steady "flow of the surplus" from poorer to richer regions without incurring the costs of administering the "cumbersome...political superstructure" of universal empire.[9]

In the late fifteenth and early sixteenth century, therefore, a new social system made its appearance: "It was not an empire yet it was as spacious as a grand empire and shared some features with it. But it was different and new. It was a kind of social system the world has not really known before and which is the distinctive feature of the modern world-system. It is an economic but not a political entity, unlike empires, city-states and nation-states. In fact, it precisely encompasses within its bounds (it is hard to speak of its boundaries) empires, city-states, and the emerging "nation-states". It is a "world" system, not because it encompasses the whole world, but because it is larger than any juridically-defined political unit. And it is a "world economy" because the basic linkage between the parts of the system is economic, although this was reinforced to some extent by cultural links and eventually...by political arrangements and even confederal structures".[10]

Wallerstein compares the capitalist world economy with two forms of economic organisation which have been prevalent throughout human history: world economies and mini-systems. World empires - such as Rome, Ancient China and Egypt - resemble capitalist world economies in two respects. A functional and geographical division of labour is common to both systems, as is the existence of a high level of cultural diversity. They share these features because their dominant classes have turned to territorial expansion and annexation in order to realise their economic objectives. On the other hand, the constituent parts of world empires are not linked together by exchange relations. The distribution of world surplus is not determined by a struggle between separate states for the control of the world economy. A world empire is distinguished by the presence of an over-arching coercive apparatus which the centre relies upon in order to appropriate the surplus produced by subject populations. The mini-systems - hunting and gathering societies for the most part - form the third dimension of Wallerstein's classificatory scheme. These systems are small-scale, culturally homogeneous societies with a simple social division of labour. In the modern period they have rarely been strong enough to offer significant resistance to the West. Most were destroyed as the capitalist world economy expanded to embrace all parts of the earth.[11]

The existence of multiple centres of political power - independent territorial states - is one of the main characteristics which distinguishes the capitalist world economy from other economic systems. Indeed, by definition, a capitalist world economy and an international states-states are one and the same thing. Wallerstein's thesis that the states-system is the political organisation of the capitalist world economy assumes that global economic relations determine the issues at stake in relations between states. Throughout his analysis, Wallerstein focuses on the state's role in creating the context in which domestic producers can maximise profit from the sale of their commodities in the world market. Each state's attempt to weaken actual and potential competitors in the world market is therefore thought to be the key to the system of international relations.[12]

It will be evident that this approach to the states-system is diametrically opposed to conventional forms of international political analysis. As noted earlier, the classical theorists of international relations argue that world-systems theory fails to deal with the realm of strategic interaction.[13] The same point has been developed in the sociological literature which stands in opposition to the world-systems perspective. These approaches point to the reductionism of the claim that the states-system is the political organisation of the capitalist world economy. They argue that this formulation obscures the real historical connections between the system of states and the development of a global economy.[14]

The dispute between world-systems theorists and Marxists over the true nature of capitalism ultimately leads towards the same conclusion. It will be recalled that Wallerstein rejects the Marxist contention that capitalism is distinguished by its uniquely modern relations of production - and particularly by the commodification of labour. Wallerstein argues that capitalism is a world market which extends across many different forms of labour organisation. The capitalist system - as it is understood by Marxist political theory - is the form of labour organisation which emerged in the core regions of the capitalist world economy. This being the case, Wallerstein argues that capitalism was "from the beginning an affair of the world economy and not of nation-states"; from the sixteenth century onward it "never allowed its aspirations to be determined by national boundaries".[15] The Marxist response is that the capitalist mode of production, which slowly evolved within the womb of European feudalism in the fifteenth and sixteenth centuries, became the dominant economic system in Western Europe in the nineteenth century. The large-scale internationalisation of capitalism is a still more recent occurrence.[16]

From a Marxist perspective, the conceptual underpinnings of world-systems theory produce a seriously inaccurate account of the development of the modern world. The states-system was not the political organisation of the capitalist world economy, and capitalism - as Marxism defines it - did not develop in the core as a means of maximising profit from the sale of commodities in the world market. In fact, the system of states preceded the capitalist mode of production and the rise of the world economy. Strategic rivalry was often the driving force behind the state's decision to promote the internal development of the capitalist mode of production in the context of an evolving world economy. The interplay between war and capitalist development created the conditions in which the Western European states acquired the kind of global economic and military reach which made the world economic system possible.[17]

Similar problems result from Wallerstein's analysis of socialist states in the modern world system. These problems result in a failure to consider strategies for advancing international socialism in a world divided into sovereign states. As far as classical Marxism is concerned, socialism can exist in one country as long as internal property relations have been transformed. Wallerstein argues that societies cannot be regarded as socialist if they have abolished the private ownership of the means of production but still produce for profit in the world market. According to this criterion, contemporary "socialist" states have not broken free from the capitalist world economy. Socialism will only exist when global production has been completely reformed so that it is geared to the satisfaction of human needs rather than to capital accumulation and the realisation of profit.[18]

The important historical question has been how world socialism can be advanced if not through the prior establishment of separate state structures which are committed to domestic change and to the transformation of the international economic and political relations which exist around them. The socialist reconstruction of economic and political relations at the national level and the attempt to formulate a socialist approach to foreign economic and political relations would therefore appear to be the two overlapping steps in the development of world socialism. Paradoxically, the world-systems approach brings the state and international relations within its analysis of world inequalities and their conceivable reduction only to fail to address the question of what "socialist" states can and should do to realise their commitment to world socialism. This failure is unavoidable if socialist states are presumed to be capitalist by virtue of their continuing involvement in the world economy.

POLITICAL DYNAMICS OF THE CAPITALIST WORLD ECONOMY

This section shifts attention from the conceptual to the substantive dimensions of world systems theory. We may begin by exploring some of the similarities between Wallerstein's approach to world economies and Wight's inquiry into systems of states. Wallerstein and Wight claim that international states-systems are relatively uncommon in world history. They are agreed that these unusual periods in which the world is divided into a number of independent states seldom survived for more than a few centuries. They note that these precarious forms of world political organisation collapsed in the past in one of two ways: either because a member state overturned the balance of power or because an outside power incorporated the multi-state system within its empire. The notion that empire has been the predominant form of world political or economic organisation in recorded history is common to these perspectives.[19]

Wight argued that the study of international relations should be concerned with the development of a comparative sociology of the origins, reproduction and transformation of systems of states. Wallerstein's perspective possesses the foundations for a similarly comparative sociology of economic systems although it is the evolution of the modern world system which has been the central object of his analysis. In an attempt to understand the main stages in the development of the modern states-system, Wight analysed the history of principles of international legitimacy. Wallerstein's account of the modern capitalist world economy has a similar interest in historical periodisation. Four stages in the evolution of the modern capitalist economy have been identified for this purpose: the emergence of the modern world-system between 1450 and 1640; its consolidation between 1640 and 1815; its global expansion between 1815 and 1917 and its increased susceptibility to challenge in the period which begins with the Bolshevik Revolution.[20]

Although Wight and Wallerstein have a common interest in understanding the evolution of state structures and the development of world culture, they offer conflicting accounts of the nature and dynamics of the modern states-system. Wight's analysis of international politics attached very little importance to the connections between states, world order and economic forces. The relationship between these phenomena only became important in rationalism when Bull began to analyse the way in which increasing disparities of power and wealth endanger the sense of membership of an international society. The world-systems perspective has been clearly concerned with understanding the connections between the state, world order and the evolution of global norms by developing a political economy of the rise of a European-dominated international

economy. But as the critics have argued, an understanding of the state
and the international political system cannot be achieved by focusing on
the dynamics of the capitalist world economy alone. On the other hand,
the world-systems perspective raises the important question of whether an
analysis of the state and world order which ignored these global economic
dynamics would be any more complete. The upshot of these points is that
world-systems theory and rationalism offer rival yet hardly irreconcilable
accounts of the evolution of the modern states-system.

The world-systems approach endeavours to provide a new account of
the reasons for the economic development of the West. Wallerstein argues
that economic development in the West occurred as a result of Europe's
dominance over the world economy. The struggle for profit in the world
market - coupled with capital movements to areas of maximum
profitability - allowed the core regions of Europe to surpass the economic
achievements of all previous economic systems. The use of the market as
an instrument of surplus-appropriation freed the core from the overhead
costs which it would have incurred if the ruling classes had opted for
world empire. Moreover, by relying on the market rather than coercion to
bring about economic redistribution, the core could allocate resources to
productive endeavour which would otherwise have been expended in the
physical repression of labour.[21]

The rise of the West also occurred because of a "series of geographical
expansions to encompass the whole globe".[22] Territorial expansion enabled
the core to increase the number of exploited regions and to expand the
area in which the process of unequal exchange was free to operate.
Wallerstein maintains that it is not the case that territorial expansion
necessarily prevented the subsequent development of peripheral and
semi-peripheral societies. Nevertheless, he argues that the level of
exploitation of labour has probably increased in the past few centuries in
the areas which have experienced significant economic development.[23] The
crucial point is that the physical expansion of the world economy allowed
the majority of core states to achieve economic development with the
minimum of international conflict. They were able to restrict the rivalries
which inevitably occur during more typical periods in which the growth
of some states reduces the amount of wealth available to others. This is
the context for Wallerstein's observation that the "outer expansion" of
the world economy "has undoubtedly reached its limits" although "inner
expansion has still some small distance to go".[24] The exhaustion of
unoccupied territory which is available for annexation or informal
domination therefore increases the likelihood of inter-state rivalries. The
additional presence of anti-systemic forces which challenge the structure
of international inequality accentuates this trend and increases the threat
to the long-term reproduction of the capitalist world economy.

These remarks form the background to Wallerstein's analysis of the
state and external relations. On the question of how the state and the
world economy are related, Hopkins and Wallerstein offer this comment:
"Because of the structure of the capitalist world economy (one economy
but multiple states), there are not one but two sets of conflicting
relationships: (1) the economic core regions in relation to the economic
peripheral regions; (2) the dominant states in relation to the dominated

states. These two subantinomies relate to each other and tend to correlate with each other, but they are not identical and it would be well to analyse each antinomy successively".[25] As a general rule, the differences between core and periphery explain the uneven distribution of state capabilities although inequalities of military and political power also help to preserve the subantinomy between the central and peripheral economies. The use of military power for this purpose is one of the hallmarks of the foreign policy of core states.

The world-systems approach maintains that all core states intervene in the world market to reproduce the antinomy between dominant and dependent states. No matter how much they uphold the doctrine of laissez-faire economics in the domestic sphere, core states always adopt interventionist policies in the world economy. In one sense, their advocacy of free trade is no less interventionist since it is one of the devices by which the powerful ensure that the principles of international economic relations disadvantage their competitors. The core may bring its power to bear upon peripheral states in a far more direct manner. It may affect the latters' ability to appropriate world surplus by colluding with comprador elites in the periphery. The policy of ensuring that the political arena in dependent societies remains highly susceptible to external interference is one means by which the subantinomy between dominant and dependent states reproduces the subantinomy between core and peripheral economic regions.[26]

The relationship between core and periphery is not the only important dynamic in the capitalist world economy. Conflict in the core gives rise to two dynamics which are equally important: the ascent and descent of hegemonic powers, and the shift from unicentric to multicentric distributions of power. Chase-Dunn and Rubinson refer to these processes in these terms: "The distribution of power among core states varies from unicentric in which there is a single hegemonic core state, to multicentric in which the power is more evenly distributed among core states. A shift from one to the other is produced by the tendency for economic competitive advantage to become concentrated in a single state, causing its rise to hegemonic power and to a central position in the world economy. Its power advantage gradually changes from one based on production to one based on the state's financial position in the world monetary system and on its centrality in the maintenance of world political stability (through military and political means). This shift from productive to financial and political hegemony allows other core states to incorporate new productive technology and to avoid the overhead costs of maintaining stability in the system. They grow rapidly and overtake the original hegemonic power in productivity, and a period of competition between core states ensues...The multicentric periods are characterised by intense economic competition and military conflict between core states and by competition for access to peripheral areas. Unicentric periods are characterised by relatively peaceful economic competition in a relatively integrated world economy supported by the institutional framework based on the hegemonic core state in international agreements".[27]

These remarks indicate that hegemony is the result of the state's successful passage through a seemingly fixed sequence of stages of development. The first of these is the attainment of dominance in the sphere of industrial production. Supremacy in this realm is then extended to supremacy in the realm of finance with the result that the national currency of the core becomes the leading currency internationally. (Wallerstein adds that financial hegemony is preceded by the control of the international transportation of commodities). These stages are followed by the state's assumption of the responsibility for the maintenance of world economic and political order and by its control of the means of disseminating the core's dominant ideas and culture.[28] A hegemonic power is then able to impose "a sense of inferiority" on the societies of the periphery.[29] Although it may lack the capacity to impose a similar sense of inferiority upon the populations which inhabit the more powerful regions, the "cultural explosion" which results from the advent of "liberalism" in the core ensures that it is regarded as the chief model of social and political, as well as technological, development.[30] A hegemonic power protects its interests by defining the dominant principles of world politics, and specifically by pressing others to recognise the necessity for free trade and the unqualified evils of colonialism. When a state realises this objective, its hegemony is said to be complete.

These "moments of hegemony have been historically rare" during the period in which the modern world-system has been in existence.[31] Only three powers have attained hegemony, and only then for relatively short periods. These were the United Provinces between 1625 and 1650/72; Great Britain from 1815 to 1850/73; and the United States from about 1945 to 1967.[32] As with the process of ascent, descent was sequential. The hegemonic power first lost its advantage in the sphere of production and then witnessed the erosion of its power over the financial, commercial, military and cultural realms of the world system. Its decline became irreversible as competitors turned to mercantilist strategies in order to promote their economic development, when low wage rates in the periphery acted like a magnet on capital in the core, and when other states started to reap the benefits of technology transfer and technological imitation.[33] Chase-Dunn argues that the additional cost of maintaining world political order usually quickened the momentum of descent.[34]

Hegemonic powers have never remained passive in the face of decline, however inevitable it may have been. In the past, they have resorted to protectionism and colonialism in an effort to reverse or arrest the process of decline. When they could no longer rely on the market to provide them with their accustomed share of world surplus, hegemonic powers did not hesitate to use "political coercion" as an instrument of "accumulation".[35] (Wallerstein cites the phenomenon of "preemptive colonialism" in the nineteenth century as evidence of the increased tolerance of violence which accompanies hegemonic decline.)[36] The shift from a unicentric to a multicentric system was not only a change in the distribution of political power: it was the cause of a major transformation of the principles of world politics as the emergence of increasingly particularistic state structures most clearly revealed. In previous periods, this development resulted from the tension between the universal interests which the hegemonic power claimed to represent and the particularism which ran through its own behaviour. Wallerstein argues that contemporary international developments suggest that this tension might at last be resolved in favour of universal interests.[37]

On this very subject, Wallerstein maintains that the radicalisation of the semi-periphery signifies that the recurrent pattern of hegemonic ascent and decline, the cyclical movement from unicentric to multicentric configurations of power and parallel changes in the nature of global norms may be about to come to an end. In short, the capitalist world economy now faces a profound political challenge as the semi-peripheral regions seek to delegitimate and to transform exploitative global economic structures. The impact of the principle of international social justice on global norms reveals that the modern world is in the throes of the transition from a capitalist to a socialist form of world political organisation.[38]

Whether or not this last proposition is correct, there certainly has been a (partial) "transformation of global values" of the kind to which Wallerstein refers. It is not at all clear, however, that the process of international normative and cultural change can be explained by a perspective which imputes dominance to the capitalist world economy. It would be more accurate to claim that the emphasis on international social justice in contemporary diplomacy is the result of the interaction between the internationalisation of the capitalist mode of production, the diffusion of its dominant cultural forms and the global expansion of the European system of states. Marx's observation that capitalist social relations comprise the "real basis" of "equality and freedom" in the modern world is worth recalling here.[39] As Marx argued, the tension which is central to capitalism - the tension between the universalistic nature of its moral discourse and the coercive and unequal nature of its dominant structures and relationships - has created the setting for demands for global reform. As for the system of states, it is necessary to remember that nation-states are members of an international society and not merely participants in the competition for capital accumulation or opponents in the struggle for military power and security. More specifically, the idea of the equality of states has been a crucial theme in the modern society of states. In the present century, the conflict between the legal equality of states and the social and economic plight of the more recent members of the states-system has contributed to the demand for the structural reform of the international economy. The internationalisation of capitalism and the expansion of the European system of states (rather than the development of a world-wide network of commodity relations) are the two phenomena which have brought about the transformation of global norms.

It would be wrong to assume that this is the only - or even the dominant - trend taking place in the modern culture of world politics. In this context, it is worth recalling Bull's comment that Third World leaders often couched their claims in nationalist rhetoric because they were obliged to use a language with maximum "resonance" in the West. As they became stronger, many Third World states were able to adopt a language which "sets Western values aside, or...places different interpretations upon them".[40] Consequently, the long-term trend may be away from rather than towards any universal consensus about the terms of international political discourse.

What holds for nationalism may also hold for the language of socialism in the Third World. Wallerstein argues that the revolt of the semi-periphery reveals that the modern world is now in the throes of a transition from a capitalist to a socialist form of world economic order. But peripheral or semi-peripheral industrialisation and state formation do not offer unqualified support for the proposition that the world is on the verge of reaching a consensus about the nature of global norms. In fact, it may be more accurate to regard the more powerful states which are emerging in peripheral and semi-peripheral regions not only as new centres of economic and political power but as new centres of cultural power which may develop along diverse and conflicting lines. The supposition that the semi-peripheral challenge to the capitalist world economy foreshadows the development of a universal consensus on the need for a socialist world system smacks of the assumption that world history will be shaped, as the nineteenth century theories of social progress had assumed, by principles which have grown out of the Western European historical experience. Consequently, although the world-systems approach has highlighted the importance of normative and cultural forces in world politics, its assumption that the capitalist world economy is the privileged sphere of social and political life prevents it from developing a sophisticated account of international cultural change. A more complex approach to the interplay between economic and political factors is needed to decide the extent to which regimes and their populations are being socialised into a common way of life, and the extent to which they are being drawn towards diverse paths of cultural development.

THE QUESTION OF THE STATE AND GEOPOLITICS

By denying the existence of separate societies which are governed by internal logics of development the world-systems perspective clearly takes issue with mainstream sociology. By denying that these societies are involved in a discrete realm of external relations it also rejects the idea of a separate study of international relations. The claims and counter-claims which have arisen in conjunction with this second theme are the main concern of this section.

In an essay which considers these points in some detail, Christopher Chase-Dunn has argued that neither the classical political economy of international trade nor the classical theory of international politics understands the relationship between economic and political factors in the modern world-system. The first perspective fails because "the world market is not simply composed of a trade network between equal partners, but is instead an institutional cover for structured inequalities based on the use of coercive political and economic power".[41] For its part, the classical theory of international relations analyses coercion in world politics but fails to understand the relationship between the state and uneven economic development. Chase-Dunn argues that world-systems theory avoids the problems which are inherent within conventional approaches to international relations. Whereas the classical tradition "has understood the global system as a set of relationships among relatively separate entities (hence the term "international"), the world-systems perspective posits the existence of a much more integrated...entity with a logic and structure of its own".[42] From this vantage-point, world-systems theorists analyse "the states-system (which) is virtually the same as the international system" in classical international theory, but they also recognise that "its dynamics are the result of its interaction with the processes of capital accumulation and class formation in the context of the hierarchical core-periphery division of labour".[43] In contrast with the classical theory of international relations, the world-systems approach therefore endeavours to construct a "reintegrated interdisciplinary science of political economy".[44]

The question raised by the critics is whether this attempt to restore a reintegrated study of international political economy is anything more than a modified form of economic reductionism. To use Chase-Dunn's terminology, the key question is whether the modern world has been governed by "one logic or two": by a dominant logic of capital accumulation which pervades all realms of human conduct or by the interaction between the process of capitalist development and an independent realm of competition between nation-states.[45] Most of the critics of world-systems theory correctly regard the contention that states are principally responsible for appropriating the optimum level of world surplus as a crude and simplistic analysis of inter-state relations. Almost all reject the tendency to stretch the perfectly valid point that economic competition has frequently been the cause of strategic rivalries to the point where strategic interaction seems to verge on the epiphenomenal. Consequently, much of the critical literature tries to rescue the autonomy of diplomatic-strategic interaction from the reductionism of world-systems theory. This is the basis for Theda Skocpol's contention that Wallerstein reduces "socio-economic structures to determination by world market opportunities and technological production possibilities; and second, (reduces) state structures and policies to determination by dominant class interests".[46] Similar considerations underlie Roger Dale's argument that world-systems analysis develops a "base-superstructure model" of the relationship between economics and politics on a "world scale".[47] Most of the critics trace this failure to deal adequately with the state and its external relations to Wallerstein's initial premise that the international states-system is the political organisation of the capitalist world economy.

Some parts of Wallerstein's writings tend to suggest that this charge of reductionism does not hold. One such part is Wallerstein's discussion of the reasons for the triumph of the modern territorial state. At the beginning of the modern period, all of the main political actors were engaged in a process of territorial expansion, and the two most important states - France and Spain - were locked in a struggle for imperial domination. The Italian city-states were unable to compete effectively in this struggle for territory and power. While they were sufficiently compact to be administered from a central point, they were too small to be militarily viable. On the other hand, France and Spain so overreached themselves in the course of the sixteenth and early seventeenth centuries that they could no longer be administered effectively from a central point. The fiscal burden of imperial expansion also took its toll on their military capabilities. The modern sovereign state succeeded where other forms of political organisation had failed because it solved the problem of scale. It was large enough to compete in the struggle for physical survival, but it was not so large that it could not be controlled from a central administrative point. The quest for a practicable solution to the problem of scale was an important aspect of the development of the capitalist world economy. Solving the problem of scale was the key to significant influence over world market forces. It was also a precondition of survival in war.[48]

Other references to the autonomy of the state exist in Wallerstein's writings. Wallerstein has maintained that skill in the art of state-building often acted like a "tipping mechanism" which allowed a dominant class to realise its potential in the world economy.[49] He has argued that state managers, especially in the core, have the power to pursue ends which may clash with the objectives of the dominant class.[50] However, Wallerstein does not deal with the question of how far the state's responsibility for defence and security explains the autonomy of the state. Nor is there a more general assessment of the role of war in the modern history of state-formation. Wallerstein has referred to the need to analyse class relations and production in conjunction with the "terribly meaningful...abstraction" of international relations.[51] But the precise meaning of this statement, and its implications for future directions in world-systems analysis, remain tantalisingly obscure.

Many of Wallerstein's critics find his approach to the state and international relations either incomplete or unconvincing. Some of them draw upon realism (or construct arguments which are akin to realism) in order to challenge the world-systems approach to the origins and reproduction of the modern world and to criticise Wallerstein's claim that the capitalist world economy is now in the process of transformation. Although many critics employ realism to challenge Wallerstein's notion of system-dominance, their position is distinguished from realism by an emphasis on the need for a two logic explanation of the modern world which analyses the relationship between social and economic development and strategic interaction.

Aristide Zolberg's essay on the origins and survival of the European multi-state system is instructive in this regard. Whereas Wallerstein claims that the states-system emerged because the ruling classes in Western Europe attempted to solve their economic crisis by establishing an exploitative international division of labour, Zolberg argues that strategic factors were the primary determinants of the structure of early modern Europe. The states-system survived because of a balance of military force involving one power which was outside the boundaries of the capitalist world economy as Wallerstein defines it. France maintained equilibrium in Europe by establishing an alliance with Turkey to counterbalance the power of Spain. Zolberg does not contend that the strategic dimensions of European international relations can be analysed in isolation from the struggle to control trade routes and from rivalries to acquire wealth by exploiting weaker regions in an emerging world economy. These factors were always interconnected. More importantly, however, the strategic relationship involving powers inside and outside of Europe cannot be regarded as the by-product of the evolution of a capitalist world economy. The military balance in Europe not only preceded the economic linkages which Wallerstein regards as the main feature of the international states-system – it was the military balance which made these economic linkages possible.[52]

The European system survived because of a "fortuitous" balance of power, to borrow Hedley Bull's phrase. But as rationalists have argued, and as Zolberg recognises, member states subsequently developed means for ensuring that the persistence of the balance of power did not depend on chance alone or result from the inevitable process of hegemonic decline. The practice of permanent ambassadors, for example, permitted states to coordinate their actions in order to "contrive" international equilibrium. Their willingness to cooperate to preserve the balance of power demonstrated their commitment to the principle that the states-system was worth preserving from the threat of empire. The reproduction of the states-system has depended upon a diplomatic culture in which there is a high level of consensus about the legal rights and duties of sovereign states.[53]

It is clear that Zolberg accepts Wallerstein's point that sociologists have been overcommitted to the analysis of the internal processes of change which have shaped the evolution of notionally separate societies. Zolberg notes that a more comprehensive sociology must consider the international systemic forces which fuelled, amongst other things, capitalist or industrial development. But the system which Zolberg analyses include the geopolitical forces analysed by realists and the social-cultural phenomena which have fallen within the orbit of rationalist explanation.

The strategic dimensions of the world system form an important part of Skocpol's critique of Wallerstein's notion of system-dominance – the supposition that the properties of the capitalist world economy shape the main developments in the social relations which exist inside the boundaries of individual territorial states. In her review of the first volume of Wallerstein's *The Modern World-System*, Skocpol took issue with his claim that the state is an instrument which the locally dominant class employs in order to influence the functioning of the world market. Skocpol's response to this claim is similar to Hintze's criticism of Marx's notion of the class-state. As Skocpol sees it, Wallerstein fails to recognise that the state is a military-bureaucratic structure with specific responsibility for the preservation of public order and for the organisation and conduct of war. The world-systems perspective underestimates the importance of the state's monopoly of control of the instruments of violence and the extent of its autonomy from the forces which comprise the locally dominant class. On this basis, Skocpol argues – as Hintze had observed earlier – that the modern world has been profoundly affected by a logic of strategic competition which arises from each state's attempt to ensure its physical security and survival. This dynamic has been at least as influential as the struggle for wealth in the capitalist world economy, and perhaps even more so.

Skocpol therefore rejects the proposition that the states-system is the political superstructure of the capitalist world economy. The remark that the international states-system is a "transnational reality interdependent in its structure and dynamics with world capitalism, but not reducible to it" clearly distinguishes two of the state's most important locations.[55] The further comment that the "state...is fundamentally Janus-faced, with an intrinsically dual anchorage in class-divided socio-economic structures and an international system of states" has the same effect.[56] It is evident from these formulations that Skocpol believes that the assumption that these domains are isolated from one another is as one-sided as the tendency to confuse them. By virtue of confusing them, however, world-systems theory fails to appreciate the "independent efficacy" of the state.[57] Contrary to the world-systems approach, states do not only enjoy discretion within the parameters laid down by their specific locations in the capitalist world economy and by the efforts of the ruling class. State managers articulate their own interests and objectives, and they can frequently secure them by overriding, where necessary, the preferences of the locally dominant class.

This theme is central to Skocpol's analysis of social revolutions. From an examination of three case-studies, Skocpol concludes that exogenous forces started a chain of events which ended in revolution. Faced with the serious financial burden of competing with neighbouring states, each of the regimes in question (pre-revolutionary France, Russia and China) diverted a significant proportion of wealth from the dominant class towards its own military needs. In response to the state's actions, the dominant class sought to shift its increasing economic burden onto subordinate class forces by increasing the level of exploitation. This decision ushered in a period of social and political revolution which culminated in the emergence of new political forces. These endeavoured to resolve the crisis, which had overturned the previous social and political order, in two ways: firstly, by strengthening the position of the state within the international configuration of military power; and secondly, and in order to achieve this aim, by consolidating the power of the state vis-a-vis other domestic political actors. It will be noted that to account for this sequence of events Skocpol distinguishes between the state's relationship with domestic class interests and its interaction with other strategic actors within the international states-system. This explanation of revolution rejects the "one logic" approach to domestic historical developments which is proffered by the world-systems approach.[58]

What Skocpol's analysis brings out is the relationship between international geopolitical competition and the rise of new centres of military power. This theme is considered at greater length in George Modelski's "long cycles" approach to world politics which analyses the relationship between the state, the projection of military power and the emergence of a global economic and political system. Modelski disputes Wallerstein's contention that the various parts of a world empire are linked together by an overarching military and political apparatus while the main elements of a capitalist world economy are linked together by a system of exchange relations. Modelski proceeds to argue that the main epochs in the evolution of the modern world system have been held together by networks of global strategic and political linkages established and built on in turn by a succession of hegemonic world powers: by Portugal, Holland, Britain and the United States. Each power emerged as the dominant state after a period of systemic warfare, and each proceeded to impose its vision of world order on other societies. Dominance in the realm of trade and communications reinforced the instruments of political and military control. By virtue of serving the interests of the hegemonic power, the global political and economic framework was inevitably challenged by subordinate powers. Their resistance to the world order system marked the emergence of a new phase of international politics which culminated in the outbreak of major war. A further cycle began when a new hegemonic power inherited and enlarged its predecessor's apparatus of global control. Four of these cycles, each lasting about one hundred years, have been completed in the modern system of states. A fifth is now under way.[59]

Modelski regards "the long cycle of global politics" as ample evidence of the modern state's extraordinary capacity to project its power beyond its narrow territorial confines. Its unrivalled success in this regard is the key to the dominant logic in world politics. The global reach of the modern state has compelled the weak to emulate the strong by establishing the same form of political organisation. The world-systems perspective has failed to recognise that, as a result, the state has been the chief architect and beneficiary of the economic and political integration of the species during the last five hundred years. The former has overlooked the evidence that the global diffusion of the territorial state, and the development of increasingly sophisticated instruments of global control and violence, have formed the central dynamic of world politics. As Modelski suggests, the formation and consolidation of states rather than the transition from a capitalist to a socialist form of world economy is the dominant feature of the modern age. But the number of global problems which require international approaches and solutions is likely to increase in conjunction with the global diffusion of the state and the states-system. For Modelski, it is the growing tension between the emerging crises which have accompanied the economic and political unification of the species and its continuing fragmentation into a number of competing and self-interested sovereign states which creates possibilities for major structural change.[60]

Modelski's focus on the growth of state power is a further variation on the theme that Wallerstein underestimates the importance of geopolitical factors in his account of a world system. It is an approach which would seem far closer to state-centric realism with its one logic interpretation of international politics. In a more recent paper, Modelski argues that the state ought to be analysed in conjunction with the "mutually reinforcing" realms of "world order" and "world development".[61] Still more recently, William Thompson has emphasised the need to consider the interplay between the strategic and the economic because "long cycle analysts, in contrast (to world-systems theorists) have not yet decided what the system's fundamental motors of change" actually are.[62] Zolberg notes that an analysis of the system of states which presumed that it was "totally

independent of the level of technological and economic development"
would be as one-sided as world-systems theory.[63] Skocpol's notion of the
state's dual anchorage further emphasises the need to analyse the way in
which the interaction between social and economic development and
strategic rivalry has shaped the development of the modern world. Each
of these authors argues that a political economy of the modern world
(the project which world-systems theory promises but which it has failed
to deliver) would start with the recognition that the world-system has
been shaped by the interaction between these two dominant logics.

In an attempt to defend world-systems theory Christopher Chase-Dunn
has argued that it is a major step beyond "two logic" accounts of the
history of the modern world. Chase-Dunn maintains that the states-system
and the capitalist world economy have reinforced each other's existence.
For this reason it is convenient to think in terms of a single "integrated
logic" of global development.[64] The balance of military power, for
instance, has contributed to the survival of the world capitalist system by
preventing "any single state from controlling the world economy, and
from imposing a political monopoly over accumulation".[65] In this context,
"factors of production (have not been) constrained to the degree that
they could be if there were an overarching world state...Thus the state
system provides the political underpinning of the mobility of capital, and
also the institutional basis for the continuing expansion of capitalist
development".[66] In addition, the international mobility of capital and the
inevitable decline of hegemonic power because of "the spread of
production techniques" have contributed to the preservation of the
international system of states.[67] This relationship has been reinforced by
the economic calculation of the "potential allies" of an aspiring world
imperial power. They have usually been concerned about "the extent to
which their interests would be protected under the new imperium".[68]
Their self-interest has motivated them to uphold the balance of power,
thereby preserving "the path of capitalist growth in the context of the
multicentric system".[69]

Although Chase-Dunn reaffirms Wallerstein's thesis that the capitalist
world economy and the international states-system are one and the same
thing,[70] the observation that the "geopolitical strategies of the competing
states are not entirely determined by economic desiderata" might seem to
invalidate any charge of reductionism.[71] But if this is so, the argument
that the states-system and the capitalist world economy have been
mutually reproducing does not seem to be sufficient to justify the case
for a "one logic" account of the development of the modern world.

It is arguable that Chase-Dunn's approach does not overcome the
limitations which result from the initial identification of these two
domains. It is far from obvious that states must form a capitalist world
economy, or that the state's domestic production must aim at maximising
profit in the world market. The possibility of a system of states in which
there is no such thing as economic exchange seems to be excluded a
priori by the world-systems perspective.[72] The world-systems approach
regards these characteristics as the necessary attributes of a system of
states, whereas a more accurate approach might argue reveal that they
are the result of the particular social and political relations which exist

in the most powerful regions of the world system. Worsley's argument that the modern international system consists of several "worlds" (the worlds of dominant and dependent states and the worlds of capitalist and socialist societies) is significant in this regard precisely because it notes that these separate worlds display different levels of tolerance towards the mobility of capital, international exchange-relations, capital markets and so forth. And Worsley's notion that the world system is shaped by the dynamics which operate within and between these sub-systems - and especially by the political and ideological differences between the major powers - might be said to offer a far more promising approach to the study of the relationship between the states-system and the world economy.[73]

Given Chase-Dunn's contention that the states-system is the political structure of the capitalist world economy it is curious that he should argue that "multistate systems exhibiting some of the tendencies of the European balance of power existed prior to the emergence of the capitalist mode of production".[74] If this has been the case then the claim that the states-system and the capitalist world economy are mutually reproducing cannot be a necessary truth. It applies only to specific historical epochs. Chase-Dunn proceeds to argue that earlier "states systems were unstable...and tended either to become world empires or to disintegrate".[75] The survival of the modern states-system, on the other hand, is explained by the development of the capitalist world economy. In response to Zolberg's argument that world-systems theory has underestimated the role of the balance of power in the evolution of modern Europe, Chase-Dunn makes this point: "It is true that this alliance (the alliance between the French and the Ottoman empire), and other less important ones between European states and states located in areas outside the capitalist division of labour, affected the course of development of the modern world-system. It may even be true that without this outside alliance the emergence of capitalism in Europe would have been long postponed. But, again, this argues that the state system is important to the capitalist world economy - on this everyone agrees. But what would have happened to the European interstate system if the capitalist world economy had not survived? Probably, it would have become a world empire."[76] This formulation subverts the world-systems claim that there is a necessary relationship between the states-system and the capitalist world economy. It makes an important concession to "two logic" modes of explanation.

The "two logics" approach recognises that strategic competition may not be reducible to economic relations. It is aware that the struggle for military power and security helped to promote capitalist development (in each of its current meanings on the Left) although it does not underestimate the impact that economic and technological change have had upon international political relations. Furthermore, it reveals that Wallerstein's account of global transition displays the same neglect of the state and war which characterised nineteenth century sociology. More importantly, the debates which have arisen in response to the world-systems approach reflect a more general pattern in the literature: the pattern which leads towards a conceptual framework which goes beyond realism and Marxism.

CONCLUSIONS

The inclusion of realist themes in contemporary sociology marks an important watershed in modern social theory. It is an attempt to ensure that sociology finally comes to terms with the nation-state and violence. This trend is most pronounced in the literature that deals with the strengths and weaknesses of world-systems analysis. Although the influence of realism has increased in current sociology there is very little support for the methodological principles which are present in its most recent formulation.[77] None of the major critics of world-systems theory defends the method of abstracting the states-system from domestic economic structures or from international economic and social change. Recent sociology may appeal to statecentric realism in order to underline the weaknesses of the classical tradition. But, it is committed - implicitly if not explicitly - to a new project in social and political theory which would unite the study of society and the study of international relations in a new theoretical framework.

The approaches discussed in the preceding section have not considered the significance of these developments for the critical theory of society. Were they to do so, they would have to stress the necessity of reflecting upon the possibility of emancipation in a world which is divided into sovereign states. To put this matter differently, they would have to recover the critical project which existed prior to the rise of classical social theory - the project which is exemplified by Kant's analysis of the possibility of realising the moral life in an international system of states. In this context, some previous comments about the implications of realism for the critical theory of society may be worth restating. It is essential to reconstruct critical social theory in light of the realist analysis of the reproduction of the system of states. But, as a counter-balancing measure, it is equally necessary to avoid the realist neglect of the possibilities of international structural change. The emancipatory interest which distinguishes the critical approach makes it essential to analyse the interplay between the logics of systemic reproduction and modification. The question of how to develop this mode of analysis is the main issue now facing the critical theory of international relations.

The main objective is to link the analysis of these logics with a critical theory of state structures. Of the perspectives surveyed in the present work, rationalism comes closest to revealing how one might begin to develop such a research project. It will be recalled that Wight argued that recurrent patterns of development existed in all systems of states. By the same token, the different periods in the development of the modern states-system displayed several commonalities. These comments reveal the extent of Wight's agreement with realism. On the other hand, Wight's sociology of the evolution of modern international society demonstrated fundamental differences with the realist tradition. Wight analysed the phenomenon of change by identifying the principal epochs in the development of the European states-system. These were delineated according to the state structures and concepts of international legitimacy which prevailed at different periods in the history of European international relations.[78] To some extent, Wallerstein brings similar concerns to bear upon the analysis of unicentric and multicentric states-systems. Extending this approach to the study of the prospects for the extension of moral and political community in different historical periods may prove to be an effective means of developing a critical account of international relations. An historical sociology of the forces which determine the boundaries of community may be one of the most illuminating ways in which sociologists can show how a critical-theoretical engagement with realism can differ from the dominant versions of realism in the study of international relations.

7 Class and State in International Relations

The renaissance of the theory of the state is the single most important development in social and political thought in the past twenty years. This development is a reaction to the enormous expansion of state power which has occurred in the twentieth century. It is a response to the greater range of domestic economic and social responsibilities which the state has assumed in this period and a reflection of the state's increased power to monitor and control civil society. The central place of the state in recent social theory is also a function of the greater importance which is attached to the relationship between the continuing revolution of military technology and the nature of society and politics. This in turn has prompted the development of more wide-ranging inquiries into the role of the state and war in earlier periods of human history. What began as an attempt to correct the classical sociological account of the modern period has now started to evolve into a more comprehensive survey of the impact of the state and war on the development of human society as a whole.[1]

These themes can be developed more fully by considering the recent history of Marxist theories of the state. Until the late 1960s, the dominant strands of historical materialism regarded the state as an instrument of class rule. As a result of its notion of the class-state, Marxism was ill-equipped, according to its critics, either to anticipate or to explain the autonomy of modern state structures and the increasing importance of international relations. The earliest attempts to reshape the Marxist theory of the state argued that the level of the state's autonomy was determined by the structural requirements of the social relations of production. The idea that the capitalist mode of production requires a relatively autonomous political apparatus was one of the most important themes in this line of argument.[2] Some of the main critics of this approach argued that the attempt to explain state autonomy in terms of the functional requirements of the relevant mode of production did little to answer the charge of economic reductionism. One of the central problems in Marxist explanation had been obscured rather than solved.

As far as present purposes are concerned, the important point to come out of these debates was the claim that Marxism had failed to come to terms with the state's monopoly of control of the instruments of violence and with the implications of its specific responsibility for the formulation and implementation of national security policy. What is more, Marxism had failed to recognise the need for an emancipatory politics which dealt directly with both the domestic and the international dimensions of the state's use of violence. This critique of the Marxist approaches to the autonomy of the state suggested the need for an analysis which moved beyond a one-dimensional form of inquiry into the state's relationship with the dominant class forces and with the constraints inherent in the mode of production. In fact, the gap between Marxism and the classical theory of international relations did start to narrow when the former began to develop analyses of the state which took account of the specificity of geopolitics and the autonomy of the system of states.[3]

An argument for reconsidering traditional approaches to the state also appeared in the international relations literature during the same period. In the first instance, this development expressed the belief that the growth of international interdependence had already brought about some important changes in the character of the modern state. According to this approach, the realist claim that the state was a monolithic actor pursuing an objective national interest was no longer tenable. At the very least, the growth of interdependence simply accentuated the fact that the state was an aggregate of different bureaucratic actors advancing their own sectional interests or reacting to powerful clients in civil society. In their critique of realism, therefore, the main writers on interdependence advanced a liberal-pluralist interpretation of the state which argued that foreign policy was the result of competition between numerous governmental and non-governmental actors.[4] Whereas social theory now emphasised the autonomy of the state, the theory of international relations increasingly stressed the need to analyse the connections between the state and civil society. The former began to converge with classical realism in some important respects; and by taking the class analysis of the state and society more seriously, the latter started to draw upon the Marxist literature to a degree which would have been unimaginable only twenty years earlier.

Thus the state emerged as a central problem across the whole of the social sciences. In some analyses, the state was regarded as the main problem area for contemporary political thought: as the area which most clearly demonstrated the extent to which the dominant strands of modern social theory had exhausted their potential to explain some of the most profound trends in the modern world. Several accounts of the state recognised (often implicitly) that a critical theory of the state and international relations would have to build upon the main strengths of the Marxist and realist traditions.[5] Even so, critical analyses of the state which consider the economic and strategic dimensions of the state's behaviour in conjunction with the class context of political power have been slow to develop either in sociology or in international relations.

A number of approaches to international relations are, nevertheless, plainly relevant to such an inquiry. The rationalist analysis of the different stages in the history of the modern states-system is salient because it reveals how the development of the modern state and the evolution of principles of international legitimacy have been interconnected. The liberal study of international interdependence with its analysis of the relationship between global social and economic change and the tendency for modern states to formulate policy within the context of international organisations and regimes is also relevant. The literature on world-systems theory and the analysis of long cycles is significant for its attempt to explain the relationship between the rise and fall of particular state structures and the changing tolerance of force in international relations. Nonetheless, an analysis of the origins, reproduction and transformation of the states which have shaped the dominant principles of foreign relations in the different epochs into which the modern states-system can be divided has yet to be attempted within the field of international relations.

Developments in Marxism, for their part, gave rise to a vast array of analyses of different forms of state: the absolutist, the capitalist, "actually existing" socialist states, dependent or peripheral state structures and so forth. But in Marxism too there has been very little analysis of the external relations of the dominant states in the main epochs which comprise the modern states-system. If there is one important exception to this claim, it is Anderson's analysis of the absolutist state, the rise of capitalism and corresponding developments in the sphere of international relations.[6]

We shall consider Anderson's work in more detail in the next section. The important point at this stage is Anderson's claim that the incidence of conflict and war in the absolutist states-system was especially high for two main reasons. Firstly, these states were involved in a relentless struggle to expand their territorial power in order to increase their chances of survival; secondly, the military and strategic causes of violence were reinforced by the survival of the feudal belief that economic growth and the conquest of land were manifestly inseparable. Anderson adds that the problem of insufficient fiscal reserves compelled the absolutist state to support the merchant class and to encourage the development of capitalist relations of production. The state's response to the fiscal crisis which resulted from endemic warfare therefore strengthened the class forces which eventually destroyed the absolutist state. Capitalist state structures emerged with a less conflictual orientation towards the conduct of foreign policy. It was in this context, one might add, that political theories which affirmed the possibility of creating an extended moral and political community developed.

This approach analyses the nature and consequences of the "dual anchorage" of the early modern European state.[7] It clearly takes account of the realist's point that there is an irreducible realm of strategic competition whenever there is an anarchic system of states. There are interesting affinities, too, with the rationalist tradition in that Anderson argues that the absolutist system of states generated distinctive principles of international relations. The method of historical materialism is employed in Anderson's account to reveal that an appreciation of the class context of political power makes possible a deeper understanding of the relationship between the development of the modern state and changes in international relations. Anderson's approach to the dual anchorage of the absolutist state therefore identifies the main factors which were responsible for the particularistic nature of the state in the age of absolutism; and it further relies on the notion of dual anchorage to explain the rise of the capitalist state and the concomitant development of new principles of international relations.

These comments invite the further suggestion that it might be possible to develop a critical theory of the modern states-system which has two main tasks: to understand the changing ways in which states and their citizens have defined the moral and political principles which underlie their separation from the rest of the world;[8] and to understand the forces which strengthened or weakened the sense of belonging to a society of states or a community of humankind at different points in the evolution of the modern states-system. Quite clearly, this task is too involved to be attempted here. The sections to follow have the more modest aim of outlining this project in greater detail by considering the literature on three forms of state. These are the absolutist state, the capitalist state and what have been regarded as the actual or potential counter-hegemonic states in the modern world system.

THE ABSOLUTIST STATE

As previously indicated, Anderson's work is an important illustration of the reconsideration of the state and international relations which has been taking place in contemporary Marxism. It should be noted from the outset that Anderson is at odds with earlier Marxist accounts of absolutism. The majority of these maintained that the absolutist state was an agent of bourgeois domination. Some cited absolutism as evidence that the state can acquire significant autonomy when the power of the main social classes (in this case the bourgeoisie and the aristocracy) is evenly balanced. Anderson argues that the historical evidence demonstrates that the feudal aristocracy was the dominant economic and political class in the period in question.[9] The aristocracy responded to the crisis of European feudalism by establishing centralised institutions of power and control in the place of the traditionally local forms of surveillance and coercion. This solution to the crisis of feudalism, in conjunction with the strategic rivalries between the territorial states into which Europe was divided, gave birth to absolutism. When the bourgeoisie embarked on its struggle for ascendancy, it did so within a pre-existent international system of absolutist states.[10]

The nuances of Anderson's analysis of the feudal crisis, and of other studies devoted to this subject, cannot be considered here. It is sufficient to concentrate on those areas which are relevant for the issues which were raised in the introduction to the present chapter. It is generally agreed that feudalism became incapable of satisfying the growing material demands of the ruling class because of serious labour shortages brought about by a host of factors including the plague and the flight of the peasantry to the towns.[11] At this point, as Anderson puts it, the feudal system had arrived at the "barrier point of its ultimate capacities".[12] The social and political consequences of its "seizure" were, firstly, "an unprecedented wave of warfare as knights everywhere tried to recoup their fortunes with plunder" and, secondly, the establishment of new instruments of political oppression to "reinforce servile conditions and make the producing class pay the costs of the crisis".[13] These developments provoked intra-class conflict within the nobility and "wild, violent resistance" on the part of an oppressed peasantry.[14] The struggle between the two main social classes was influenced by a flourishing urban sector within the interstices of the feudal economy which made the "flight from serfdom a permanent possibility for discontented peasants".[15] The gravitational attraction of the towns, which acted as a major "solvent" of traditional social arrangements, forced the aristocracy to reconstitute its domination by establishing a centralised apparatus of social and political control.[16]

The diffuse nature of political power in the feudal world had therefore become a fetter upon the continuing dominance of the aristocracy. Its response to economic crisis and social breakdown was to promote the "displacement of politico-legal coercion upwards towards a centralised, militarised summit" which was "the Absolutist State".[17] This new apparatus of control altered the relationship between the nobility and the monarch although it perpetuated the dominance of the traditional ruling class. The state, in other words, was a "redeployed and recharged apparatus of feudal domination designed to clamp the peasant masses back into their traditional social position".[18]

In Eastern Europe the emergence of absolutist state structures followed a somewhat different path of historical development. By contrast with Western Europe, feudalism in the East had not reached its optimum level of production. But the East faced a similar problem of labour shortage as the peasantry fled from exploitation. The latter fled not to the towns, which were undeveloped compared with their counterparts in the West, but to the refuge provided by open and unsettled regions. In its response to this crisis, the aristocracy empowered absolutist state structures to tie the peasantry to the land, so establishing what has come to be known as the second serfdom.[19] The internal impetus behind the establishment of centralised territorial states in the East was reinforced by the need to respond to the process of state-formation and territorial expansion which originated in the more advanced regions of Western Europe. In fact, the intra-regional dynamic which encouraged the development of absolutism in Eastern Europe was less important than the inter-regional consequences of state-formation, territorial expansion and war. It "was the international pressure of Western Absolutism, the political apparatus of a more powerful feudal aristocracy, ruling more advanced societies, which forced the Eastern nobility to adopt an equivalently centralised state machinery to survive".[20] As a result, "the birth of a multilateral political order, as a single field of competition and conflict, was...both cause and effect of the generalisation of Absolutism in Europe".[21] It was the process of state-formation in the West, then, which compelled the nobility in Eastern Europe to follow the Western path of political development. As a result, when similar military and bureaucratic structures were established in the East, "the international state-system that defined and demarcated the continent as a whole was complete".[22]

Although the crisis of feudalism was the main reason for the emergence of a multi-state system, the latter gave rise to an irreducible process of state-formation and strategic competition. Yet Anderson does not argue that an explanation of absolutism and its transformation must simply add the logic of strategic interaction to the conventional materialist investigation of conflict between social classes. Nor does Anderson argue that the economic was the primary causal phenomenon because it was determinant in the last instance. One of Anderson's main points is that the notion of primacy (whether it is attached to economic or strategic factors) is meaningless when applied to the period in question. The relationship between feudal social relations of production and the state's conduct of external relations was such that it is necessary to conclude that the economy and the polity were inextricably tied together.

Anderson argues that Marxism has failed to construct a general "theory of the variant social functions of war in different modes of production".[23] It is clear though, as far as Western feudalism is concerned, that there was a very close relationship between war and production. The dominant strata believed that warfare was "possibly the most rational and rapid single mode of expansion of surplus extraction available for any given ruling class".[24] In practice, the assumption that territorial expansion was a necessary condition of economic growth ensured that violence was endemic in the absolutist system of states. The mercantilist analysis of the relationship between power and wealth was emphatic about the zero-sum nature of international political and economic interaction: "The mercantilist theories of wealth and of war were, indeed, conceptually interlocked: the zero-sum model of world trade which inspired its economic protectionism was derived from the zero-sum model of international politics which was inherent in its bellicism".[25] The historical record provides ample evidence of the consequences of these ideas about the connections between territorial expansion, war and economic growth. Throughout the sixteenth century only twenty five years passed without major war. There were seven such years in the whole of the seventeenth century.[26]

Anderson's approach to the dual anchorage of the state explains why it was that "the typical medium of inter-feudal rivalry" was "military". The same method is employed to explain the emergence of a new condition of "inter-capitalist competition" in which the typical form of rivalry was "economic" and in which all "rival parties" could "expand and prosper", albeit "unequally".[27] By placing the emphasis on the processes which resulted from the dual anchorage of the state, Anderson's explanation departs from mainstream Marxist explanations of the transition from feudalism to capitalism. The latter have invariably centred their explanation on the internal contradictions of the feudal mode of production.

Anderson rejects the traditional Marxist argument that capitalism emerged as a consequence of a fundamental contradiction in the feudal mode of production. According to the classical Marxist explanation, feudalism collapsed because the social relations of production had become a fetter upon the further development of the forces of production. The capitalist system overcame this contradiction by introducing new social relations which made further technological development possible. According to the dominant explanation offered by non-Marxist historians - an explanation which Anderson shares - the reality was quite different. The absolutist state encouraged new relations of production in order to achieve a higher level of economic and technological progress. Its main objective was to strengthen its fiscal base in order to contend with internal and external challenges to its power and authority. The state required additional reserves of wealth to compete with neighbouring states, yet its policy of raising additional reserves by encouraging the increased exploitation of the peasantry simply provoked a series of crippling tax revolts. In order to consolidate its military and bureaucratic power, the state threw its weight behind a small but important mercantile capitalist class in what was predominantly an agrarian economy.[28] In a more detailed analysis, North and Thomas describe the pattern of change in this way: "facing continual fiscal crises, the embryonic competing nation-states soon found that survival demanded ever larger revenues which could only come from new sources. Those political units which were relatively more efficient at solving their fiscal problems survived; the relatively inefficient were absorbed by their rivals".[29] The absolutist state was the major initiator of economic and social change in the attempt to ensure its own military survival. Mercantilism with its emphasis upon the interdependence of state power and economic growth matured in a context in which the state was caught between the pressures of domestic conflict and international rivalry.

For mercantilism, the outward projection of military power was essential for overcoming the fiscal crisis of the absolutist state: "conquest was an obvious way to accomplish this end and two centuries of warfare was the result".[30] As for the relationship between the state and society, mercantilism advocated the use of state power to create "national" economies which would support the state's effort to increase its power and wealth.[31] To this end, mercantilism was concerned with the elimination of feudal barriers to the mobility of labour and commodities and with the establishment of a national currency. In addition, the state conferred special rights and privileges on the merchant class. It sought to harness its economic activity in order to increase its military and bureaucratic power. In his famous work on mercantilist economic policy, Heckscher maintained that the state was less concerned with increasing its own "activity in economic affairs" than with reaping the benefits of the "private initiative and acquisitiveness" which its policies were designed to stimulate.[32] It is generally agreed that this symbiotic relationship between the state and mercantile capital created the environment in which the emergence of industrial capitalism became possible. As George Lefebvre noted: "The merchant community and the State furnished each other with mutual assistance: the former as creditor and supplier of public contracts (particularly for the army), the latter as distributor of privileges, prizes and monopolies. Besides, rulers favoured commerce and manufacture in the interests of taxation as well as preservation of the country's monetary stock; mercantilism and colonial exploitation, erected into systems, profited the merchant. Thus the latter had no thought of overturning the social and political order; it was predictable that he would take the part of the king if the monarchy was threatened. On the other hand, the symbiosis between the State and the merchants was a grievance to those early capitalist producers who did not enjoy the same advantages as the privileged merchants, and had to rely on their own resources...Nevertheless, it is impossible to deny that the collusion between commerce and the state promoted the development of capitalism..."[33]. Some absolutist states squandered their fiscal reserves in the pursuit of adventurous overseas policies. This behaviour brought ruin to several lending institutions and hindered capitalist development. As a general rule, however, the domestic and foreign policies of the absolutist powers promoted rather than hindered the development of capitalism in Western Europe. In due course, new state structures emerged proclaiming their allegiance to new and more democratic principles of domestic and international politics.

Anderson attempts to explain the connections between the crisis of feudalism and the emergence of the modern system of states. The analysis seeks to uncover an internal thread running between feudal conceptions of economics and politics and the international relations of absolutist states. It then sets out to explain a further relationship between strategic rivalries and war and the emergence of an international system of capitalist states. Impressive as the argument is, the question arises of whether Anderson has drawn out the main implications of his critique of traditional Marxist accounts of the transition from feudalism to capitalism. There are three dimensions to this question: firstly, is Anderson's analysis of the interconnections between class conflict, state-building and warfare in early modern Europe compatible with any conventional understanding of Marxism as the class analysis of politics and history? Secondly, can the analysis account for the evolution of the European international society of states? And, thirdly, by emphasising the role of state-building and war in early modern European history, does it not begin to create serious problems for the traditional Marxist account of the privileged role of class conflict in the struggle for human emancipation?

Giddens is one of the main advocates of the view that an adequate explanation of the state and war cannot be constructed within the Marxist tradition. In part, Giddens and Anderson are agreed that the "breakthroughs in military technology" which made the city "largely obsolete" were amongst the most important reasons for the emergence of the absolutist state.[34] Yet Giddens wishes to place greater emphasis on military developments in order to explain the period in question: "technological changes affecting warfare were more important than changes in techniques of production".[35] Moreover, the development of the instruments of violence was "substantially separate from...production, which it affected much more than the other way around".[36] Indeed, contemporary social theory should recognise, in Giddens' view, that what was true for absolutism may be true for human history as a whole: "In accounts of social change linked to, or influenced by, historical materialism, it is often suggested that technological innovations bring about the transformation of societies through their direct effect on production. A more accurate emphasis would be upon the application of technological development of weaponry".[37] Whether one presses this point or not, an answer to the first question raised above might be that Marxism cannot emphasise state-building, geopolitical rivalry and developments in the sphere of military technology as Anderson does without sacrificing what has been distinctive about its account of politics and history, namely the supposition that it is class and production which have been most important.

As for the second question posed earlier, Anderson's account of the rise of absolutism has significance for Habermas' observation that it was in this period that the idea of a "state of war, universal and in principle irremovable (came to be) recognised...as the fundamental presupposition of politics".[38] This was the period in which "a modern physics of human nature replace(d) the classical ethics of Natural Law", and the epoch in which the classical idea of politics as an activity orientated towards the perfection of human life gave way to a technical or instrumental understanding of political action.[39] But as Hinsley has argued, "Machiavellism" was in conflict with "the medieval understanding of international society as a single society in which the natural divine law imposed a network of common legal rights and duties on the component states".[40] Furthermore, although "the revival of empire was...the ambition of every state whose relative power rose above the average",[41] the states of Europe finally reached an agreement about the rights and duties which linked them together in a society of states. Although Anderson recognises the importance of this development, it is far from clear that his explanation of the rise and fall of absolutism can explain it. To do so, it would be necessary to accept rather more of the rationalist argument that "international political life, including its normative or institutional dimension, has its own logic and is not to be understood simply as the reflection of economic interests or productive processes".[42]

As for the third question raised earlier, it is clear that the rise of capitalism was accompanied by the "revolutionist" idea that the element of society in international relations could be significantly extended. The supposition that the international political and economic environment could be brought under human control was linked with the conviction that the spread of commerce would undermine the zero-sum conception of international politics which had typified the foreign policy of the absolutist state. In short, the emergence of a critical approach to international relations was connected with the evolution of a new combination of capitalist nation-states. It may be useful to suggest that a developmental logic was at work here in which the European states agreed that the exercise of power should be circumscribed by the need for international order. The rise of bourgeois society then fostered the belief that it was possible to create a new international order which was compatible with the demand for human freedom. Anderson's analysis of the dual anchorage of the modern European state invites the observation that Marxism has failed as a critical international theory because it has not considered the need for a practice which could promote the transition from power to order and from order to emancipation.

THE CAPITALIST STATE

While absolutism prevailed it seemed inevitable that international relations would be governed by the dominant logic of systemic reproduction. The rise of capitalism engendered the belief that it might be possible to supersede the classical system of international relations. At this juncture, the idea of progress was thought to be applicable to relations between as well as to relations within nation-states. Initially, this approach to international relations evolved out of the liberal critique of the mercantilist's zero-sum conception of economic growth. By rejecting this premise liberals denied the mercantilist belief that conflict between nation-states was natural and inevitable. Instead liberals envisaged an international society in which economic activity would be free from the arbitrary constraints which absolutism had imposed upon it. They argued that the international application of free market principles would allow all human beings to enjoy the benefits of material progress and to enlarge the sphere of social interaction which was subject to individual consent.[43] Richard Cobden summarised the moral vision at the centre of the liberal theory of international relations in this way: "I see in the Free Trade principle that which shall act on the moral world as the principle of gravitation in the universe, - drawing men together, thrusting aside the antagonism of race, and creed, and language, and uniting us in the bonds of eternal peace".[44] And in the socialist tradition Saint-Simon observed that the "most salient fact observable in history is the continual extension of the principle of association, in the series of family, city, nation, supernatural Church. The next term must be a still vaster association comprehending the whole race".[45]

The belief that capitalist civilisation would bring about an expansion of moral and political community was therefore central to liberal and socialist approaches to political economy in the nineteenth century. This assumption was present in the earliest versions of functionalism which maintained that new forms of international political organisation were necessary to manage the social and economic relations which cut across the boundaries separating sovereign states. Twentieth century functionalists have continued to discuss the need for new forms of international administration which would erode "sovereignty by installments" and slowly weaken the bonds which connected the citizen to the state.[46] More recent developments have usually dispensed with the optimism which pervaded earlier accounts of the universal potential inherent in capitalism or industrialisation. The former are more often inclined to emphasise the extent to which international regimes can reduce the political uncertainties and instabilities which accompany interdependence. And they are far more likely to comment on how the state and the states-system continue to impede fundamental change in the international political system. Continuities with earlier theories of capitalism and industrialisation are nonetheless perfectly apparent. They are evident in the claim that interdependence may generate powerful transnational and transgovernmental coalitions which can erode the coherence of the state and increase the importance of consensual as opposed to coercive means of managing an interdependent world order.[47]

Most of these analyses pay tribute to realism as they examine the meaning of international interdependence. The realisation that Marxist theories of the connection between class and state might deepen the analysis is a more recent theme in the discussion. The need for a more serious dialogue with Marxism is suggested by Keohane's claim that contemporary international regimes are so biased towards the dominant economic and political interests in the West that they are unable to command international legitimacy.[48] The need to understand rather more about the relationship between class and the state is further underlined by one contemporary realist analysis of international political change. Robert Gilpin has argued that the state's internal function of upholding "the property rights" of its citizens inevitably influences its "primary external function" of defending "property rights and personal security" in relations with "other states". Furthermore, the structure of civil society "sets the constraints upon and may even determine the actions of state authority".[49] The main issue to be considered here is McGowan and Walker's question of whether the relationship between class and state in the leading capitalist states obstructs the development of transnational and transgovernmental coalitions which are committed to removing the economic and political biases which are inherent in the modern world economy.[50]

The nature of the relationship between the state and civil society has been the primary focus of Marxist political theory in recent years. What has to be determined for present purposes is how far Marxist political theory deepens our understanding of the constraints and possibilities which are inherent in the international relations of capitalist states. For this purpose it is convenient to use a familiar classification of Marxist approaches which distinguishes between the instrumentalist, structuralist and Hegelian-Marxist approaches to the capitalist state.

Ralph Miliband's *The State in Capitalist Society* was the first major formulation of the instrumentalist approach to the state. This work was designed to rescue Marxism from the economic reductionism of the Second and Third Internationals. Its attempt to repair Marxist political theory was connected with a critique of the dominant liberal-pluralist theories of the state. According to the latter approaches, the state is an impartial referee presiding over the contest between competing interests in civil society. Miliband's critique of the liberal claim that no single set of interests controlled the state emphasised the conventional Marxist point that each state was embedded in, and constrained by, the system of unequal ownership and control of the means of production. But whereas the class character of the state had become virtually axiomatic in historical materialism, Miliband set out detailed empirical evidence of the means by which social and economic inequalities were converted into inequalities of political power. Miliband argued that earlier versions of Marxism were superseded, just as pluralism was refuted, by the evidence that there were three main links between the state and civil society. Interpersonal ties between members of the capitalist class and the managers of state power - ties which had deepened because of the increased integration of the private and public sectors - were one reason for the state acting as the representative of the dominant interests in civil society. Secondly, the fact that business and governmental personnel were recruited from the same social stratum, and invariably possessed similar ideological preferences, reinforced the state's class character. Finally, the experience of social-democratic governments revealed that their political options were seriously restricted by the need to preserve business confidence and to maintain conditions which would encourage continuing capital investment. Unless it worked within these constraints the state would not be assured of the economic growth on which its public expenditure was ultimately dependent.[51]

Miliband began with the assumption that the state and civil society are separate from one another. The problem was then to explain how the ties between them worked to the advantage of the dominant interests in civil society. Structural Marxists such as Poulantzas reversed the starting point of the analysis. They argued that it was necessary to understand why it was that the state and civil society had to appear to be separate in the first place. Poulantzas argued that capitalism was distinguished from pre-capitalist modes of production by the existence of free labour. In the capitalist system of production the dominant class did not use the coercive power of the state to force the exploited class to surrender control of its labour-power. Instead, the subordinate class agreed to alienate control of its labour-power in exchange for wage payment. Because production was based upon contracts between the bourgeoisie and the proletariat, capitalism necessarily stressed the freedom and equality of all citizens and defended its claim to legitimacy in these terms. The dominant ideology made it essential for the state to avoid too close an identification with the interests of any single class.[52]

The apparent separation between the state and civil society did not alter the fact that the state was crucial for the reproduction of capitalism. Indeed, the absence of direct class control of the state was essential for the state to perform its functions effectively. Poulantzas argued that the bourgeoisie consisted of various "fractions" which lacked a common strategy for ensuring the survival of capitalism. The pursuit of some of the short-term economic and political objectives of these fractions could conceivably jeopardise the survival of capitalism itself. Because of the fragmented nature of the bourgeoisie, and because of the tension between some short-term interests and the long-term survival of the bourgeoisie as a whole, the state was empowered to maintain the preconditions for future capitalist development. Its "relative autonomy" from the dominant class allowed the state to contain any fraction which posed a threat to the survival of capitalism. The relative autonomy of the state enabled it to act as the "factor of cohesion" in capitalist society: on one level, the state attempted to minimise conflict within the dominant class while, on another level, it sought to maximise division within the working class and to counter the atomistic tendencies inherent in civil society by disseminating the symbols of national unity.[53]

Poulantzas argued that the class character of the state was evident from the functions it performed in capitalist societies. This removed the need for an empirical search for interpersonal connections between the state and members of the dominant class. Where such ties existed, they were an effect rather than a cause of an objective relationship between the state and civil society.[54] In responding to this argument, Miliband accused Poulantzas of "structural super-determinism" which assumed that individuals were simply "bearers" of pre-established social roles.[55] Other critics noted similarities between Poulantzas' structural Marxism and functionalist approaches to politics which had been influential in bourgeois social science especially in the United States.[56] However valid these points may have been, structural Marxism was undoubtedly important for "bringing the state back" into contemporary social theory. It encouraged the analysis of various state structures and the extent of their autonomy from dominant class forces. In fact, Gilpin's comments on the way in which the state is constrained by civil society reveal that these concerns have surfaced in the wider literature.

Miliband and Poulantzas agreed that the state acted to promote the legitimacy of capitalist society. For writers within the Hegelian-Marxist tradition, it is the state's role in the process of legitimation which discloses the real nature of its relationship with civil society. Gramsci was one of the first Marxist theoreticians to develop this approach to the state. In *The Prison Notebooks* Gramsci argued that most accounts of capitalism had failed to explain the real secret of its survival. Neither the observation that the state would defend capitalism by force nor the allegation that the proletariat had been diverted from its revolutionary path by false consciousness fully captured the reasons for its reproduction. Its survival ultimately depended on a complex mix of coercion and consent in which dominant interests met some of the demands issuing from subordinate social forces. That did not mean that the dominant class would be prepared to compromise its most basic class interests. All it revealed was its understanding that it would more likely to realise its class objectives in the context of popular rule.[57]

Gramsci maintained that the dominant class exercised hegemony when it could rely on the voluntary compliance of subordinate groups. It was essential for the state to use its "moral and political leadership" to incorporate the elements of different class viewpoints within an overarching "national-popular will".[58] The state's role in constructing a national ideology which encompassed and transcended different class perspectives was crucial for the survival of capitalism. Consequently, although the state was undeniably constrained by the dominant forces in civil society, it had to be sufficiently autonomous to enact its role as the guardian of political legitimacy.

The matter of the state and foreign policy has been at the margin of these inquiries. Nevertheless, most of them suggest that an understanding of the class-state relationship will cast as much light on foreign policy as it does on domestic politics and policy-making. Apart from noting that the "supra-national character of the capitalist mode of production" constrains all modern state structures, most inquiries point to the state's direct role in promoting the internationalisation of capitalism.[59] Miliband and Poulantzas regarded the establishment of a supranational political structure in the European Economic Community, and attempts to perpetuate dependent post-colonial state apparatuses in the Third World, as ample evidence of the state's class role.[60] According to this argument, international interdependence ought to be regarded as the expression of specific class interests which obstruct the development of a universal social and political consensus. This being so, one might presume - to return to the main theme of the section - that all capitalist international organisations reflect the domestic class interests in the most powerful capitalist states and complement their efforts to perpetuate global inequalities of economic and political power.

It is unclear whether or not the exponents of the Hegelian-Marxist approach to the state would be willing to embrace these conclusions in their entirety. They are equally emphatic about the class nature of the capitalist state, although they argue that the state must represent a broad range of social interests in order to legitimate the capitalist order. It is arguable that similar processes may exist in international organisations. If so, the state might be said to have a dual function of promoting specific class interests while acting to establish principles of international relations which can command the widest possible legitimacy. This second function might be regarded as necessary because capitalist states have been unable to proclaim the universal validity of freedom and equality without creating subsequent expectations that the international economic system will be modified to meet the needs of weaker societies. If this analysis of the class context of political power is correct, it might seem unlikely that capitalist states will ever initiate fundamental change in international organisations and in the structure of global economic relations more generally. By the same token, it would appear to be inevitable that these organisations will continue to represent the most powerful interests in the dominant capitalist societies. On the other hand, it would be a mistake to suggest that the class structure of capitalist society prevents the state from exercising any autonomy from dominant class forces; and it would be just as wrong to underestimate the state's capacity to reach a compromise, however limited, with the political representatives of subordinate class and state interests.

All of these approaches aim to reveal that class analysis can explain the main functions of the modern capitalist state. But all of them are acutely aware of the need to free Marxism from economic reductionism. The Hegelian-Marxist approach attempts to reconcile these points by arguing that the state must represent a range of political interests and perspectives if it is to perform its class role effectively. For those who adopt this perspective - indeed for Marxists more generally - there is no contradiction between reaffirming the class nature of the state and conceding the (relative) autonomy of the state and "politics".

The issue, of course, is whether these responses go far enough to dispel the suspicion that Marxists have simply invented another form of class reductionism. The contention that Marxism has consistently failed to understand the nature of state autonomy - especially with regard to the formulation and implementation of national security policy - remains a powerful argument in the theory of international relations for precisely this reason. The charge of reductionism persists because Marxism has rarely addressed the relationship between the citizen's concern for territorial security and the state's claim to represent the national interest in its conduct of foreign policy. This accusation is also prompted by the absence of any significant Marxist analysis of the part that national security fears play in the development of national ideology. What is more, it will no doubt continue to prevail in international relations circles as long as Marxism seems to be resistant to two propositions: to the fact that the state's national security role may bring it into conflict with members of the dominant class; and to the proposition that this is a conflict which members of the dominant class may find themselves unable to win.

In short, the crux of the realist argument against Marxism, and against radical theories of foreign policy more generally, is that they have yet to produce a comprehensive analysis of the autonomy of the state. This argument has been developed in two stages. It began with the realist critique of the revisionist histories of American foreign policy from the Cold War to the period of intervention in South East Asia. These were the first approaches to international relations to take the class-state relationship seriously. The second stage of the argument has been concerned with contemporary Marxist theories of the state, and with the critique of structural Marxism in particular. It is useful to consider each stage in turn, beginning with the debate which surrounded Gabriel Kolko's revisionist approach to American foreign policy.

Kolko's analysis of the foreign policy of the United States is similar to subsequent Marxist critiques of the pluralist theory of the modern state. Kolko argued that the pluralists were wrong to assume that the corporate sector was no more powerful than any other organised group in American society. Given the "grossly inequitable distribution of wealth and income", the corporate sector was uniquely placed to shape "the essential preconditions and functions of the larger American social order".[61] The immense pressure which this sector could bring to bear on the state apparatus was only one instance of its political dominance. The extent to which bourgeois ideology also pervaded the entire "socio-economic framework" often made it unnecessary for the corporate sector to resort to the direct exercise of its economic and political power.[62] The dominant ideology was sufficiently powerful within the state apparatus to prevent the recruitment of individuals whose decisions might be "dysfunctional" for the system as a whole.[63] In the same way an ideological consensus defined the boundaries of acceptable political choice.

For these reasons, Kolko rejected the realist argument that foreign policy-makers acted to protect transcendent national interests. The case of American raw materials foreign policy provided clear evidence of the state's explicit support for the dominant interests in civil society. Moreover, the main global aspirations of the foreign policy-making establishment clearly reflected the ideological preferences of the dominant class. It was the dominant ideology in civil society which explained the vision of world order which the United States attempted to impose upon other societies in the 1950s and 1960s. When the United States adopted the policy of "countering, neutralising and containing...disturbing political and social trends" in the Third World which challenged its right to "define the course of global politics", it did so in direct response to internal social-structural imperatives.[64]

It is perfectly possible that the dominant ideology in foreign policy is one of the principal embodiments and expressions of class power - and the dominant ideology in international organisations might be considered in the same way. Nevertheless, the revisionists almost certainly underestimated the extent of the state's autonomy from civil society, as the realist critique of revisionist historiography was quick to emphasise. In his critique of revisionism, Robert Tucker argued that the role of global vision in American foreign policy could be explained without introducing "problematic assumptions about the effects of social structure upon state behaviour".[65] The decisive factor was American military power which allowed the state to step beyond the limited concern with security and survival which typically dominated the foreign policies of less powerful states. It was this relative freedom from the tyranny of national security politics which allowed the United States to act to implement its vision of world order.[66] The same freedom explained its willingness to use force to squash those revolutionary movements which challenged its endeavour to "define the course of global politics".

Tucker's main contention was that capitalist states resist international institutional reform because they are states and not because they are capitalist. A major socialist power would act no differently.[67] Taken literally, this argument would seem to suggest there is nothing in the structure of society to prevent the United States, say, from attempting to construct a socialist world order if it believed that this would enable it to advance its security interests more effectively. Of course, the claim that strategic factors have to be addressed in any explanation of the United States' resistance to global economic reform is the chief merit of Tucker's argument. But it is scarcely credible that the state possesses as much freedom from social-structural forces as Tucker suggested, and it is hardly likely that social-structural forces in the United States would allow an American government to make a foreign policy commitment to the establishment of a socialist world system - which is, on Tucker's argument, at least a logical possibility. What Tucker's argument lacks is an account of the forces which determine the ideological dimension of foreign policy. An emphasis upon the state's superior military power does not explain the content of its global ideology. And although this may seem to be less problematic, it is far from self-evident that superior military power explains the state's willingness to impose its global vision on other societies. For these reasons, there are good grounds for examining social and economic structures to ascertain how far, and in what way, they influence foreign policy. It might then be suggested that while revisionism erred by reducing the state to social structural forces, Tucker's realist critique erred in an opposite direction by overestimating the state's freedom from social structural influences. If this is so, neither perspective can explain the relationship between class, state and foreign policy.

To put the point another way, it may be essential to work towards an account of the state and foreign policy which builds on the respective strengths of Marxism and realism. Stephen Krasner puts this issue to the test in his work on American raw materials foreign policy. According to Krasner, decision-makers in this area have consistently pursued three main policy goals. They are in ascending order of importance: the maintenance of competition between the most important sources of supply, the guarantee of American access to important raw materials and the "general policy objective" of preventing communist expansion into regions which are economically or strategically vital to the United States.[68] Krasner argues that the pluralist perspective suggests that interest group competition is the reason this hierarchy of policy objectives exists. Its hypothesis is disconfirmed by the evidence that the state acted autonomously in deciding to pursue these goals.[69] The dispute between realism and structural Marxism cannot be resolved so simply as neither perspective underestimates the significance of state power.[70] Their differences can be resolved, however, on strictly theoretical grounds.

The argument is as follows. For structural Marxism, the autonomy of the state is essential for the reproduction of the capitalist system. As far as realism is concerned, the state enjoys its autonomy from civil society because of its special responsibility for the management of national security policy. On Krasner's interpretation of structural Marxism, the capitalist state cannot pursue objectives which would undermine internal social cohesion.[71] Realism is bound by no such assumption. In fact, realists maintain that the conflict between private and public interests is an ever-present possibility because of the state's role as a strategic and diplomatic actor. This conflict between dominant societal interests and the state can become pronounced in the case of great powers which enjoy sufficient military strength to attempt to impose their preferred vision of world order on others. In this context, the state can initiate what the structural Marxist would regard as "non-logical" action which threatens the stability of the capitalist social order.[72] Krasner regards American policy towards Vietnam as a striking illustration of a possibility which structural Marxists seem to exclude a priori. Because the Vietnam War placed considerable "strain on domestic social cohesion" it was "the very opposite of what a structural Marxist expects from the state or the dominant ideology".[73]

Krasner argues that the pursuit of non-logical foreign policy goals is a function of the great power's dominant position in the international system. This theme, which restates Tucker's argument against revisionism, may be just as vulnerable to the criticism that it exaggerates the state's capacity to determine the ideological objectives of foreign policy. Krasner's defence of realism also rests on a limited or ungenerous reading of structural Marxist thought. It is true that structural Marxists argue that the capitalist state is obliged to promote the long-term reproduction of the capitalist mode of production. Whether they must therefore deny that the state can act non-logically is open to question. To concede the relative autonomy of the state is presumably to allow for the possibility of political irrationality, albeit with the added qualification that class forces will mobilise to pull the state back into line.

The important question is whether or not it is inevitable that these class forces will be successful. The quasi-functionalist overtones of structural Marxism would seem to assume that they will. Some strands of recent Marxist political theory which are critical of the implicit reductionism of this view steer well clear of this conclusion. Fred Block, for example, endorses the structuralist point that "the exercise of state power occurs within particular class contexts, which shape and limit the exercise of that power. These class contexts in turn are the products of particular relations of production".[74] But because the state possesses a monopoly of control over the instruments of violence, "state managers" are able to act "in ways that violate both the existing political rules and the normal constraints of class relations".[75] The growth of state power in Nazi Germany in the 1930s provided incontrovertible evidence of this possibility. The fact that the state can turn civil society into an instrument for the realisation of its own purposes is not, for Block, a sufficient reason for abandoning class analysis. What this possibility does reveal, as Miliband and others have suggested, is the need to close the gap between Marxism and the Weberian approach to the state and violence and the need therefore to analyse the connections between the state's position vis-a-vis domestic class forces, the world economy and - not least - the international states-system.[76]

It is necessary to reject the claim that the state is primarily an instrument of class rule, just as it is necessary to reject the argument that it is largely immune from social structural influences. An analysis of the possibilities which are inherent in the international system of capitalist states would therefore require a more complex understanding of the relationship between class and state than either realism or Marxism can provide. This brings the discussion back to McGowan and Walker's question of "whether or not any U.S. foreign economic policy can be formulated that can help to establish an international economic regime which meets the interests of all parties to such a degree as to preserve itself from challenge and collapse".[77] McGowan and Walker argue that "radical" analyses of the capitalist state explain why it is unlikely that the American state apparatus will construct a foreign economic policy which meets the demand for structural change. In the first place, the "internalisation of the liberal economic paradigm" which protects the interests of the dominant class has "disposed policy-makers to resist proposals for a New International Economic Order, and instead adopt policies that reproduce the existing system". Secondly, even if the internalisation of this dominant ideology had not occurred, the state would pursue similar policies because of the pressure applied by the central "network of special interests". And finally, state managers cannot escape the structural constraints imposed by the capitalist system: the "capitalist structure of the U.S. economy and the world system limits the nature of U.S. economic policy and the modal choices of the state, so that policy outcomes tend to reproduce the capitalist features of the domestic and international system".[78]

McGowan and Walker maintain that "radical" theories of the state are useful for explaining decisions which produce an unequal distribution of costs and benefits for different groups within the community. Tariff policy is one area where gains are clearly "divisible", and where the class actors which are most seriously affected mobilise to stave off any threats to their interests.[79] In contrast, the costs and benefits of decisions affecting "power, security and prestige" are usually "indivisible".[80] In this domain where all citizens stand to gain or lose to the same extent, the policy process tends to conform with the "rational actor model" developed by conventional theories of international relations. These dimensions may interact to exclude foreign policies which might be concerned with achieving major international economic redistribution. There are fractions of the dominant class in capitalist societies which reject Third World claims for the reform of the international economic system. Further opposition to these claims stems from those parts of the state apparatus which have a specific interest in the maintenance of national power and prestige. Subordinate class interests may also oppose a redistributive foreign policy out of economic self-interest, because of ideological hostility to the idea of international redistributive justice or because they believe that there may be a national security cost. In this case, a combination of radical and conventional modes of analysis is necessary to unravel the connections between class, state and foreign economic policy.

McGowan and Walker develop a powerful case for moving beyond Marxism and realism. The concluding issue is how their argument could be extended to produce a more comprehensive understanding of the historical possibilities which are inherent in the international relations of capitalist states. Goran Therborn's analysis of the "four axes of determination" of the power of the bourgeoisie suggests one possible way to proceed. The level of capitalist development in any society and its relationship with earlier modes of production are two crucial axes. Its "central or peripheral position" in the international capitalist system is a third determinant of bourgeois power, and "the international configuration of harmonious or conflicting forces" more generally (to which presumably the international states-system belongs) is the fourth determinant of class power. Therborn's argument that these four axes are the main influences determinants of the power of the state in capitalist societies certainly smacks of class reductionism.[81] A more successful approach which draws elements from Marxism and realism would distinguish between the determinants of class power and the determinants of state power. Such an approach would facilitate the development of a taxonomy of capitalist state structures. It would cast light on the numerous domestic and international relations which exist between different fractions of the dominant class and the various organs of each state apparatus. And it would clarify the context in which the state approached the question of foreign economic policy-making and the extent to which it could satisfy demands for international economic redistribution.

As far as this last point is concerned, there is every reason to suppose that radical proposals for reducing international inequalities will continue to be opposed by the dominant classes of the capitalist societies. In some cases, these interests may have the support of powerful allies in the state apparatus. However it would be wrong to assume that the state's opposition to international redistributive policies is simply a manifestation of its role as an instrument of class power. As realists have argued, the state's independent concern with changes in the international configuration of power is an additional reason for its resistance. Apart from that, there are elements in the state apparatus which neither reflect specific class interests nor respond simply to strategic imperatives. Whether they are motivated by considerations of social justice or conscious of the long term problem of maintaining consensus in world politics, these actors are often more willing to reach a compromise with the representatives of subordinate interests.[82] These are the agencies of the state which have to respond to one demand for change which distinguishes the international system in which capitalism is dominant from the system in which the absolutist state prevailed. This is the demand that the tension between the normative code which proclaims freedom and equality as universal values and actual international economic constraints and inequalities ought to be abolished. The interplay between different class forces and the various organs which comprise the capitalist state will determine the extent to which the dominant capitalist societies can or cannot satisfy this demand for the extension of international community.

THE COUNTER-HEGEMONIC STATE

Marx believed that counter-hegemonic socialist states would emerge out of the conflicts and crises which were peculiar to the bourgeois world. Although Marx foresaw the destruction of capitalist states and the establishment of socialism on a world scale, he did not predict the stages which the species would pass through in its journey towards socialism. Marx did indicate that in the first instance the class struggle would have to be national in form. Each national proletariat would have to wrestle control of the state from the national bourgeoisie before it could begin its project of socialist transformation.[83] But the emergence of new socialist state structures in the more advanced regions of the world system was simply the first step in a journey which would end when socialism had been established across the world at large. Marx evidently believed that the modern state and classical power politics would be superseded in the course of this transition.

The inadequacies of Marx's notion of an imminent world-historical transition soon became transparent. Not only did the majority of the advanced capitalist states survive their internal contradictions, but socialist movements quickly succumbed to nationalism while socialist regimes gravitated towards the foreign policy agenda of the classical sovereign state. At this stage, it became essential to regard the transition to socialism as a two-dimensional enterprise. The first problem was how to promote socialism within the existing post-revolutionary societies; the second and novel issue was how to realise socialist internationalism in a world which was divided into socialist as well as capitalist states. Although these questions might be regarded as equally central, the Marxist tradition has tended to regard the second problem as less important than the first.

To many observers, the supposition that Marxists must aim to realise socialism on a world scale may seem a distraction from the central task of transforming the class structure of specific capitalist and pre-capitalist societies. If radical change in the structure of international relations is improbable or remote, then there would seem to be no choice but to work towards socialism at the level of the individual nation-state.[84] When formulating the doctrine of "socialism in one country", Bukharin therefore argued that Russian Marxists had no alternative but to create socialism on the "wretched technical base" of Soviet society before they could begin to contemplate world socialist revolution.[85] The process of global revolution would inevitably be a "gigantic process" stretching over many "decades".[86]

In his defence of permanent revolution, Trotsky warned the advocates of socialism in one country against the dangers of "national messianism".[87] The phenomenon of "red brotherhood at war" has confirmed Trotsky's contention that the appearance of socialist states might not be a significant advance beyond the old international system.[88] Trotsky's critique of the idea of socialism in one country rested upon the tenuous assumption that an embryonic international community already existed in the ranks of the working class movement. Since the move beyond exclusive national identities had already occurred, there was no need to consider the question of whether it was capitalism or the nation-state which had to be abolished in order to promote human emancipation.[89] In more recent periods in which the internationalism of the proletariat no longer has any meaning, and in which the power of the sovereign state is undiminished, this question can no longer be avoided. Not only is it abundantly clear that a universal society cannot be constructed without the prior transformation of state structures. It is also evident that Marxism, or any other approach to critical social theory, must explain how internationalism can be advanced in a world which consists of separate states. The thesis that socialism must first be established in separate countries has still to explain how these countries might conduct their external relations in order to advance the cause of internationalism. This is a question for which Marxism was unprepared and for which it has still to find an answer.

Marxists began to analyse the prospects for counter-hegemonic movements and regimes in the periphery when revolution in the advanced capitalist countries began to seem increasingly remote. As we noted in previous chapters, the Marxist theories of nationalism and imperialism were the first to examine the peripheral challenge to metropolitan capitalism. Analysts such as Trotsky suggested that a world-wide socialist revolution might be triggered by events in the periphery. Lenin argued that progressive national movements in the periphery were the natural allies of the main revolutionary force in the more advanced capitalist societies. It became necessary, however, to break with the assumption that the periphery had a supporting role to play in the more central European conflict when alliances between the oppressed groups of the centre and the periphery also began to seem unlikely. The contention that the industrial proletariat had been corrupted by the system of global dominance and dependence raised the important question of whether counter-hegemonic state structures might be more likely to emerge in the periphery rather than in the core.

The context for this discussion of the peripheral counter-hegemonic state was analysed in the chapter on international inequality. In the first place, dependency theorists observed that the penetration of peripheral state structures - the "transnational integration and national disintegration" of the periphery as Sunkel called it - would remain as long as world capitalism continued to exist.[90] This being the case, the periphery had to withdraw from the capitalist world economy in order to take possession of its own sovereignty. Secession would enable the periphery to construct socialism on the national level. If socialism was to be realised on a global scale, it could only be through the efforts of counter-hegemonic peripheral state structures.

In his critique of dependency theory, Warren denied that peripheral societies were powerless to improve their position within the existing capitalist world system. Warren argued that the evidence revealed that powerful state structures had already emerged in the periphery. Connections with the capitalist world promised to bring cultural modernisation and more democratic forms of polity to the periphery. Warren argued that the internal class dynamics of these societies would determine the nature of the post-colonial state. Continuing involvement in, rather than secession from, the capitalist world economy was a necessary if not a sufficient condition for the development of powerful counter-hegemonic states.[91]

An analysis of the prospects for the emergence of new counter-hegemonic states must take account of two other factors, the first being the "socio-cultural" effects of joint ventures between the managers of the peripheral state and the managers of foreign capital.[92] It has been argued that these partnerships are evidence of a logic of "transnational class formation" which disseminates the dominant capitalist ideology of the core.[93] These partnerships reinforce "immanent tendencies towards the embourgeoisement of the state bureaucratic elite" and encourage the spread of bourgeois civilisation across the world as a whole.[94] Whereas some accept Marx's argument that the diffusion of bourgeois civilisation is a progressive development which dissolves archaic and oppressive social relations and promotes economic and political development, others maintain that the transmission of core ideology simply reinforces peripheral dependence and strengthens the position of the dominant capitalist states.[95] If the second perspective is correct, the chances that new counter-hegemonic regimes will emerge in the periphery are indeed remote.

The second factor which is crucial has been analysed at length in the theory of the "post-colonial state". One of the main themes of this literature is that the colonial powers left behind an "overdeveloped state" in which "the excessive enlargement of power of control and regulation that the State acquires extends far beyond the logic of what is necessary in the interests of the orderly functioning of the peripheral capitalist economies".[96] Managers of the state apparatus therefore "enjoy a relative autonomy vis-a-vis the dominant classes", and "even the metropolitan bourgeoisie...and the metropolitan States (which act) on their behalf must now negotiate their demands with post-colonial States".[97] The question is whether the overdeveloped state apparatuses of the periphery are a likely source of significant counter-hegemonic strategies.

In an argument which owes more to Pareto, Mosca and Michels than to Marx, Meillassoux has argued that state managers possess many of the characteristics of a dominant class. They are not a dominant class in the conventional Marxist sense because they do not own the instruments of production. But their military and bureaucratic power enables them to control, if not to own, the forces of production. Their class character stems from their role as the "managerial board of a kind of state corporation".[98] The members of this state-class employ the language of socialism and nationalism to legitimate the claim that they represent the wider societal interest. In fact, their alliances with foreign capital have the opposite effect of incorporating the domestic labour force within new international relations of oppression and exploitation. The principal benefits of these arrangements have been appropriated by state managers who have attained a higher international rank albeit "under the rule of the old master".[99]

By this account, the nature of state formation in the periphery does little to increase the likelihood that progressive state structures will emerge there. This theme is especially pronounced in analyses of the high incidence of state terrorism and military repression in several Third World societies. The contention that state managers enjoy considerable autonomy from internal social forces because they inherited highly developed military and bureaucratic structures from the colonial powers is relevant in this context. Given this legacy, state repression is not a means of preserving the privileges of the dominant class: it is a response to the internal (and external) challenges or threats to the regime's own power and security.[100]

These dimensions of state-formation in the periphery necessitate a new definition of the counter-hegemonic state. In classical Marxism, a counter-hegemonic state is one which has embarked on the transition from capitalism to socialism on the domestic level and which is committed to the establishment of socialism on a world scale. The rise of the authoritarian state in the Third World indicates the need for a broader notion of counter-hegemony which aims to protect the freedom of citizens from the potentially repressive state. Moreover, as Wallerstein has argued, by concentrating on the "withering away of the state" Marxists for the greater part of this century failed to raise the crucial question of how to encourage the "withering away of states".[101] For this reason, a critical theory of state structures ought to be as concerned with the particularism of the nation-state as classical Marxism was with the particularism of class forces and relations. The idea of counter-hegemony might be extended still further to include opposition to the deleterious ecological consequences of the industrial mode of exploiting nature. The upshot of these points is that the Marxist notion of counter-hegemony assumed that the dominant logic in the modern world was the transition from capitalism to socialism. The main conclusion which emerges from this discussion of recent theories of the state is that this is no longer the context in which to understand the counter-hegemonic state.[102]

CONCLUSIONS

Recent developments in the theory of the state reveal what is meant by the decline of the classical tradition of sociology.[103] They may well signify the end of the tradition of social inquiry which treated particular societies as if they were isolated from the effects of state-formation, strategic competition and war. In the same way, these developments confirm the need for a move beyond the conventional theory of international relations. They suggest that the evolution of the system of states cannot be considered without taking account of economic and social phenomena which were once held to fall within the province of sociology. The study of international relations and sociology have begun to converge as a result of recent debates about the nature of the state. For the first time it is clear why two regions of social and political inquiry which evolved in comparative isolation from one another ought to develop a common research agenda.

The argument for convergence can be defended on a number of different grounds. The significance of Marxism for the critique of conventional international political theory has already been acknowledged in some quarters. Although the case for reassessing the strengths and weaknesses of historical materialism is not linked with the defence of a critical theory of international relations in all cases,[104] those who do make this connection argue that the emancipatory project has been flawed precisely because of its failure to deal with the persistence of the system of states. For this reason, as we noted in the first chapter, a critical theory of international relations should be concerned with the realities of power, order and emancipation in the system of states. It must be aware of the phenomenon of "recurrence and repetition" in international relations and of existing or conceivable logics of change within the states-system. More specifically, critical approaches to international relations which recognise the strengths of Marxism and realism might endeavour to understand how far the dominant forms of state in each epoch obstruct or permit the extension of moral and political community.

This in turn invites the question of whether the move beyond realism and Marxism strengthens the case for a new "empirical philosophy of history".[105] Habermas has presented the case for a new philosophical history in his argument for the reconstruction of historical materialism. According to Habermas, Marx's analysis of the role of the labour-process in the self-creation of the species no longer provides the foundations for an empirical philosophy of history. A narrative which aims to explain how "freedom was sought out and won" must explore the evolution of moral-practical reasoning as well as the evolution of the relationship between society and nature.[106] More specifically, in the course of executing the first of these tasks it must explain the evolution from customary and particularistic to rational and universalistic ethical world-views.[107]

Habermas argues that the development of moral reasoning cannot be reduced to the development of production and industry. Indeed at one point Habermas suggests that the need for order between independent political communities has been just as important an influence on the moral development of the species.[108] One might develop this point further by suggesting that Marx's attempt to explain the gradual unification of the species and the widening of community was one of the major achievements of historical materialism. The main problem with the approach was the supposition that a sociology of the universalising process should concentrate on modes of production and their external relations. The Marxian approach to the universalising process was incomplete because it failed to include political and cultural relations between independent communities in its account of the moral and political development of the human race. As a result, a contemporary critical theory of international relations requires what Bull has called "a general historical analysis" of the evolution of the "political structure of the world as a whole".[109] What a "post-Marxist critical theory" or an "empirical philosophy of history with a critical intent" would bring to this project is a particular focus upon the origins and development of universal moral norms in the sphere of intersocietal relations.[110]

A critical sociology of moral development in the sphere of intersocietal relations may be regarded as post-Marxist for the following reasons. Marx's social theory pointed to tensions between universal norms and particularistic practices in production relations. At no point did Marx develop an account of how similar tensions developed in other social relations involving the sexes, races, nations or ethnic groups, states and other independent political communities. Nor did Marx consider the modes of political conduct which would free subjects from the tensions which existed in these spheres of social interaction.[111] The crucial point for present purposes is that Marx did not consider how the tension between universalism and particularism emerged in relations between independent political communities; and his social and political theory made no comment on how this tension might be resolved. For this reason Giddens is right to argue that Marx's thought is the starting-point for an emancipatory politics - nothing more and nothing less.[112] The significance of this remark is only now being recognised in the field of international relations. When its full import has been recognised, the study of international relations and critical social theory may merge in a comprehensive historical analysis of the struggle between universalising and particularising processes.

Conclusions

There are three major approaches to the conflict between realist and Marxist theories of international relations. According to the first of them, the traditional realist explanation of world politics remains valid and its renowned critique of historical materialism still holds. A second perspective contends that Marxism is capable of developing an accurate account of international economic and political relations. The most important formulation of this approach maintains that a reconstructed historical materialism should incorporate elements of realism within its account of history and politics. A third approach - the one defended in the present work - agrees with the argument for combining elements of realism and Marxism within the one conceptual framework. This approach is distinguished from the others by the further observation that a critical theory of international relations can only be developed by moving beyond the realist and Marxist perspectives. Let us now consider each of these positions in turn.

The realist tradition, as it is exemplified by Waltz's major theoretical work on international relations, argues that strategic interaction determines the nature of world politics. From this angle, the struggle for power and security is the overriding concern of each sovereign state and the logic of reproduction is the dominant logic in international relations. Waltz reaffirms the classical realist argument that it is futile to construct idealised visions of alternative world orders and utopian to suppose that any of these visions will ever be realised in practice. The attempt to understand the means by which states protect their national security and uphold order is the proper task of international theory.

Realists therefore repudiate the political aspirations of the Enlightenment and the internationalism or cosmopolitanism of its principal heirs: liberalism and Marxism. Moreover, they argue that their dispute with Marxism about the extent to which it is possible to transform world politics can be resolved by considering their respective analyses of capitalism, the states-system and war. Realism emphasises the fact that Marx and early twentieth century Marxism believed that capitalism would erode the differences and divisions between nations and states. The establishment of world socialism would then complete the great ascent towards internationalism. Realism argues that the primacy of geopolitics explains why capitalism has failed to weaken and why socialism has failed to abolish the power and appeal of the sovereign nation-state. Furthermore, since the 1930s and 1940s realists have regarded the national fragmentation of Marxism and the process by which socialist states became involved in the world of power politics as added confirmation of the superiority of the realist interpretation of international relations. To the realist the transformation of Marxism is sufficient evidence that world socialism cannot be achieved in an international system of states.

The compelling features of the realist analysis of world politics have long been recognised within the study of international relations. In recent years they have acquired new forms of support especially in the sociological literature on the state. The realist critique of Marxism which has been prevalent in international relations for almost forty years now has a counterpart in sociology. In the same period, Marxists have become aware that studies of the exogenous realm of strategic interaction can correct their traditionally endogenous and class-reductionist account of state-formation and state behaviour. It is all the more significant therefore that one of the most recent developments in international theory calls for a fundamental reassessment of Marxism in order to criticise and correct realism. There are two main reasons for the decision to review the classical verdict on historical materialism and to invoke Marxist themes in the critique of realism. First of all, since the 1970s a growing body of theoretical literature has argued that Marxist and neo-Marxist analyses of the state and the world economy have opened up new possibilities in the theory of international relations. The main works to develop this theme argued that Marxism can explain important connections between class and the state and crucial linkages between the international states-system and the world economy which mainstream international theorists have largely ignored. These works have concluded that Marxism has a major contribution to make to the emerging "post-realist" theory of international relations.

The development of new methodological and epistemological disputes about the nature and purpose of international relations theory has been a second reason for the reassessment of Marxism. The influence of dependency theory in international relations was especially important in this regard. Dependency theory had the effect of inviting the argument that the classical theory of international relations was preoccupied with a limited and conservative range of normative issues. The classical tradition was accused of privileging the goals of national security and international order and of ignoring the relationship between global economic and political structures and international inequalities of power and wealth. This was the context in which the argument for a critical theory of international relations began to be developed.

The analysis of the knowledge-constitutive interests which underlie the three sociologies and the three main schools of international theory has helped to explicate the issues which are at stake in this dispute. The influence of Marxism is evident in recent challenges to technical and practical forms of problem-solving theory. Its influence is visible in the critical turn in international relations which argues for a theoretical position which is committed to the goal of human emancipation. In short, Marxism has acquired its current and unprecedented level of influence in the theory of international relations for two reasons: because it is a major tradition of international political economy and because it is the dominant form of critical sociology.

There are good reasons for claiming that Marxism can correct realism, as Cox and others have observed, and there is much to be said for the argument that the analysis of the interplay between "state-building" or "geo-political aggrandisement" and "the logic of capital accumulation" should occupy a more central place in the study of international relations than it presently does.[1] If this is so, the future of international relations theory certainly does not lie with realism. The question which immediately arises is whether a critical theory of international relations which preserves elements of realism either falls squarely outside the Marxist tradition or represents Marxism in a reconstructed form.

John Hall's solution to this problem raises the crucial question of how many relative autonomies Marxism can concede before it has abandoned its distinctive approach to history and politics.[2] Taking this as one's point of departure, one could argue that the use of the term "Marxism" to describe a perspective which adds the state and war (among other things) to its traditional inventory is permissible if the following conditions hold: if the influence of production on history far outweighs the combined influence of all other logics of social and political interaction; and if the struggle between classes has contributed (and seems certain to continue to contribute) more than the cumulative effect of all other forms of struggle to human emancipation. As already noted, several approaches to the reconstruction of historical materialism appear to assume that these conditions hold.[3] The fact that the Marxist emphasis on the centrality of class and production no longer neglects the importance of other processes such as the logic of state-building and strategic competition is, then, an indication of the intellectual vitality of Marxism and evidence of its continuing theoretical evolution. The opposing view which is represented by Pettman, and Kubalkova and Cruickshank in the study of international relations and by Giddens and Mann in sociology, argues that the notion of the primacy of class conflict and production can no longer be sustained. The argument for a post-Marxist critical theory denies that there are grounds for concluding that the two propositions mentioned above are (or ever were) true.

These issues have been explored at length in recent sociology. The critique of Marxism in sociology maintains that human history is the product of several interacting logics which include the labour-process stressed by Marxism, state-building and war, and developments in the realm of culture and ideology.[4] None of these phenomena has been dominant throughout the whole of human history although any one of them can be the pacemaker of historical development at any particular time. The Marxist tradition committed the mistake of assuming that class conflict and industrial development had this primary role not only in the nineteenth century but throughout the whole of human history.

Put another way, Marxism cannot justify the claim that the self-formation of the human race can be explained by a political economy which sets out the development of the major modes of production. There are no grounds for arguing that state-building and war have been less important than class conflict and the evolution of the forces of production in human history. And there is no reason to suppose that the basic categories of Marxist explanation (classes and class conflict, the mode of production, the social division of labour, alienated labour and so forth) are primary and self-sufficient. As an explanation of the rise of capitalism in the West clearly reveals, the decision to impute primacy to economic forces in this period is entirely arbitrary. What is true of this epoch is true of recorded history more generally: developments within the sphere of production cannot be explained without taking account of the state, war and culture - and developments in these other spheres cannot be understood in isolation from the level of economic and technological development.

Furthermore, the idea that class conflict has been the driving force behind the main advances in social and political development must be rejected precisely because it privileges antagonisms within the sphere of production and undervalues other political arenas in which the struggle for emancipation has been conducted. In the modern world this struggle is undertaken in a number of different arenas in which social movements and political groups attempt to bring an end to racial, national or ethnic and gender-based forms of discrimination and domination. To the conflicts which take place in these arenas it is necessary to add the struggle to limit the power of the state to control the lives of its own citizens and the attempt to reduce the potential for violence which is inherent in the international system of states. Given these multiple arenas, Marxism can no longer defend the claim that it has uncovered the reasons for the evolution of human powers and needs to their present level; and it cannot defend the claim that it is the theoretical and practical key to their further development.[5]

The realist dimension of this critique of Marxism is present in the claim that war and international conflict have been far more important determinants of world history and social evolution than Marxism has allowed. Echoes of realism are also present in the contention that there is nothing in the Marxist idea of an emancipatory politics which is likely to reduce the incidence of violence in relations between states. Although this approach has similarities with the earlier realist critique of Marxism, it is not a defence of realism. Giddens' rejection of Marxism, for example, is undertaken in a spirit of agreement with Marx's contention that social and political theory has a critical function of promoting the enlightenment and emancipation of human beings. The point then is to understand the significance of realist themes for critical social theory rather than to defend "state-reductionism"[6] or to support an exclusively "problem-solving" conception of theory.

On the basis of these arguments it is impossible to accept the traditional realist critique of Marxism without serious qualification, but it is also impossible to assume that the reconstruction of historical materialism can develop an effective alternative to realism: in which case the future of international relations theory clearly does not lie with Marxism either. But if it is wrong to "anticipate" the future of critical international theory "dogmatically", if it is necessary to "find (it) through criticism of the old", then it is essential to begin by analysing the strengths and weaknesses of the Marxist tradition.

With this in mind, let us recall Marx's attempt to understand the development of the notion that human beings are the authors of their own history and his attempt to explain the evolution of their need to imprint their reason and will on "unmastered practice".[7] Let us recall Marx's analysis of the forces which brought about the economic, technological and cultural unification of the species, and his belief that for the first time in human history it had become possible for human beings to create a universal society of free and equal producers. Three questions have been raised by Marx's analysis of the species' long historical journey towards universal emancipation: firstly, did Marx defend this vision of universal freedom and did he provide even a broad description of the structure and organisation of future communist society?; secondly, did the materialist interpretation of history account for the complete range of factors which affected the evolution of human freedom either by precipitating its further development or by standing in its way?; and thirdly, to what extent did Marx's approach to the politics of universal emancipation ever come to terms with the unyielding power of nationalism and the state?

The answer to the first question is necessarily brief. Marx did not think it was necessary to provide an elaborate justification for the idea of a universal society of free and equal producers; nor did he think it proper that a scientific socialism should offer detailed blue-prints for the society which represented the emergence of the "kingdom of freedom". Although Marx argued that individuals could not realise their capacity for self-determination until they had constructed a society which included the whole human race, and although he commented on some of the practices which would enhance human freedom in the post-revolutionary age, his more fundamental concern was to demonstrate that the project of universal emancipation was no longer "quixotic". As Anderson has noted, the "post-classical tradition of Western Marxism did nothing to remedy these deficiencies".[8]

As for the second question: although Marx realised that war and conquest had contributed to the unification of the species, commerce and production remained central to his inquiry. Marx emphasised the way in which pre-capitalist modes of production had contributed to the emergence of world history. His analysis highlighted the contribution that capitalism had made to the integration of the species and its effect of frustrating the realisation of a universally free and equal form of life. On the other side of the ledger, Marx took very little account of the relationship between the struggle for military power and the extension of political control over space. Nor did he consider the role that state-building, the creation of empires and the search for order between independent political communities had played in the universalisation of norms.[9] Further, there was no analysis of the relationship between international military rivalries and the production and reproduction of "closed" moralities in Marx's writings. Marx's "paradigm of production" also underestimated the extent to which the symbolic and cultural dimensions of social organisation have inhibited or encouraged the emergence of universalistic social relations.

The limitations of Marx's theory of history were reflected in his account of revolutionary practice. There is no doubt that Marx believed (at least in his early writings) that the unification of the human race was imminent. Although his subsequent writings on nationalism and Engels' later reflections on strategy and war began to rethink this assumption they did not reconsider the significance of the nation-state for the politics of critical social theory. Marx and Engels did not offer a vision of an alternative world order which took issue with the particularistic nation-state; they did not explain how the move beyond the nation-state could be achieved in practice; and, given their belief in the integrative effect of capitalism, they did not identify the need for a specific practice for superseding nationalism and the state.

Marx's writings do not contain an adequate answer to the three questions discussed above. With the possible exception of Austro-Marxism, subsequent theories of nationalism and imperialism did little to enlarge upon Marx's socialist vision. These were the first theories, however, to recognise the need to revise Marxism so that it took account of the particularism of the nation-state. These approaches extended Marx's analysis of the relationship between the state and mode of production and they produced more complex analyses of the state's position in the unevenly-developing world economy, but they failed to provide an explanation of the "anchorage" of the state which included the international system of states. Marxism in the early part of the twentieth century still did not possess an adequate understanding of the prospects for realising the objectives of critical social theory in the modern world. These limitations continued to impoverish the Marxist idea of a politics of universal emancipation. Almost all of the principal statements of Marxism reaffirmed the claim that the proletarian revolution would remove the main obstacles to the development of a world socialist society. There was no awareness of the possibility that the politics of emancipating the subordinate classes from economic exploitation might do little to diminish rivalries between nation-states.

Important as the more recent developments in the Marxist and neo-Marxist literature undoubtedly are, they have also failed to confront these difficulties. Structuralist analyses of the capitalist world economy have produced more sophisticated analyses of the tension between the unifying and the divisive properties of the modern world system. They have shed considerable light on the nature of the economic and technological integration of the species. Significant debates have developed around the question of whether peripheral entanglement within a Western-dominated capitalist system will bring about the progressive transformation of these societies or block their further development. Much of this literature has analysed the connections between the uneven development of the world economy, peripheral nationalism and the radicalisation of Third World states and societies with enlightening results.

But, in general, this literature suffers from the same problems which were encountered in earlier accounts of nationalism, imperialism and the state. Approaches to nationalism which argue that it is, above all else, a demand for justice in a world of unequal economic development overlook the relationship between nationalism and international insecurity and political distrust. Analyses of the manner in which various modes of production are articulated to form the world economy generally ignore the non-economic dimensions of relations between states. Most of the approaches to the uneven development of the world economy are guilty of ignoring inequalities of political and military power. The relationship between international anarchy and oligarchy is seldom discussed in Marxist analyses of the world system as a result. Although recent developments in the Marxist theory of the state increasingly emphasise the autonomy of the state and the irreducibility of strategic interaction they have yet to make any significant progress in creating a critical theory which deals directly with the sovereign state.

In the end, the case for a post-Marxist critical theory of international relations rests on two grounds. First of all, whether one analyses the literature on nationalism, imperialism, international inequality, the world-systems perspective or the state itself, the same pattern emerges: that it is necessary to acquire a more sophisticated analysis of the anchorage of the state than the Marxist tradition has provided. In the second place, (and as a result of this) a critical theory of international relations must regard the practical project of extending community beyond the nation-state as its most important problem - and not just as the backdrop to the allegedly more basic struggle between antagonistic social classes.

Despite its assorted shortcomings, Marxism foreshadowed a project which is superior to realism: a project which brings an emancipatory interest to the analysis of the factors which have been responsible for the expansion and contraction of human community. The main question is how to reconstruct this project. In the first place, the normative interest in defending the extension of moral community deserves rather more discussion than it has received within the Marxist tradition.[10] In the second place, this project requires a more complex sociology of how production, state-building, international relations and developments in the realm of culture and ideology have shaped and reshaped the moral frontier at different points in human history. This task may be conducted on several different levels. An inquiry into the history of political community in the modern system of states which addresses present trends and future possibilities is crucial to the whole exercise. This project can be linked with Wight's notion of a comparative sociology of international systems in order to explain the processes which shaped the prevalent beliefs about the boundaries of moral community in earlier systems of states. And this in turn may form part of a larger sociological enterprise which considers the history of the universalisation of norms in relations between societies.[11]

Whether one is concerned with the modern states-system, with systems of states more generally, or with international relations in the broadest sense, war and production emerge as major determinants of the moral boundaries which separate communities. War and production are also important for any analysis of how these boundaries have been redrawn at various stages in human history. Accordingly, realism and Marxism have an important place in the sociological project outlined above. But neither perspective contains a comprehensive analysis of the expansion and contraction of moral community. An inquiry into the widening of moral and political community in particular has to take account of two phenomena which realism and Marxism have ignored. The means by which

independent political communities have established the principles of their
co-existence is the first of these phenomena. The second is the means by
which moral principles have been universalised in the course of human
history. The interplay between these four phenomena is the starting-point
for a critical theory of international relations.[12]

Finally, neither realism nor Marxism answers the question of how
political action might extend the moral communities with which citizens
identify in the modern world. Indeed, it is not at all clear that any
strand of social and political thought provides a compelling account of
"strategies of transition".[13] Perhaps this is an unrealistic test of social
and political theory, and an especially unrealistic test of critical theory
given that its role is not to offer instructions on how to act but to
reveal the existence of unrealised possibilities. Even so, the contention
that it is possible to move beyond realism and Marxism not only as
theories of the world but as commentaries on practice has to be subject
to a similar empirical test. In this case, the success or failure of the
critical theory of international relations will be determined by the amount
of light cast on present possibilities and not just by its performance in
the spheres of philosophy and historical sociology alone.

Notes and References

INTRODUCTION

1. Butterfield and Wight (1966) pp. 17-34.
2. See Horkheimer (1972) for the distinction between traditional and critical theory; on its significance for international relations, see Cox (1981) Ashley (1981), Linklater (1986) and Hoffman (1987).
3. Horkheimer (1972).
4. See Marx's *The Eighteenth Brumaire of Louis Bonaparte* in Marx (1977) p. 300; and J.J. Rousseau, *The Social Contract* (translated with an introduction by G.D.H. Cole) (London, 1968), p. 12.
5. This phrase is borrowed from Peter Singer, *The Expanding Circle: Ethics and Sociobiology*, (Oxford, 1981).
6. For a recent discussion, see Kubalkova and Cruickshank (1985).
7. Giddens (1981).
8. Two of the most important works are R.O. Keohane and J.S. Nye (1977) and E. Morse (1976).
9. For a statement of this argument, see Cox (1981). p. 129.
10. Keohane and Nye (1977) p. ix.
11. See, for example, R.O. Keohane, *After Hegemony: Discord and Collaboration in the World Political Economy*, (London, 1984) p. 256. M. Smith, R. Little and M. Shackleton (eds.) *Perspectives on World Politics* (London, 1981) remains one of the best introductions to realist, liberal and Marxist approaches to international relations.
12. Pettman (1979) remains important in this regard.
13. See Bernstein (1976), Benton (1977), Fay (1975) and, of course, Habermas (1972).
14. Ashley (1981). Ashley's more recent writings have taken a different direction. See "The Geopolitics of Geopolitical Space: Towards a Critical Social Theory of International Politics", *Alternatives*, 12 (1987).
15. Cox (1981). See below ch. 1, pp. 27-30.
16. Hoffman (1986) p. 244.
17. Giddens (1982) p. 227.
18. For an analysis of Marxism on the state, see B. Jessop, *The Capitalist State* (Oxford, 1982) and M. Carnoy, *The State and Political Theory* (Princeton, 1984). On the need to deal with military factors, see Anderson (1974), Brucan (1978) Skocpol (1979), Zolberg (1981), Block (1980) Shaw (1984) and Giddens (1985).
19. Giddens (1986).

20. See Mann's essay in Shaw (1984) p. 28, and his more recent *Sources of Social Power: From the Beginning to 1760 A.D.*, (Cambridge, 1986).
21. Giddens (1985).
22. Carr (1939), ch. 14. The same theme arises in R.C. Johansen, *The National Interest and the Human Interest: An Analysis of U.S. Foreign Policy* (Princeton, 1980) ch. 6.
23. Habermas (1979).

CHAPTER 1: POWER, ORDER AND EMANCIPATION IN INTERNATIONAL THEORY

1. See Wight (1987) p. 227. For a discussion of Wight's perspective, see H. Bull, "Martin Wight and the Theory of International Relations", *British Journal of International Studies*, 2 (1976).
2. Wight (1987).
3. See Bernstein (1976).
4. Ashley (1981). See Habermas (1972) op. cit. For an interpretation of Habermas, see T. McCarthy (1982) ch. 2.
5. Bernstein (1976). See the introduction and pp. 225-36.
6. Ashley (1981). Also Herz's reply in the same issue of *International Studies Quarterly*.
7. On the positivism of modern realism, see Ashley (1981) and the more extensive discussion in "The Poverty of Neo-Realism", *International Organisation*, 38 (1984) pp. 225-86. See also Waltz (1979) ch. 1, esp. p. 6. M. Smith, *Realist Thought from Weber to Kissinger* (London, 1986) makes that useful point that the differences between "neo-realism" and past versions of realism should not be overestimated.
8. Waltz (1979) esp. chs. 1-4. On "constraining conditions", see p. 73.
9. Waltz (1979) pp. 8, 46 and 79.
10. Waltz (1979) p. 88. On self-help, see ch. 6.
11. H. Butterfield, *History and Human Relations* (London, 1951) pp. 9-36.
12. Waltz (1979) pp. 96-7 and 104-7.
13. Waltz (1979) p. 66. The earlier work is, of course, Waltz (1959).
14. Waltz (1979) pp. 127-8.
15. Ashley (1981) p. 219.
16. Waltz (1979) ch. 6.
17. See Ashley (1981) and (1984), op. cit.
18. H. Morgenthau, *Politics Among Nations: The Struggle for Power and Peace* (New York, 1973) p. 541, and H. Kissinger, *The White House Years* (London, 1979).
19. Carr (1939) pp. 10, 12 and 239; Hans Morgenthau "The Intellectual and Political Foundations of a Theory of International Relations" in *Politics in the Twentieth Century* (Chicago, 1971) pp. 286-7 and 295-8.
20. Giddens (1985).
21. Giddens (1981) and (1985).
22. Cox (1981) esp. pp. 128-30.
23. Wight (1981) p. 23.

24. These would appear to be the main practical concerns of Bull (1977) notwithstanding the comments on pp. 319-20. These themes are developed further in Bull (1983) and in Bull and Watson (1984).
25. See the concerns raised in Bull and Watson (1984) esp. chs. 8, 14 and the conclusion.
26. Wight (1977) p. 22.
27. Wight (1977) ch. 1. The idea of a "sociology of states-systems" appears on p. 33.
28. Wight (1977) p. 43.
29. Wight (1977) p. 33.
30. Bull (1977) pp. 13-16.
31. Bull (1977) pp. 316-17.
32. ibid.
33. Bull (1977) pp. 5-6, and pp. 16-20.
34. See H.L.A. Hart, *The Concept of Law* (Oxford, 1961) pp. 189-95. For further discussion, see H. Suganami, "The Structure of Institutionalism: An Analysis of British Mainstream International Relations", *International Relations*, 7 (1983) pp. 263-81.
35. See H. Butterfield and M. Wight (1966) ch. 2.
36. Bull (1977) chs. 1-3.
37. Bull (1977) ch. 4.
38. See Ashley (1984) op. cit.
39. Wight (1977) ch. 6.
40. Bull and Watson (1984) p. 223.
41. Wight (1977) p. 153.
42. Wight (1977) p. 154.
43. Wight (1977) p. 105.
44. Wight (1986) ch. 7.
45. Wight (1986) p. 82.
46. It "is not possible to understand international politics simply in terms of mechanics." Wight (1986) p. 81.
47. On states as "like units", see Waltz (1979) pp. 9 and pp. 104-7.
48. Bull (1977) pp. 315-7.
49. Bull (1983).
50. Bull (1977) pp. 316-7.
51. Bull and Watson (1984) p. 435.
52. Bull (1983) pp. 6 and 10.
53. Bull (1977) ch. 4.
54. Bull and Watson (1984) p. 429.
55. Bull (1983) p. 18.
56. Bull (1983) pp. 11-12 and 14.
57. Bull (1977) pp. 275-6.
58. Bull, in the introduction to Wight (1977) p. 19.
59. Bull (1977) pp. 78, 126 and 319-20.
60. Bull (1977) ch.4. Compare, moreover, pp. 152 and 289. R. J. Vincent, *Human Rights and International Relations* (Cambridge, 1986) addresses these themes.
61. Wight (1977) p. 38.
62. Bull (1977) p. 26.
63. Bull (1977) pp. 238-40.

64. On Kant, see Gallie (1978) and Linklater (1982).
65. For a fuller discussion, see S. Lukes, *Marxism and Morality* (Oxford, 1985).
66. For an introduction, see Bottomore (1984), Held (1980), Friedman (1981), Connerton (1980) and Geuss (1981).
67. See p. 173 fn.4.
68. Bottomore (1984) p. 49.
69. Horkheimer (1972) p. 233.
70. Habermas (1973) p. 253.
71. ibid.
72. Horkheimer (1974) p. 182.
73. Horkheimer (1974) p. 178.
74. See L. D. Easton and K. H. Guddat, *Writings of the Young Marx on Philosophy and Society* (New York, 1967) p. 212.
75. Horkheimer (1978) p. 9.
76. Horkheimer (1978) p. 21.
77. For a discussion, see Kolakowski (1978). esp. vol. 3.
78. For a discussion, see M. Jay, *The Dialectical Imagination: A History of the Frankfurt School and the Institute of Social Research, 1923-50* (Boston, 1973) esp. ch. 8.
79. See A. Wellmer, *Critical Theory of Society* (New York, 1975) esp. ch. 2.
80. For a discussion, see Connerton (1980).
81. See Friedman (1981) p. 35.
82. M. Horkheimer (1972) p. 53. See also Horkheimer (1978) pp. 157-8.
83. Friedman (1981) p. 36.
84. Giddens (1985) esp. ch. 11.
85. See P. Connerton ed. *Critical Sociology* (Harmondsworth, 1976) pp. 217-18.
86. Horkheimer (1972) p. 53, and Horkheimer (1974) pp. 66-7.
87. See Friedman (1981) p. 216.
88. Connerton (1980) p. 114.
89. See Held (1980) p. 26.
90. See the preface to Horkheimer (1974).
91. Bottomore (1984) pp. 62 and 64.
92. Quoted in Bernstein (1976) p. 199.
93. Habermas (1979) p. 95.
94. J. Habermas, "A Reply to My Critics", in J. B. Thompson and D. Held (eds.) *Habermas: Critical Debates* (London, 1982) p. 221.
95. See Giddens (1982) chs. 7-8.
96. Habermas (1979) pp. 97-8, 120 and 160.
97. J. Habermas, "History and Evolution", *Telos*, 39 (1979) esp. pp. 30-44.
98. For further discussion, see McCarthy (1982) pp. 232-71. In addition, see R. Roderick, *Habermas and the Foundations of Critical Theory* (London, 1986) esp. chs. 3-4.
99. For further discussion, see McCarthy (1982) ch. 4.
100. For discussion, see McCarthy (1982) ch. 4.
101. Habermas (1973) p. 251.
102. Habermas (1979) pp. 114-15.

103. See Habermas (1979) pp. 196-7. Also "What Does A Legitimation Crisis Mean Today? Legitimation Problems in Late Capitalism", in W. Connolly (ed.) *Legitimacy and the State* (Oxford, 1984) esp. pp. 140-2.
104. Quoted in McCarthy (1982) p. 133.
105. ibid.
106. Habermas (1973) p. 251.
107. Cox (1981) pp. 136-7.
108. Cox (1981) pp. 128-9.
109. Cox (1981) p. 130.
110. ibid.
111. Cox (1981) pp. 129 and 132.
112. Cox (1981) p. 130. For further consideration of Cox's position on realism, see the comments by Cox and Waltz in R. O. Keohane (ed.) *Neo-Realism and its Critics* (Princeton, 1986).
113. Cox (1981) pp. 133-5.
114. Cox (1981) p. 140.
115. Cox (1981) pp. 150-1. For further discussion, see R. W. Cox, *Production, Power and World Order: Social Forces in the Making of History* (New York, 1987).
116. ibid.
117. ibid.
118. Cox (1981) p. 137.
119. Cox (1981) p. 130.
120. See Giddens (1982) ch. 4.
121. Giddens (1981) p. 23.
122. Giddens (1985) pp. 22-31.
123. Giddens (1981) ch. 10 and (1985) p. 5.
124. Cox (1981) p. 128.
125. Giddens (1985) pp. 334-5.

CHAPTER TWO: MARX AND THE LOGIC OF UNIVERSALISM

1. See the extracts from *The German Ideology* in Marx (1977), p. 171 for example.
2. Butterfield (1951) op. cit. ch. 3.
3. This is the import of Wight's comment on Marx: "Neither Marx, Lenin nor Stalin made any systematic contribution to international theory." See Butterfield and Wight (1966) p. 25.
4. See *The New Science of Giambattista Vico* (translated by T. G. Bergin and M. H. Fisch (London, 1970) p. 51.
5. See Colletti (1979) ch. 12.
6. See E. Kamenka, *The Ethical Foundations of Marxism* (London, 1972) p. 123.
7. Marx (1973) p. 101.
8. Marx (1973) p. 158.
9. Marx (1973) p. 84. See also *Capital* (London, 1970) vol. 1, p. 334.
10. Marx (1973) p. 490.
11. Marx (1973) pp. 474 and 491.

12. Marx (1973) pp. 97 and 141.
13. Marx (1973) p. 103.
14. Marx (1973) p. 159.
15. Marx (1973) pp. 156-7.
16. Marx (1973) pp. 163 and 237.
17. Marx (1973) p. 158.
18. Marx (1973) p. 184.
19. Marx (1973) pp. 159 and 650.
20. Marx (1973) p. 243.
21. Marx (1973) pp. 225-7.
22. Marx (1973) p. 225.
23. Marx (1973) p. 245.
24. ibid.
25. Marx (1973) p. 243.
26. ibid.
27. Marx (1973) p. 248.
28. Marx and Engels (1974) pp. 85-7.
29. ibid. p. 40.
30. See S. Avineri, *The Social and Political Thought of Karl Marx* (London, 1968) ch. 6. See also Marx (1973) p. 161.
31. Marx (1973) p. 539.
32. Marx, *The German Ideology*, in Marx (1977).
33. Marx (1973) pp. 161-2.
34. Marx (1973) p. 158.
35. ibid.
36. Marx (1973) p. 159.
37. Marx (1973) p. 410.
38. Marx (1973) p. 750.
39. See M. Fleischer, *Marxism and History* (New York, 1973) pp. 18-19, 32-3, 65-6 and 70. See Ollman (1977) on the development of a universal language, albeit alongside local languages, and complete racial integration as crucial steps in the eradication of barriers between members of the species.
40. Marx, *A Contribution to the Critique of Political Economy* (London, 1904) p. 209.
41. See Bloom (New York 1941) and Lowy (1981). On the Austro-Marxists, see below pp. 58-60.
42. Marx to Annenkov, Dec. 28, 1846 in *The Poverty of Philosophy* (Moscow, 1966) p. 159.
43. Marx, *The German Ideology*, in Marx (1977) p. 161.
44. Marx, quoted in R. Luxembourg & N. Bukharin, *Imperialism and the Accumulation of Capital* (London, 1972) p. 58.
45. Brewer (1980) ch. 8.
46. See M. Nicolaus in the introduction to Marx (1973) pp. 52-4.
47. See Marx, *Capital* (London 1970) vol 1., ch. 6.
48. See Lukes (1985) op. cit.
49. See fn. 44 above.
50. Marx (1970) op.cit., pp. 8-9.
51. See M. Evans, *Karl Marx* (London, 1975) p. 74.
52. Marx and Engels (1974) p. 85.

53. Marx and Engels, *The Communist Manifesto* (Moscow, 1966) p. 12.
54. See Marx and Engels (1971) pp. 280-1.
55. Quoted in Cummins (1980) p. 23.
56. Giddens (1985) pp. 287-8.
57. See Anderson (1974) pp. 113-21 and Nairn (1981) pp. 88-9.
58. See Giddens (1981) pp. 249-50 and Giddens (1985) introduction.
59. Anderson (1983) especially the postscript, and Nairn (1981).
60. Giddens (1982) p. 227.
61. Marx, *Critique of Hegel's Philosophy of Right*, edited with an introduction by J. O'Malley (Cambridge, 1970) pp. 139-42.
62. Eaton and Guddat (1967) op. cit. p. 299.
63. See *The Communist Manifesto*, in Marx (1977) p. 236.
64. For Marx's views on this matter, see "Confidential Communication", in Marx and Engels, (1971) pp. 160-3. See also Cummins (1980) ch. 5.
65. A. Gilbert, "Marx on Internationalism and War", *Philosophy and Public Affairs"*, 7 (1977-78) p. 359.
66. Marx and Engels (1971) pp. 292-3.
67. See M. MacDonald, "Marx, Engels and the Polish National Movement", *Journal of Modern History"*, 3 (1941) pp. 321-34.
68. Marx and Engels (1971) p. 332.
69. See A. Smith, *Nationalism in the Twentieth Century* (Canberra, 1979) pp.132 and 142.
70. See W. O'Connor, *The National Question in Marxist-Leninist Theory and Strategy* (Princeton, 1984) p. 13. On the subject of "historyless peoples", see Lowy (1976) pp. 84-5, and Cummins (1980) pp. 36-46.
71. Engels, *The Origin of The Family, Private Property and the State*, in Marx and Engels (1968) pp. 585-7.
72. See *The Marx-Engels Reader*, edited by R. C. Tucker (New York, 1972) p. 187.
73. ibid.
74. Quoted by Petras (1971) p. 803.
75. See Skocpol (1979) pp. 30-1 where Hintze is cited to highlight weaknesses in the construction of historical materialism. On "excessively endogenous" explanation, see Foster-Carter (1976) p. 18.
76. Preface to *The Contribution to the Critique of Political Economy*, in Marx (1977) pp. 388-91.
77. G. A. Cohen, *Karl Marx's Theory of History: A Defence* (Oxford, 1978). In addition, see Cohen's later argument in *Nomos*, vol 26 (New York, 1983).
78. A. Swingewood, *Marx and Modern Social Theory* (London, 1975). Engels, Letter to J. Bloch, in Marx and Engels (1968) pp. 692-3.
79. B. Ollman, *Alienation: Marx's Conception of Man in Capitalist Society* (Cambridge, 1976).
80. M. Rader, *Karl Marx's Interpretation of History* (Oxford, 1979).
81. For a discussion, see Carnoy op. cit., ch. 2. In addition, see Engels' comments in Marx and Engels (1968) p. 588.
82. Marx, *Capital* (London, 1970) vol. 1, p. 82.
83. Marx, *Capital* (London, 1970) vol. 3, p. 791-2.
84. ibid.
85. See Hintze (1975) chs. 4 and 5.

86. Hintze (1975) for example pp. 181-3.
87. Hintze (1975) p. 452.
88. Skocpol (1979) pp. 30-32.
89. Gallie (1979) pp. 67-9.
90. Gallie (1979) p. 76.
91. Marx (1973) p. 128.
92. Gallie (1979) p. 93.
93. Gallie (1979) p. 88.
94. This term is derived from W. McNeill, *The Pursuit of Power* (Oxford, 1983).
95. Gallie (1979) p. 91.
96. Gallie (1979) pp. 86-8.
97. Gallie (1979) pp. 69, 83-8 and 94-5.
98. See Cummins (1980) p. 177.
99. Gallie (1979) p. 69.
100. Trotsky (1969) pp. 40ff.
101. An interesting interpretation of the process can be found in Gouldner (1980) esp. part 3.
102. Gallie (1979) p 69.
103. Giddens (1986) p. 222.
104. See Giddens (1982) esp. pp. 56-60.
105. On Polanyi, see T. Skocpol (ed.) *Vision and Method in Historical Sociology* (Cambridge, 1984) ch. 3.
106. Gallie (1979) p. 68.
107. Marx (1973) p. 109.
108. Brucan (1978) pp. 11-13.
109. Skocpol (1974) pp. 30-1 where Skocpol describes her position as "realist". For further reference to Hintze, see Zolberg (1981) pp. 277-80.
110. Anderson (1974). Anderson's discussion of the formation of the European multistate system will be considered in more detail in ch. 7. See also Nairn (1981).
111. E. P. Thompson, "Notes on Exterminism: The Last Stage of Civilisation", in *Exterminism and Cold War* (London, 1982) p. 2.
112. Giddens (1985) ch. 11.

CHAPTER THREE: THE NATION AND THE SPECIES

1. R. Aron, *Progress and Disillusion* (Harmondsworth, 1968) part 3.
2. E.H. Carr, *Nationalism and After* (London, 1945) pp. 1-26.
3. Carr (1945) ibid., and Morgenthau (1973) op. cit., chs. 16 & 20.
4. Nairn (1981) p. 329.
5. Debray (1977) pp. 25, 27-8, 30 and 34-5.
6. Nairn (1981) p. 90.
7. See J. Plamenatz "Two Types of Nationalism" in E. Kamenka (ed.) *Nationalism: The Nature and Evolution of an Idea* (London, 1973) p. 27.
8. K. Deutsch, *Nationalism and Social Communication* (London, 1953) p. 191.

9. See the essay on nationality in Lord Acton, *Essays on Freedom and Power* (Boston, 1948) and E. Kedourie, *Nationalism* (London, 1960).
10. This is the position taken by Hobsbawm (1977) pp. 9-10, 14 and 17-18.
11. For a discussion of the Congress, see R. A. Kann, *The Multinational Empire: Nationalism and National Reform in the Habsburg Monarchy* (New York, 1964).
12. Bottomore and Goode (1978) pp. 102-25.
13. Bottomore and Goode (1978) pp. 109-25.
14. Stalin (1953) pp. 309-13.
15. Pipes (1954) p. 26. See also E. Nimni "Marxism and Nationalism", in Shaw (1985) esp. pp. 125-32.
16. Pipes (1954) p. 25.
17. On Vico, Herder and historicism, see I Berlin, *Vico and Herder* (London, 1976). On convergence, see Nimni in Shaw, op. cit.
18. Bottomore and Goode (1978) p. 106.
19. Bottomore and Goode (1978) pp. 107 and 110.
20. Bottomore and Goode (1978) p. 107.
21. Bottomore and Goode (1978) pp. 108 and 111.
22. Bottomore and Goode (1978) pp. 108-9. For a discussion of Schiller and Hegel on the "recreation" of "political community", see R. Plant, *Hegel* (London, 1973) ch. 1.
23. Bottomore and Goode (1978) p. 56.
24. Bottomore and Goode (1978) pp. 113-17.
25. Bottomore and Goode (1978) pp. 116-17. The concept of a new "medievalism" is derived from Bull (1979) pp. 254-5. It should be noted that Bauer denied the medieval analogy - see Bottomore and Goode (1978) p. 117.
26. J. P. Nettl, *Rosa Luxembourg: A Biography* (Oxford, 1966) p. 862.
27. Nettl (1966) p. 849.
28. ibid.
29. Lenin, *Collected Works*, vol. 22 (1964) p. 24.
30. This is the main task of Lenin (1964) vol. 22, see pp. 34-5.
31. See Pipes (1954) p. 28.
32. See Pipes (1954) p. 36.
33. Lenin (1964) vol. 22, p. 25, and Lenin (1964) vol. 20, p. 172.
34. Lenin (1964) vol. 20, pp. 405-6.
35. Lenin (1964) vol. 20, p. 27.
36. Lenin, quoted in Pipes (1954) p. 43.
37. Lenin (1964) vol. 20, p. 290.
38. Plekhanov is quoted in Stalin (1953) p. 354. See also p. 343.
39. See Pipes (1954) p. 45.
40. Stalin (1953) pp. 323-4.
41. Stalin (1953) pp. 353-4, 364. See also Lenin (1964) vol. 20, pp. 40-4.
42. Stalin (1953) pp. 315-17 and 319.
43. Lenin (1964) vol. 20, p. 423.
44. Lenin (1964) vol. 20, pp. 40-4.
45. See Pipes (1954).
46. Lenin (1964) vol. 20, p. 45.
47. Lenin (1964) vol. 20, pp. 222-3.

48. Lenin (1964) p. 222.
49. Lenin (1964) vol. 20, p. 35.
50. Borochov (1973).
51. Borochov (1973) pp. 141 and 151-9.
52. Borochov (1973) p. 159.
53. Borochov (1973) pp. 136-7.
54. Borochov (1973) p. 144.
55. Borochov (1973) pp. 135-6.
56. Borochov (1973) p. 161.
57. See p. 36 above.
58. See pp. 50-2 above.
59. Marx and Engels, *The Communist Manifesto*, in Marx (1977) p. 230.
60. Quoted in G. Mayer, *Friedrich Engels: A Biography* (New York, 1969) p. 151.
61. On the development of Bukharin's thought, see especially S. F. Cohen, *Bukharin and the Bolshevik Revolution: A Political Biography, 1888-1938* (Oxford, 1980) esp. pp. 66-7 and 187-8.
62. Cohen, ibid., pp. 148-9.
63. Cohen, ibid., p. 188. For Trotsky's warnings against the dangers of national messianism, see C.C. Lee, "Trotsky's Theory of the Permanent Revolution", *Issues and Studies*, (1972) pp. 60-76. On "Marxist" realism, see Kubalkova and Cruickshank (1980).
64. Giddens (1981) p. 250.
65. Waltz (1979) p. 128.
66. For a discussion of the emergence of national rivalries between socialist states in South East Asia, see G. Evans and K. Rowley, *Red Brotherhood at War: IndoChina since the Fall of Saigon* (London, 1984).
67. Linklater (1982) pp. 28-32.
68. See Deutsch, op. cit., Aron, op. cit., and Gellner (1964).
69. Gellner (1964) p. 148. For a critical account of the "modernity of nationalism", see A. Smith, *The Ethnic Origins of Nations* (Oxford, 1986).
70. Nairn (1981) p. 341.
71. Nairn (1981) pp. 335-6.
72. Nairn (1981) p. 353.
73. Nairn (1981) pp. 71-2, 329-31, 335 and 355.
74. Nairn (1981) p. 340.
75. Nairn (1981) pp. 348-9.
76. Nairn (1981) pp. 89 and 350-6. See also Debray (1977) p. 33: "...I would maintain that it is better for a national identity to be affirmed against an existing socialist order than not, because this leaves open some possibility for future socialism, while in the other case socialism becomes a foreign body to the nation."
77. Smith (1981) p. 40.
78. Gellner (1964) pp. 147-8 and 172; Gellner (1983) p. 12. See also Gellner's *Spectacles and Predicaments: Essays in Social Theory* (Cambridge, 1979) p. 270.
79. Gellner (1983) p. 17.
80. Gellner (1983) p. 16.

81. Gellner (1964) p. 154.
82. Gellner (1964) pp. 152 and 171-2.
83. Gellner (1974) p. 151. On the distinction between high and low cultures, see Gellner (1983) ch. 1.
84. For further discussion, see Gellner (1974).
85. Gellner (1964) pp. 155 and 158-64. Gellner (1974) pp. 146-51.
86. Gellner (1983) p. 52.
87. ibid.
88. ibid.
89. Gellner (1964) pp. 167 and 172.
90. Gellner (1964) pp. 166-8.
91. Gellner (1974) p. 153.
92. ibid.
93. Gellner (1964) pp. 167-8.
94. ibid.
95. Gellner (1964) pp. 175-6.
96. Bull and Watson (1984), especially the editors' introduction and conclusion.
97. Gellner (1964) p. 169.
98. S. Krasner, "Transforming International Regimes: What the Third World Wants and Why", *International Studies Quarterly*, 25 (1981) 119-48.
99. Smith (1983) p. 160.
100. Emmanuel (1972) p. 263.
101. Emmanuel (1972) pp. 178-84.
102. Emmanuel (1972) p. 179.
103. Hobsbawm (1977) pp. 9-10 and 14-15.
104. Nairn (1981) pp. 72 and 203-5.
105. Nairn (1981) pp. 348-9 and 372.
106. Nairn (1981) p. 87.
107. Bull (1983) p. 6.
108. R. Tucker (1977); R. Higgott & R. Robinson (1985) p. 35.
109. E. Nimni, in Shaw (1985) pp. 135-7.
110. Smith (1981) p. 40, and Orridge (1981) p. 182.

CHAPTER FOUR: THE THEORY OF CAPITALIST IMPERIALISM

1. H. Magdoff, "Militarism and Imperialism", *American Economic Review*, 60 (1970) p. 237.
2. Lenin (1968) pp. 18 and 83-4.
3. S. Avineri (1970) op. cit. pp. 174-84.
4. Hilferding (1981) p. 311.
5. Hilferding (1981) ch. 22.
6. Lenin (1968) p. 59; Hobson (1938) p. 86.
7. Lenin (1968) pp. 70-1 and 88. See also Kautsky, "Ultra-Imperialism", *New Left Review*, 59 (1970).
8. Bukharin (1972) pp. 127-8.
9. Bukharin (1972) p. 73.
10. Bukharin (1972) pp. 120-1.

11. Lenin (1968) p. 8.
12. Bukharin (1972) p. 28.
13. Bukharin (1972) p. 53.
14. Bukharin (1972) pp. 17-18.
15. ibid.
16. ibid.
17. Bukharin (1972) pp. 147 and 161-2.
18. Bukharin (1972) p. 109.
19. Bukharin (1972) pp. 161-2 and 166.
20. Bukharin (1972) p. 166.
21. Lenin (1968) pp. 12 and 102.
22. Lenin (1968) p. 102.
23. Bukharin (1972) p. 167.
24. ibid.
25. ibid.
26. Waltz (1979) ch. 2 and Fieldhouse (1976) pp. 48-9, 51 and 54-9. See Lenin (1968) for statistical evidence regarding capital flows in 1910.
27. Stokes (1969) p. 301.
28. ibid.
29. ibid.
30. Stokes (1969) p. 289; see Lenin (1968) p. 57.
31. Lenin (1968) p. 60; Stokes (1969) p. 290.
32. N. Etherington, *Theories of Imperialism: War, Conquest and Capital* (New Jersey, 1984) p. 273.
33. ibid.
34. ibid., p. 274.
35. ibid.; For Fischer's argument, see *World Power or Decline: the Controversy over Germany's Aims in the First World War* (London, 1975).
36. See the comments in W. Berghahn (ed.) *Germany and the Approach of War in 1914* (New York, 1973) pp. 79-81.
37. ibid., p. 84.
38. ibid., p. 259.
39. Lenin (1968) p. 13.
40. Etherington (1982) p. 33.
41. This is the impression conveyed by Waltz (1979) ch. 2.
42. Marx, *Capital*, vol. 1 (London 1970) ch. 26.
43. James Joll, *Europe Since 1870* (1973) pp. 38 and 93-5.
44. Choucri and North (1975) pp. 1 and 16.
45. G. Lichtheim, *Europe in the Twentieth Century* (New York, 1974) chs. 1-3.
46. Pettman (1979) p. 12.
47. See above, pp. 28-30.
48. Gramsci (1971) p. 176: "Do international relations precede or follow (logically) fundamental social relations? There is no doubt that they follow. Any organic innovation in the social structure, through its technical-military expressions, modifies...the international field too...although it also reacts back upon them to a certain extent (to the extent precisely to which superstructures react upon the structure, politics on economics, etc.)." In addition, see pp. 84, 116,

182 and 264.

49. Waltz (1979) ch. 2, and Cohen (1973).
50. J.Schumpeter, *Imperialism and Social Classes* (New York, 1951).
51. See Wehler "Industrial Growth and Early German Imperialism", in Owen and Sutcliffe (1972) ch. 3; and Wehler (1970).
52. Fieldhouse (1976) and Robinson "Non-European Foundations of European Imperialism: sketch for a theory of collaboration", in Owen and Sutcliffe (1972) ch. 5.
53. Stokes (1969) p. 301. Also, Doyle (1986) for an empirical defence of the need to include "metrocentric", "pericentric" and "systemic" factors in an explanation of colonialism.
54. Lenin (1968) pp. 81 and 112.
55. ibid.
56. Hopkins and Wallerstein (1977) p. 31. See Doyle (1986) pp. 246 and 343.
57. Lenin (1968) p. 86. See also pp. 78-9 and 81.
58. Lenin (1968) pp. 73-4.
59. ibid.
60. Waltz (1979) pp. 27 and 36.
61. For the weaknesses in systemic explanation, see Doyle (1986) pp. 146 and 196-7.
62. Compare Waltz (1979) pp. 25-7 with Lenin (1968) p. 77 and Bukharin (1972) pp. 112-13.
63. Cohen (1973) and P. Darby, *Three Faces of Imperialism: British and American Approaches to Asia and Africa* (New Haven, 1987) pp. 13-21.
64. Cohen (1973). See also Pettman (1979).
65. Lenin (1968) pp. 73-4 and 79-80.
66. Wehler, in Owen and Sutcliffe (1972) pp. 74-5.
67. Wehler, in Owen and Sutcliffe (1972) pp. 77-8.
68. ibid.
69. ibid.
70. ibid.
71. ibid.
72. ibid., p. 81. See H.U. Wehler, *The German Empire 1871-1918* (Leamington Spa, 1985) pp. 172-3 and 178 where it is claimed that "economic interests in the narrow sense" were always involved in the process of annexation.
73. Wehler, in Owen and Sutcliffe (1981) p. 81. Wehler (1985) ibid., p. 175.
74. Wehler, in Owen and Sutcliffe (1981) p. 82. Wehler (1985) ibid.
75. Robinson, in Owen and Sutcliffe (1972) p. 130.

76. Robinson, in Owen and Sutcliffe (1972) p. 139; Fieldhouse (1976) pp. 8-9.
77. Fieldhouse (1976) pp. 35 and 475. And R. Robinson, "The Excentric Idea of Imperialism, with or without Empire", in W. Mommsen and O. Osterhammel, *Imperialism and After: Continuities and Discontinuities* (London, 1987).
78. Fieldhouse (1976) p. 35.

79. Robinson, in Owen and Sutcliffe (1972) p. 120.
80. Fieldhouse (1976) pp. 77 and 460-3.
81. Robinson, in Owen and Sutcliffe (1972) p. 121.
82. Fieldhouse (1976) p. 463; Robinson, in Owen and Sutcliffe (1972) p. 140.
83. Robinson, in Mommsen and Osterhammel (1987) op. cit., p. 271.
84. Brewer, in Mommsen and Osterhammel (1987) op. cit., p. 329.
85. Doyle (1986) p. 229.
86. See fn. 81 above.
87. See Robinson and Gallagher, "The Partition of Africa", in W. R. Louis (ed.) *Imperialism: The Robinson and Gallagher Controversy* (London, 1976) p. 100. See the editor's comments on p 4 on the need to distinguish the strategic "motives" for expansion from the actual "causes" of colonialism which were located in the periphery.
88. Fieldhouse (1976) pp. 35-7 and 64-6.
89. W. Baumgart, *Imperialism: The Idea and Reality of British and French Colonial Expansion* (Oxford, 1982) p. 183.
90. Doyle (1986) p. 336.
91. Doyle (1986) p. 19.
92. Mann, in Shaw (1984) pp. 28 and 45.
93. ibid., p. 45.
94. ibid., p. 31.
95. J. S. Mill, *Essays on Sex Equality*, edited by A. S. Rossi (Chicago, 1970) pp. 152-3.
96. Hobson (1938) p. 234.
97. G. Lichtheim (1972) op. cit., p. 13.
98. See above, p. 24.

CHAPTER FIVE: THE PROBLEM OF INTERNATIONAL INEQUALITY

1. Lenin (1968) p. 9.
2. Bukharin (1972) pp. 20-1.
3. For a discussion, see Knei-Paz (1978) pp. 89-107.
4. Pettman (1979) pp. 75-6 sets out the normative and empirical significance of this remark. And see Pettman's introduction to *Moral Claims and World Affairs* (London, 1979) pp. 26-9.
5. ibid., especially the conclusion.
6. Brewer (1980) p. 272.
7. Bull (1977) p. 96; Waltz (1979) p. 132; Tucker (1977) pp. 175-7.
8. Waltz, ibid.
9. Tucker (1977) pp. 51-72.
10. Tucker (1977) p. 61.
11. ibid.
12. Tucker (1977) p. 58.
13. Tucker (1977) pp. 200-1.
14. See the discussion of Cox on p. 28 above. For a related argument, see C. G. Murphy, "What the Third World Wants: An Interpretation of the Development and Meaning of the NIEO

Ideology", *International Studies Quarterly*, 27 (1983) 55-76.
15. Bull and Watson (1984).
16. Bull (1977) pp. 240-3.
17. See the argument of chapter one.
18. Bull (1977) p. 290.
19. See p. 183, fn. 100.
20. Hopkins and Wallerstein (1977) p. 112.
21. See A. Gerschenkron, *Economic Backwardness in Historical Perspective* (Cambridge, Mass. 1962).
22. Frank (1967) pp. 146-50, and Frank (1969) ch. 1
23. Frank (1967) see pp. 115-20, and Frank (1969) ch. 2. For a critical analysis see Higgott and Robinson (1985) introduction.
24. Frank (1967) pp. 7-8 where it is suggested that some of the economic surplus is absorbed by the dominant groups in each metropolis.
25. Frank (1967) pp. 11-12.
26. See Higgott and Robison (1985).
27. See D. Booth, "Marxism and Development Sociology", in Shaw (1985) p. 74.
28. Laclau (1977). Brewer (1980) pp. 167-174.
29. Brewer (1980) pp. 171-4.
30. G. Kay, *Development and Underdevelopment: A Marxist Analysis* (London, 1975) p. x.
31. See Warren (1980).
32. Brewer (1980) p. 174.
33. Brewer (1980) pp. 230 and 249.
34. Warren (1980) part 2.
35. Warren (1980) pp. 18-25 on "cultural progress".
36. Warren (1980) pp. 10, 164 and 176.
37. See Higgott and Robison (1985) and P. Evans, *Dependent Development: The Alliance of Multinational, State and Local Capital in Brazil* (Princeton, 1979). Booth's essay in Shaw (1985) and S. Corbridge, *Capitalist World Development: A Critique of Radical Development Geography* (New Jersey, 1986) pp. 144-5 are two of many sources which claim that the Warren thesis goes too far.
38. See Higgott and Robison (1985) and Leaver's essay in the same volume.
39. Wallerstein (1979) p. 136.
40. Wallerstein (1983) ch. 1.
41. Wallerstein (1977) p. 24.
42. Fitzgerald (1981) p. 11.
43. Wallerstein (1974) chs. 1-2.
44. Wallerstein (1979) ch. 1.
45. Hopkins and Wallerstein (1977) pp. 128-9.
46. Chase-Dunn and Rubinson (1977) pp. 472-3.
47. Wallerstein (1979) pp. 23 and 69-70.
48. Brewer (1980) p. 208.
49. Emmanuel (1972) ch.2, and Hopkins and Wallerstein (1977) pp. 117-18.
50. Wallerstein (1979) p. 70.
51. Wallerstein (1979) ch. 1.

52. Frobel, Heinrichs and Kreye (1980).
53. Frobel et al (1980) pp. 9-15.
54. Frobel et al (1980) pp. 45-8.
55. Frobel et al (1980) pp. 385 and 404.
56. ibid. For contrasting arguments, see V. Bornschier "Multinational Corporations in World System Perspective", in Mommsen (1987) op. cit., p. 261, and Corbridge (1986) op. cit., p. 187.
57. Wallerstein (1979) ch. 1.
58. Wallerstein (1979) p. 35.
59. See Pettman (1979) pp. 40 and 154; Cox (1982) and Sklar (1976). For an opposing perspective which emphasises the "universalisation of the neo-mercantilist state", see R. Bush et al, *The World Order: Socialist Perspectives* (Oxford, 1987) p. 74.
60. See S. Eisenstadt, "European Expansion and the Civilisation of Modernity" in H. L. Wesseling (ed.) *Expansion and Reaction* (Leiden, 1978) ch. 9. Wallerstein emphasises the importance of state formation in "Dilemmas of Anti-Systemic Movements", *Social Research*, 53 (1986) 185-206. For further comments on Wallerstein on the state, see pp. 129-30 below.
61. Brewer (1980) p. 16-17.
62. Brewer (1980) p. 170.
63. Foster-Carter (1978) and Laclau (1977).
64. Brenner (1977) pp. 83-6.
65. Fitzgerald (1981) p. 13.
66. Fitzgerald (1981) p. 11.
67. See Knei-Paz (1978) ch. 3.
68. Amin (1976) pp. 191-7.
69. ibid.
70. See Brewer (1980) p. 186.
71. Petras, in Limqueco and MacFarlane (1983) pp. 206-7.
72. Petras, ibid. p. 210.
73. Petras, ibid.
74. Petras, ibid. p. 212.
75. Cox (1981) pp. 144-6.
76. Cox (1983) pp. 171-2.
77. Cox (1981) pp. 149-50.
78. Cox (1983) p. 150. See the comments on the dependent state on pp. 159-62 below.
79. As argued in Pettman (1979).
80. S. Hymer, *The Multinational Corporation: A Radical Approach* (Cambridge, 1979) p. 55.
81. Anderson (1983) p. 99.
82. See C. Chase-Dunn, *Socialist States in the World System* (Beverly Hills, 1982) introduction and conclusion.
83. See R. Ashley, *The Political Economy of War and Peace: The Sino-Soviet-American Triangle and the Modern Security Problematique* (London, 1980) p. 223.

CHAPTER SIX: THE STATES-SYSTEM AND THE WORLD-SYSTEM

1. See pp. 108-12 above.
2. See pp. 113-14 above.
3. Waltz (1979) p. 38.
4. Skocpol (1979) p. 22.
5. Hopkins and Wallerstein (1977) pp. 130-2, and Chase-Dunn and Rubinson (1977) pp. 463-4.
6. Wallerstein (1974) p. 7.
7. Wallerstein (1974) p. 24.
8. Wallerstein (1979) p. 161.
9. Wallerstein (1974) pp. 15-16.
10. ibid.
11. Wallerstein (1979) pp. 5-6.
12. See Wallerstein (1979) p. 6, and Chase-Dunn (1981) p. 25.
13. For further discussion, see pp. 130-6 below.
14. J. Baechler, *The Origins of Capitalism* (Oxford, 1975) pp. 73-8.
15. Wallerstein (1979) p. 19.
16. Brewer (1980) p. 18.
17. Giddens (1985) chs. 5-6.
18. Wallerstein (1979) pp. 73-4 and 113-15.
19. Wallerstein (1979) pp. 5-6 and Wight (1977) p. 43.
20. Chase-Dunn and Rubinson (1977) p. 458.
21. Wallerstein (1974) p. 15.
22. Chase-Dunn and Rubinson (1977) p. 457.
23. Wallerstein (1983) pp. 40 and 101.
24. Hopkins and Wallerstein (1977) p. 125.
25. Hopkins and Wallerstein (1977) p. 127.
26. Wallerstein (1979) pp. 66 and 121.
27. Chase-Dunn and Rubinson (1977) p. 464.
28. Wallerstein (1980) pp. 38-9.
29. Wallerstein (1980) p. 65.
30. ibid.
31. Hopkins and Wallerstein (1977) pp. 130-1.
32. ibid.
33. ibid.
34. See C. Chase-Dunn, "Core-Periphery Relations: The Effects of Core Competition", in B. H. Kaplan (ed.) *Social Change in the Capitalist World Economy* (Beverly Hills, 1978).
35. Hopkins and Wallerstein (1977).
36. P. C. W. Guttkind and I. Wallerstein, *The Political Economy of Contemporary Africa* (Beverly Hills, 1976) p. 38.
37. See, however, Wallerstein (1983) chs. 3-4 on the paradoxes of universalism.
38. Wallerstein (1983) p. 93.
39. See p. 38 above.
40. See p. 74 above.
41. Chase-Dunn (1979) p. 605.
42. Chase-Dunn (1979) p. 602.
43. Chase-Dunn (1979) p. 603.

44. Chase-Dunn (1981) p. 42.
45. Chase-Dunn (1981).
46. Skocpol (1974) pp. 1078-9.
47. Roger Dale, "Nation-state and international system: The world-system perspective", in McLennan (1984) p. 206.
48. Wallerstein (1974) ch. 4. For further discussion, see G. Mattingly, *Renaissance Diplomacy* (Harmondsworth, 1973) ch. 5.
49. Wallerstein (1974) p. 356.
50. Wallerstein (1974) p. 355 and Wallerstein (1979) p. 20.
51. Wallerstein (1979) p. 96.
52. Zolberg (1981).
53. This is the implication of the remark that we need to understand "a unique social formation that was simultaneously close to the war of all against all and founded on the acknowledgment of the formal equality of its collective actors". Zolberg (1981) pp. 280-1.
54. Skocpol (1974) and Skocpol (1979) pp. 19-31.
55. Skocpol (1979) p. 22.
56. Skocpol (1979) p. 32. Petras (1971) p. 815 notes that Marx possessed a related notion of dual anchorage in which the "framework of the present-day national state" was set within two other frameworks: the world market and the international system of states.
57. Skocpol (1974) p. 1080.
58. Skocpol (1979) pp. 19-31, 99, 110 and 161-2.
59. Modelski (1978).
60. ibid. See also G. Modelski (ed.) *Exploring Long Cycles* (London, 1987) pp. 234-9.
61. See G. Modelski, "Dependency Reversal in the Modern States-System: A Long Cycle Perspective", in C. F. Doran et al, *North/South Relations: Studies of Dependency Reversal* (New York, 1983).
62. See W. Thompson, "Uneven Economic Growth, Systemic Challenges and Global Wars", *International Studies Quarterly*, 27 (1983) 341-55.
63. Zolberg (1981) p. 275.
64. Chase-Dunn (1981) p. 19.
65. Chase-Dunn (1981) p. 31.
66. ibid.
67. Chase-Dunn (1981) p. 37.
68. Chase-Dunn (1981) pp. 40-1.
69. ibid.
70. Chase-Dunn (1981) pp. 19 and 24-6. But see C. Chase-Dunn and J. Sokolovsky, "InterState-Systems, World Empires and the Capitalist World-Economy: A Response to Thompson, *International Studies Quarterly*, 27 (1983)) p. 359: "In the capitalist world-economy system dynamics are produced by a single logic in which capitalist commodity production interacts with the processes of geopolitics, state formation and nation building".
71. Chase-Dunn (1981).
72. However, see Chase-Dunn and Sokolovsky (1983) op. cit., pp. 346 and 361 where it is argued that a states-system which it is not a capitalist world economy is "unlikely" - "but it would not fall outside our definition of an inter-state system".

73. Worsley (1980) pp. 301 and 316-25.
74. Chase-Dunn (1981) p. 33.
75. ibid.
76. Chase-Dunn (1981) p. 35.
77. Giddens (1985) for example, pp. 26-31 and 288.
78. See pp. 17-18 above.

CHAPTER SEVEN: CLASS AND STATE IN INTERNATIONAL RELA-
TIONS

1. See Held (1983) McLennan (1984) for an account of these
   developments.
2. Poulantzas (1975).
3. Brucan (1978) and Block (1980).
4. Keohane and Nye (1977) ch. 2.
5. Giddens (1985) esp. pp. 287-93 and 310-41.
6. Anderson (1974).
7. See p. 134 above.
8. On the idea of separateness, see J. G. Ruggie, "Continuity and
   Transformation in the World Polity: Towards A Neo-Realist
   Synthesis, *World Politics* (35) p. 274.
9. Anderson (1974) pp. 15-19.
10. ibid.
11. P. Anderson, *Passages from Antiquity to Feudalism* (London, 1974)
    pp. 197-209.
12. ibid., p. 197.
13. ibid., p. 200.
14. ibid., p. 202.
15. ibid., p. 206.
16. ibid., p. 208.
17. Anderson (1974) p. 19.
18. Anderson (1974) p. 18.
19. Anderson, *Passages*, op. cit., pp. 246-64.
20. Anderson (1974) pp. 197-8. See part 2, ch. 1 for the discussion of
    state formation in Eastern Europe.
21. Anderson (1974) p. 431.
22. ibid.
23. Anderson (1974) p. 31.
24. ibid.
25. Anderson (1974) p. 37.
26. Anderson (1974) p. 33.
27. Anderson (1974) p. 31.
28. Anderson, *Passages*, op. cit., pp. 203-4, and Anderson (1974) part 1,
    ch. 1.

29. D. C. North and R. P. Thomas, *The Rise of the Western World: A
    New Economic History* (Cambridge, 1973) p. 96.
30. ibid., pp. 80-1.
31. ibid.

32. E. Heckscher, *Mercantilism* (London, 1955) vol. 2, p. 332.
33. G. Lefebvre, in R. Hilton (ed.) *The Transition from Feudalism to Capitalism* (London, 1976) p. 125.
34. Giddens (1985) p. 97.
35. Giddens (1985) p. 112.
36. ibid.
37. ibid. p. 54.
38. Habermas (1973) p. 50.
39. ibid., p. 64.
40. See F. H. Hinsley, "The Concept of Sovereignty and the Relations Between States", *Journal of International Affairs*", 21 (1967) p. 246.
41. ibid., p. 248.
42. Bull and Watson (1984) p. 9.
43. For an analysis, see K. Kumar, *Prophecy and Progress: The Sociology of Industrial and Post-Industrial Society*, (Harmondsworth, 1968) and Morse (1976). For a critique, see Giddens (1982) ch. 4.
44. Quoted in A. Bullock and M. Shock, *The Liberal Tradition: From Fox to Keynes* (Oxford, 1967) p. 53.
45. Quoted in J. B. Bury, *The Idea of Progress* (New York, 1932) p. 287.
46. For a survey of functionalism, see A.J.R. Groom and P. Taylor (eds.) *Functionalism: Theory and Practice in International Relations* (London, 1975).
47. Keohane and Nye (1977) and Morse (1976).
48. Keohane (1984) op.cit., p. 256.
49. R. Gilpin, *War and Change in World Politics* (Cambridge, 1981) pp. 16-17.
50. McGowan and Walker (1981) p. 348.
51. Miliband (1973).
52. Poulantzas (1975) see pp. 123, 130 and 133.
53. Poulantzas (1975).
54. N. Poulantzas, "The Problem of the Capitalist State" in R. Blackburn (ed.) *Ideology and Social Science: Readings in Critical Social Theory* (Glasgow, 1972) p. 245.
55. Miliband, "Reply to Nicos Poulantzas", ibid. pp. 258-9.
56. The issue is raised in A. Callinicos, *Is There A Future for Marxism?* (London, 1982) pp. 73-5.
57. See Gramsci (1971). For a discussion, see Femia (1981) and Mouffe (1979).
58. See Mouffe (1979) pp. 183-4.
59. Miliband (1973) pp. 15 and 138-9; N. Poulantzas, *Classes in Contemporary Capitalism* (London, 1975) p. 73.
60. Miliband (1973) pp. 138-9; Poulantzas, ibid., ch. 2.
61. Kolko (1969) pp. 4-9, 15 and 26.
62. ibid., p. 7.
63. ibid., p. 14.
64. ibid., pp. 55, 85 and 132.
65. Tucker (1971) p. 71.
66. ibid., pp. 69, 107-12 and 151.
67. ibid., pp. 138-40.
68. Krasner (1978) pp. 35-6.

69. ibid., ch. 1.
70. ibid., pp. 152-3.
71. ibid., pp. 15, 33, 152, 196 and 278-9.
72. ibid., pp. 16 and 33.
73. ibid., pp. 325-6.
74. Block (1980) pp. 229-30, 232-4 and 238-40.
75. ibid.
76. See R. Miliband, *Class Power and State Power* (London, 1973) ch. 4. It should be noted that Krasner's position in "American Policy and Global Economic Stability" in W. P. Avery and D. P. Rapkin, *America in a Changing World Political Economy* (New York, 1982) emphasises the role of particularistic economic interests as do the exponents of class analysis.
77. McGowan and Walker (1981) p. 348.
78. McGowan and Walker (1981) p. 378; Walker and McGowan (1982) p. 221.
79. McGowan and Walker (1982) p. 212.
80. ibid.
81. G. Therborn, *What Does The Ruling Class Do When It Rules?* (London, 1978) pp. 162-3.
82. For a discussion which bears on this issue, see J. Ravenshill "What is to be done for Third World Commodity Exporters : An Evaluation of the STABEX Scheme", *International Organisation*, 38 (1984) 537-74.
83. See p. 65 above.
84. See Cox (1983).
85. S. Cohen (1980) op.cit., p. 187.
86. S. Cohen (1980) op.cit., p. 253.
87. See p. 66 above.
88. Evans and Rowley (1984), op. cit.
89. Waltz (1959) p. 157.
90. O. Sunkel, "Transnational Capitalism and National Disintegration in Latin America", *Social and Economic Studies*, 22 (1973) 132-76.
91. See p. 106 above.
92. On the socio-cultural dimension, see S. J. Kobrin, "Multinational Corporations, Sociocultural Dependency and Industrialisation: Need Satisfaction or Want Creation", *The Journal of Developing Areas*, 13 (1979) pp. 109-25. See also N. Janus and R. Roncaglioli, "Advertising, Mass Media and Dependency", *Development Dialogue* (1979) pp. 81-97.
93. Sklar (1976) p. 86.
94. ibid., p. 83.
95. For a discussion, see Warren (1980).
96. H. Alavi, "Class and State in Pakistan", in D. Banerjee (ed.) *Marxian Theory and the Third World* (Beverly Hills, 1985) pp. 209-10. See the same author's "The State in Post-Colonial Societies: Pakistan and Bangladesh", *New Left Review*, 74 (1972).
97. Alavi, in Banerjee, ibid.,
98. Meillassoux (1970) pp. 97 and 106-8.
99. ibid.

100. For a discussion see C. Thomas, *The Rise of the Authoritarian State in Peripheral Societies* (New York, 1984).
101. I. Wallerstein, "The Withering Away of the States", *International Journal of the Sociology of Law"*, 8 (1980) p. 372.
102. Giddens (1985) esp. pp. 310-41.
103. Giddens (1982) ch. 4.
104. Kubalkova and Cruickshank (1985) does not consider Marxism in this light.
105. For the case for an empirical philosophy of history, see Habermas (1979) chs. 3-4.
106. ibid., pp. 97-8.
107. ibid., pp.104-5.
108. ibid., pp. 112-13.
109. Bull (1977) p. 11.
110. See Linklater (1982) part 3 for a preliminary discussion.
111. Giddens (1981) ch. 10.
112. Giddens (1982) p. 227.

CONCLUSIONS

1. Kubalkova and Cruickshank (1985) p. 246.
2. J. Hall, in Shaw (1984) p. 72.
3. See P. Vilar, "On Nations and Nationalism", *Marxist Perspectives*, 5 (1979) p. 9: "The attribution of primacy signifies only that the evolution of humanity (the extension of its productive capacities and the success of its social transformations) has depended less on these great international clashes, which in fact are inter-state, than on those internal struggles at the core of organised groups - struggles between classes responsible for production and the distribution of goods."
4. Giddens (1985); see also Mann (1986) op. cit.
5. Giddens (1985) ch. 11.
6. Miliband (1983) op. cit., p. 73.
7. E. P. Thompson, cited in P. Anderson, *Arguments Within English Marxism* (London, 1980) p. 17.
8. Anderson (1983) p. 98.
9. Mann (1986) is crucial in this regard.
10. See Linklater (1982) for a normative defence of the extension of community.
11. Such a history ought to take account of the tension between critical theory and post-structuralism for the reasons outlined in the epilogue to M. Jay, *Marxism and Totality: The Adventures of a Concept from Lukacs to Habermas* (Berkeley, 1984).
12. It might be argued - to build on some central themes in Habermas's work - that this project is concerned with understanding the interplay between four "rationalisation processes" in world history. These are the rationalisation of the instruments of production and the concomitant development of human mastery of nature (Marxism); the rationalisation of the control of human beings, specifically state-

building and the development of strategic thought, military technology etc. (realism); the rationalisation of the principles of international order (rationalism); and the rationalisation of the ethical sphere (Habermas and the branch of cultural evolutionism which includes, amongst others, Green and Hobhouse). The problem of how the interaction between these processes determined the moral frontier in different historical epochs will be considered in a later work.

13. On strategies of transition, see S. Mendlowitz in the introduction to J. Galtung, *The True Worlds* (New York, 1980) p. xvii.

Select Bibliography

Amin, S., *Unequal Development: An Essay on the Social Formations of Peripheral Capitalism* (Sussex, 1976).

Anderson, P., *Lineages of the Absolutist State* (London, 1974).

Anderson, P., *Considerations on Western Marxism* (London, 1976).

Anderson, P., *In The Tracks of Historical Materialism* (London, 1983).

Ashley, R. K., "Political Realism and Human Interests", *International Studies Quarterly*, 25 (1981) 204-36.

Benton, T., *Philosophical Foundations of the Three Sociologies* (London, 1977).

Bernstein, R., *The Restructuring of Social and Political Theory* (London, 1979).

Block, F., "The Ruling Class Does Not Rule: Notes on the Marxist Theory of the State", *Socialist Revolution* (1977) 6-28.

Block, F., "Beyond Relative Autonomy: State Managers as Historical Subjects", *Socialist Register*, (1980) 227-42.

Bloom, S. F., *The World of Nations - A Study of the National Implications in the Work of Karl Marx* (New York, 1941).

Borochov, B., *Nationalism and the Class Struggle: A Marxian Approach to the Jewish Problem* (Connecticut, 1973).

Bottomore, T. B. & Goode. P., *Austro-Marxism* (Oxford, 1978).

Bottomore, T. B., et. al., *A Dictionary of Marxist Thought* (Oxford, 1983)

Bottomore, T. B., *The Frankfurt School* (London, 1984).

Brenner, R., "The Origins of Capitalist Development: Critique of Neo-Smithian Marxism", *New Left Review*, 104 (1977) 25-92.

Brewer, A., *Marxist Theories of Imperialism: A Survey* (London, 1980).

Brucan, S., *The Dialectic of World Politics* (New York, 1978).

Brucan, S., "The State and the World System", *International Social Science Journal*, 32 (1980) 752-69.

Bukharin, N., *Imperialism and World Economy* (London, 1972).

Bull, H., *The Anarchical Society: A Study of Order in World Politics* (London, 1977).

Bull, H., "Order and Justice in International Relations", *Hagey Lectures* (University of Waterloo, 1983).

Bull, H., & Watson, A., *The Expansion of International Society* (Oxford, 1984).

Butterfield, H. & Wight, M., *Diplomatic Investigations* (London, 1966).

Carr, E. H., *The Twenty Years' Crisis, 1919-39* (London, 1939).

Carr, E. H., "The Bolshevik Doctrine of Self-Determination", *The Bolshevik Revolution 1917-23*, vol. 1, (Harmondsworth, 1966).

Chase-Dunn, C., & Rubinson, R.,"Towards a Structural Perspective on the World-System", *Politics and Society*, 7 (1977) 453-76.

Chase-Dunn. C., "Comparative Research on World-Systems Characteristics", *International Studies Quarterly*, 23 (1979) 601-23.

Chase-Dunn, C., "Interstate System and Capitalist World Economy: One Logic or Two?", *International Studies Quarterly*, 25 (1981) 19-42.

Choucri, N. & North, R.C., *Nations in Conflict: National Growth and International Violence* (San Francisco, 1975).

Cohen, B. J., *The Question of Imperialism* (London, 1973).

Colletti, L., "The Idea of Bourgeois-Christian Society", in *Marxism and Hegel* (London, 1979).

Connerton, P., *The Tragedy of Enlightenment: An Essay on the Frankfurt School* (Cambridge, 1980).

Cox, R. W., "Social Forces, States and World Orders: Beyond International Relations Theory", *Millenium*, 10 (1981) 126-55.

Cox, R. W., "Gramsci, Hegemony and International Relations: An Essay in Method", *Millenium*, 12, (1983) 162-75.

Cummins, I., *Marx, Engels and National Movements* (London, 1980).

Debray, R., "Marxism and the National Question", *New Left Review*, 105 (1977) 25-41.

Doyle, M., *Empires* (London, 1986).

Emmanuel, A., *Unequal Exchange: A Study of the Imperialism of Trade* (New York, 1972).

Etherington, N. "Reconsidering Theories of Imperialism", *History and Theory*, 21 (1982) 1-36.

Fay, B., *Social Theory and Political Practice* (London, 1975).

Femia, J., *Gramsci's Political Thought: Hegemony, Consciousness and the Revolutionary Process* (Oxford, 1981).

Fieldhouse, D. K., *Economics and Empire 1830-1914* (London, 1976).

Fitzgerald, F. T., "Sociologies of Development", *Journal of Contemporary Asia*, 11 (1981) 5-18.

Foster-Carter, A., "Neo-Marxist Approaches to Development and Underdevelopment", in E. de Kadt & G. Williams (eds.) *Sociology and Development* (London, 1974).

Foster-Carter, A. "Marxism and the Fact of Conquest", *African Review*, 6 (1976) 17-32.

Foster-Carter, A., "The Modes of Production Controversy", *New Left Review*, 107 (1978) 47-77.

Frank, A. G., *Capitalism and Underdevelopment in Latin America: Historical Studies of Chile and Brazil* (New York, 1967).

Frank, A. G., *Latin America: Underdevelopment or Revolution* (New York, 1969).

Friedman, G., *The Political Philosophy of the Frankfurt School* (Ithaca, 1981).

Frobel, F., et. al., *The New International Division of Labour: Structural Unemployment in Industrialised Countries and Industrialisation in Developing Countries* (Cambridge, 1980).

Gallie, W. B., *Philosophers of Peace and War* (Cambridge, 1978).

Gellner, E., *Thought and Change* (London, 1964).

Gellner, E., *Contemporary Thought and Politics* (London, 1974).

198 *Beyond Realism and Marxism*

Gellner, E., *Nations and Nationalism* (Oxford, 1983).

Geuss, R., *The Idea of A Critical Theory* (Cambridge, 1981).

Giddens, A., *A Contemporary Critique of Historical Materialism* (London, 1981).

Giddens, A., *Profiles and Critiques in Social Theory* (London, 1982).

Giddens, A., *The Nation-State and Violence; volume 2 of the Contemporary Critique of Historical Materialism* (Cambridge, 1985).

Gold, D. A., et. al., "Recent Developments in Marxist Theories of the Capitalist State", *Monthly Review* (1975) 29-43.

Gouldner, A., *The Two Marxisms: Contradictions and Anomalies in the Development of Theory*, (New York, 1980).

Gramsci, A., *Selections from the Prison Notebooks* (edited and translated by Q. Hoare and G. Nowell Smith) (London, 1971).

Gulalp, H., "Frank and Wallerstein Revisited: A Contribution to Brenner's Critique", *Journal of Contemporary Asia*, 11 (1981) 169-88.

Habermas, J., *Knowledge and Human Interests* (London, 1972).

Habermas, J., *Theory and Practice* (Boston, 1973).

Habermas, J., *Communication and the Evolution of Society* (Boston, 1979).

Held, D., *Introduction to Critical Theory* (London, 1980).

Held, D. (ed.) *States and Societies* (Oxford, 1983).

Higgott, R., & Robison, R., *South-East Asia: Essays in the Political Economy of Structural Change* (London, 1985).

Hilferding, R., *Finance Capital* (London, 1981).

Hilton, R., *The Transition from Feudalism to Capitalism* (London, 1976).

Hintze, O., *Historical Essays* (edited with an introduction by F. Gilbert) (Oxford, 1975).

Hobsbawm, E., "Some Reflections on The Break-Up of Britain", *New Left Review*, 105 (1977) 3-22.

Hobson, J., *Imperialism: A Study* (London, 1938).

Hoffman, M., "Critical Theory and the Inter-Paradigm Debate", *Millenium*, 16 (1987) 231-49.

Hollist, W. L. & Rosenau, J., "World System Debates", *International Studies Quarterly*, 25 (1981) 5-17.

Hopkins, T. K., & Wallerstein, I., "Patterns of Development of the Modern World-System", *Review*, 1 (1977) 111-45.

Horkheimer, M., *Critical Theory: Selected Essays* (New York, 1972).

Horkheimer, M., *Eclipse of Reason* (New York, 1974).

Horkheimer, M., "Traditional and Critical Theory", in P. Connerton (ed.) *Critical Sociology* (Harmondsworth, 1976).

Horkheimer, M., *Dawn and Decline* (New York, 1978).

Keohane, R. O. & Nye, J. S., *Power and Interdependence: World Politics in Transition* (New York, 1977).

Keohane, R. O. & Nye, J. S., "Power and Interdependence Revisited", *International Organisation*, 41 (1987) 725-53.

Knei-Paz, B., *The Social and Political Thought of Leon Trotsky* (Oxford, 1978).

Kolakowski, L., *Main Currents in Marxism* (Oxford, 1978).

Kolko, G., *The Roots of American Foreign Policy: An Analysis of Power and Purpose* (Boston, 1969).

Krasner, S. D., *Defending the National Interest: Raw Materials Investments and U.S. Foreign Policy* (Princeton, 1978).

Kubalkova, V. & Cruickshank, A. A., *Marxism-Leninism and Theory of International Relations* (London, 1980).

Kubalkova, V. & Cruickshank, A. A., *International Inequality* (London, 1981).

Kubalkova, V. & Cruickshank, A. A., *Marxism and International Relations* (Oxford, 1985).

Laclau, E., *Politics and Ideology in Marxist Theory* (London, 1977).

Lenin, V., *Collected Works, volumes 20 and 22* (Moscow, 1964).

Lenin, V., *Imperialism: The Highest Stage of Capitalism* (Moscow, 1968).

Limqueco, P. & McFarlane, B., *Neo-Marxist Theories of Development* (London, 1983).

Linklater, A., "Men and Citizens in International Relations", *Review of International Studies*, 7 (1981) 23-37.

Linklater, A., *Men and Citizens in the Theory of International Relations* (London, 1982).

Linklater, A., "Realism, Marxism and Critical International Theory", *Review of International Studies*, 12 (1986) 301-12.

Lowy, M., "Marxists and the National Question", *New Left Review*, 96 (1976) 81-100.

Lowy, M., "Marx and Engels: Cosmopolites", *Critique*, 14 (1981) 5-12.

Marx, K. & Engels, F., *Selected Writings in One Volume* (London, 1968).

Marx, K., & Engels, F., *Ireland and the Irish Question* (Moscow, 1971).

Marx, K., *Grundrisse* (Harmondsworth, 1973).

Marx, K., & Engels, F., *On Colonialism* (Moscow, 1974).

Marx, K., *Selected Writings*, edited by D. McLellan (Oxford, 1977).

McCarthy, T., *The Critical Theory of Jurgen Habermas* (London, 1982).

McGowan, P, & Walker, S. G., "Radical and Conventional Models of U.S. Foreign Economic Policy-Making, *World Politics*, 33 (1981) 347-82.

McLennan G, et. al., *The Idea of the Modern State* (Milton Keynes, 1984).

Meillassoux, C., "A Class Analysis of the Bureaucratic Process in Mali", *Journal of Development Studies*, 6 (1970) 97-110.

Miliband, R., *The State in Capitalist Society* (London, 1973).

Modelski, G., "The Long Cycle of Global Politics and the Nation-State", *Comparative Studies in Society and History*, 20 (1978) 214-35.

Morse, E., *Modernisation and the Transformation of International Relations* (New York, 1976).

Mouffe, C., *Gramsci and Marxist Theory* (London, 1979).

Nairn, T., *The Break-Up of Britain* (London, 1981).

Ollman, B., "Marx's Vision of Communism: A Reconstruction", *Critique*, 8 (1977) 4-41.

Orridge, A. W., "Uneven Development and Nationalism", *Political Studies*, 29 (1981) 1-15 & 81-90.

Owen, R., & Sutcliffe B., *Studies in the Theory of Imperialism*, (London, 1972).

Palma, G., "Dependency: A Formal Theory of Underdevelopment or a Methodology for the Analysis of Concrete Situations of Underdevelopment", *World Development*, 6 (1978) 881-924.

Peet, R., (ed.) *An Introduction to Marxist Theories of Underdevelopment* (Canberra, 1980).

Petras, J. A., "Marx and Engels on the National Question", *Journal of Politics*, 33 (1971) 797-824.

Pettman, R., *State and Class: A Sociology of International Affairs* (London, 1979).

Pipes, R., *The Formation of the Soviet Union* (Cambridge, Mass., 1954).

Poulantzas, N., "The Problem of the Capitalist State", in R. Blackburn (ed.) *Ideology and Social Science: Readings in Critical Social Theory* (Glasgow, 1972).

Poulantzas, N., *Political Power and Social Classes* (London, 1975).

Roxborough, I., *Theories of Underdevelopment* (London, 1979).

Schroyer, T., *The Critique of Domination: The Origins and Development of Critical Theory* (New York, 1973).

Shaw, M., (ed.) *War, State and Society* (London, 1984)

Shaw, M., (ed.) *Marxist Sociology Revisited: Critical Assessments* (London, 1985).

Sklar, R. L., "Post-Imperialism: A Class Analysis of Multinational Corporate Expansion", *Comparative Politics*, 9 (1976) 75-92.

Sklar, R. L., "The Nature of Class Domination in Africa", *Journal of Modern African Studies* (1979) 531-52.

Skocpol, T., "Wallerstein's World Capitalist System": A Theoretical and Historical Critique", *American Journal of Sociology*, 82 (1974) 1075-90.

Skocpol, T., *States and Social Revolutions* (Cambridge, 1979).

Smith, A. D., *The Ethnic Revival* (Cambridge, 1981).

Smith, A. D., "Ethnic Identity and World Order", *Millenium*, 12 (1983) 149-61.

Stalin, J., "Marxism and the National Question", *Collected Works, vol. 2* (Moscow, 1953).

Stokes, E., "Late Nineteenth Century Colonial Expansion and the Attack on the Theory of Economic Imperialism: A Case of Mistaken Identity", *Historical Journal*, 12 (1969) 285-301.

Trotsky, T., *Military Writings* (New York, 1969).

Tucker, R. W., *The Radical Left and American Foreign Policy* (Baltimore, 1971).

Tucker, R. W., *The Inequality of Nations* (New York, 1977).

Walker, S. G., & McGowan, P., "U.S Foreign Economic Policy Formation: Neo-Marxist and Neo-Pluralist Perspectives", in W. P. Avery & D. P. Rapkin (eds.) *America in a Changing World Economy* (New York, 1982).

Wallerstein, I., *The Modern World-System: Capitalist Agriculture and the Origins of the European World-Economy in the Sixteenth Century* (London, 1974).

Wallerstein, I., *The Capitalist World-Economy* (Cambridge, 1979).

Wallerstein, I., *The Modern World-System: Mercantilism and the Consolidation of the European World-Economy 1600-1750* (London, 1980).

Wallerstein, I., *Historical Capitalism* (London, 1983).

Waltz, K. N., *Man, the State and War* (Columbia, 1959).

Waltz, K. N., *Theory of International Politics* (Reading, Mass., 1979).

Warren, W., *Imperialism: Pioneer of Capitalism* (London, 1980).

Wehler, H-U., "Bismarck's Imperialism 1862-1890", *Past and Present*, 48 (1970) 119-55.

Wight, M., *Systems of States* (Leicester, 1977).

Wight, M., *Power Politics* (Harmondsworth, 1986).

Wight, M., "An Anatomy of International Thought", *Review of International Studies*, 13 (1987) 221-7.

Worsley, P., "One World or Three? A Critique of the World-System Theory of Immanuel Wallerstein", *Socialist Register* (1980).

Zolberg, A., "Origins of the Modern World System: A Missing Link", *World Politics*, 33 (1981) 254-81.

Index

Adorno, T., on war, 25

Anderson, P., on the absolutist state, 142-8 *passim*

Ashley, R. K., on the "impossibility theorem", 13
on method, 10,

Austro-Marxism, *see* nationalism

Bauer, O., on nationalism, 58-60 *passim*

Block, F., on the state and violence, 156

Borochov, B., on nationalism, 64

Bukharin, N., on imperialism, 78-81
on international inequality, 97
on nationalism and revolution, 65-6

Bull, H., on order, 16-20
on the challenge to the West, 19-20, 74, 129
see also rationalism

Bull, H., and Watson, A., on the expansion of international society, 15

Carr, E. H., on realism and idealism, 7, 13

Chase-Dunn, C., in defence of world-systems theory, 130-1, 136-7, 191 fns. 70 and 72

Colonialism, excentric or peripheral approach, 91-3
in Lenin's thought, 86-90 *passim*
and social imperialism, 90-1
summary of non-Marxist approaches, 86
Waltz's systemic approach, 88-90 *passim*
see also imperialism

Community, expansion and contraction of as a theme in the critical theory of international relations, 6-7, 85, 89-90, 100-1, 118, 120-1, 138-9, 142-3, 158-9, 163-4, 171-2
see also rationalisation processes

Cox, R. W., on global hegemony 115-16
on problem-solving vs. critical theory 27-31
on realism and Marxism, 29-30, 85
on the state in the periphery, 112

Critical theory, applied to international relations, 3-4, 8-10, 14-15, 27-32, 138-9, 162-4
and the Frankfurt School, 22-7
as a method of social inquiry, 1-2, 9-10
see also community, Cox, Marxism, revolutionism

Debray, R., on the failure of the Marxist theory of nationalism, 56-7, 182 fn. 76

Dependency theory, 97-8, 101-7
impact on the study of international relations, 98-9, 166
Marxist critics, 102, 104-7, 112-18 *passim*
see also inequalities of development, world-systems theory

Emmanuel, A., on peripheral nationalism, 73
on unequal exchange, 110